How to Become an American

HOW TO
BECOME AN
AMERICAN

A History of Immigration,
Assimilation, and Loneliness

Daniel Wolff

THE UNIVERSITY OF
SOUTH CAROLINA PRESS

© 2022 University of South Carolina

Published by the University of South Carolina Press
Columbia, South Carolina 29208

www.uscpress.com

Manufactured in the United States of America

31 30 29 28 27 26 25 24 23 22
10 9 8 7 6 5 4 3 2 1

Library of Congress Cataloging-in-Publication Data
can be found at http://catalog.loc.gov/.

ISBN 978-1-64336-363-9 (paperback)
ISBN 978-1-64336-364-6 (ebook)

Author's note on text: There are words quoted in this book that characterize people in the crudest possible way by race, gender, and ethnic origin. They are included because they are part of our national history. If you find reading these words unnerving, I hope that is a sign that we are finally moving past the values they represent.

Author's Note

This book began forty years ago when I was asked to dispose of the contents of a household in Minneapolis. A family had lived there for six decades, and there was a lifetime of acquisitions to go through: furniture, clothing, kitchen goods, books. It was daunting to decide what "history" should be kept and what tossed, especially for someone in their midtwenties. I did the best I could.

Some stuff had to be shipped to relatives. A lot went to local thrift stores. I found a bookstore to take the modest library, mostly book-of-the-month selections, classics, biographies of important Americans like John F. Kennedy and Justice Louis Brandeis. Nothing of much value, nothing I needed to read.

I remember there were odd things I wasn't sure about like the collection of paper placemats from restaurants around the country. Of course, they just needed to be trashed, but a lot of time and energy had been put into collecting them, shouldn't I . . . ? I spent most of a week there, and the hard decisions soon got easier.

Scrapbooks, family portraits, I kept. It wasn't clear if anyone still cared (at some point, personal history loses meaning?), but I couldn't bring myself to toss them. Among the papers I found incomplete family genealogies, letters, essays, short stories, poems. Those I kept, too, with even less confidence that anyone cared. But I was throwing a lot out, and I could always go back and get rid of these, too.

Among the paperwork, I found a diary. It had been kept, briefly, by the woman of the house. I sat down and glanced through it, feeling a little like I was invading the privacy of the dead.

If there was anything special about the diary, it was how un-special it was. There was nothing notable about it. It wasn't written by a so-called important American, far from it. The writer's concerns were real but personal, and she didn't make much effort to put them in context. The events and feelings were already decades old, and almost all the people the diary mentioned had long since passed away.

But the very un-specialness of the diary struck me. It wasn't typical; it contained, after all, the facts and emotions of a particular life. On the other hand, it was a variation on a familiar, a national story. I put it on the "Save" pile along with papers and pictures that might relate to it.

When the house was empty and swept clean, I loaded up the old but barely used Chevrolet and drove back east, the diary and other papers in the trunk. They went into deep storage, occasionally moved from house to house, box to box, not taking up much room either physically or mentally.

Why did I come back to them forty years later?

For one thing, I was getting old enough where I realized that if I didn't deal with them and soon, they probably wouldn't be dealt with. Someone else would have to unpack and look through them and make the keep-or-trash decisions all over again. And that person would know even less about them than I did. If there was a story here worth telling, I'd better get to it.

For another, I'd written a series of books about American history: from a biography of soul singer Sam Cooke to a history of Asbury Park, New Jersey; from profiles of leading Americans like Ben Franklin and Rachel Carson to a history of people trying to return to New Orleans after Hurricane Katrina. Most recently there had been a dual biography of Bob Dylan and Woody Guthrie. All together, these formed (in my head, anyway) a single story. I liked to think I'd used important Americans to get at broader issues. But that still left so-called unimportant people in so-called unimportant situations.

Didn't those lives form the real bulk of history, taking place against and often overshadowed by larger events? I wondered if there wasn't a way to work at that level, to track how public and private events bounced off and reflected each other. The way your life and mine work.

I dug out the diary, the photographs, the other related papers. I thought of historians who wrote "from the bottom up:" Howard Zinn, E. P. Thompson, Staughton Lynd, Herbert Gutman. I went back to the *U.S.A.* trilogy by John Dos Passos and to Walker Evans's and James Agee's *Let Us Now Praise Famous Men*. Agee talked about "stories whose whole intention is the direct communication of the intensity of common experience."

The path the diary traced—from immigrant to citizen—certainly applied to almost all American families. In this case, it included an economic rise to middle-class status. But the more I looked through my pile of papers, the more I wondered what it meant to become an American. How did it happen? When did it happen? And once it happened, was it permanent? In my lifetime, the immigration question—who was and wasn't allowed in—stayed open. And once you were "in," what rights you had seemed to depend on property: where you lived, how much you had. As if the definition of an American was up for grabs. As if all our passports ought to be stamped "Temporary."

Could these papers shed some light on that? I thought I knew where to begin: with the woman writing her first entry in the diary. I began trying to put the story together from there, tracking what I could find of the history, using family names. It didn't work. There was something too specific, too revealing, too explicit. She and her family became specimens, pinned and lifeless. Then I tried identifying them by initials only, a sort of shorthand. That worked better but ended up feeling like a code to be broken, a tease. Finally, I came to the idea that they might be anonymous, that in the great flux of American history they already were anonymous. Not that you couldn't find out who they were if you tried: the story, after all, would come from public records as well as private. But it felt like writing the story without names, while an odd experiment, gave it a kind of power. Like the Tomb of the Unknown Soldier. This would be the story of the unknown family.

It wouldn't be history exactly, couldn't be. There were too many gaps in the record; they weren't "important" enough to be fully documented. Instead, they traveled in a half-light, leaving behind the sort of history families (American families?) often have: based on fact but vague. "I think grandma came from so-and-so. And remember she told us about that bombing she saw?" Through research, I could supply some context and detail, but like a family album, the images were bound to be faded, indistinct.

History disappears. Or gets retold with different meanings. Did that have something to do with our fluctuating national identity? And with the loneliness that ran through the diary?

It was when I got to those questions that I decided this story of an unknown family might be useful. Instead of throwing it out, I'd try to tell it.

Prelude

Man survives earthquakes, epidemics, the horrors of disease, and all the agonies of the soul, but for all time his most tormenting tragedy has been, is, and will be—the tragedy of the bedroom.

—Maxim Gorky, *Reminiscences of Leo Nikolaevich Tolstoy*

She finds the quote by Tolstoy and puts it at the start of her new diary. The diary is light green, hardbound, the pages numbered and lined, the word RECORD printed on the front. It's a commercial ledger left over from her father's business, long since closed down, a record intended for a man's world, the "real world" of commerce and action. Now it will become a different kind of record.

She starts on the first page, in pencil, in a dense script. "What do men write in their journals? Thoughts? Impressions? My one impression now is of loneliness. How cryingly lonely I am all day. Is this self-pity—miserable, decaying self-pity—weak thoughts with shallowness, shamed and painful as my hand, my arm while I write?

"I am lonely. . . ."[1]

It's January 1943. She's about to turn fifty-seven. Her sons, thirty-two and twenty-nine, are away in the war. As she writes, the British are bombing Berlin, and Russian troops have turned the tide in the long defense of Stalingrad. In Pilsen, Czechoslovakia, Nazis have begun emptying the city of Jews, transporting a large group to an "unknown destination."[2]

"Once there was a time when love created peace in me. When my boys were near I was satisfied. . . . When on his long legs, [my younger son] walked into my room, picked up a letter from the dresser. When he sat studying at the desk in the sunroom, and the radio—swing music—played on like the wind accompanying, I was at peace. . . . When [my older son] sprawled on the chaise lounge. . . ."

But the boys—now men—moved out almost a decade ago, went to college, started careers on the East Coast. Her daughter, twenty, still lives at home but is "far away in spirit, split from me by her youth, her selfishness—the selfishness of all youth that is forced by its own inner instinct to reach for its own pleasure, its own fulfillment regardless of the pain it brings others." Her husband of almost thirty-five years is off at work.

She's lonely.

She sits in her sunroom in her once-modern, prewar house, on a lot at the edge of a park in the city of Minneapolis, Minnesota. The world outside is frozen.

"Are all souls alone like me?"

Her gray-blue eyes are set behind high cheekbones; she has fine, prematurely white hair, pulled back and held tight.

"I'm homely now," she writes. She's sitting straight-backed, scratching the pencil carefully across the bound ledger. "I used to look well, to call forth praise. I look haggard, brown-skinned, unbelievably old. Maybe now I'll realize the stupidity and uselessness of spending any money on adorning myself."

It's quiet in the house. There's the sound of heat coming up through the vents.

"My greatest satisfaction and pleasure is in writing. Because writing may relieve me and may release the pent-up feeling in me. . . . To write may mean to be free."

She wants to be a published writer, but "I don't fool myself. I know I'm not a genius." She hopes keeping a diary will offer a way for "self-centeredness [to] be absorbed in charity. . . . I write words and writing these very empty words opens the flood gates. The inner torment subsides. Yet," she quickly adds, "when I read over what I have written, the page tells nothing, says nothing."

She's beginning the diary three weeks after her mother's death.

"It belongs to my grief and weight that the past is over, gone, flitting from me. It is part of her—my mother. In its inner room lies the happiness I felt when my children were here, young, lovely, revolving around me.

"And out there in the cold ground she is sleeping, no not sleeping; that is too metaphysical a word. Her shell is there. . . . How she dreaded just that that has come to her."

Mother was impulsive, emotional, charged. She, on the other hand, is more like Father, the cautious businessman. She has what she calls a "will to logic."

She sits in her geometric, modern house surrounded by dark, nineteenth-century furniture. Some of these pieces were passed on from Mother—who got them from Grandmother—and she, a good daughter, has made a point of keeping these connections to the past dusted and waxed. That is, she has a cleaning woman come in once a week, a Swedish girl.

Past the furniture, past her reflection in the sunroom's window, is their small yard. And the wooden fence. And then the neighbor's house, followed by the house after that, and the one after that. Winter in Minnesota: ice on the eaves, snow in the backyard, a gray sky, and a chill wind coming in off the lake.

"Love," she writes, returning to her mother, "—was ever anyone so loving? She had sympathy for each—too much. So much she wanted you and me happy, tho I took from you, or you cheated me and wronged me. No one ever lived who forgave so easily, so generously. . . ."

When she reads over what she's written, it seems to say nothing.

"I had such love for my mother. . . . It's all hard and inflexible inside me now. There is no pleasure, no peace, no movement of love."

Fifty-seven, white-haired, the mother of three grown children, her marriage intact. And when she looks inside: no movement of love.

Where did this loneliness come from? She who had renounced other faiths still had faith in the logic of history. Never mind what men wrote in their journals; she'd use her diary to look inward and backward, to relive the events that had led her here, back to before her family's arrival in America, how they had made their way and what that had to do with this loneliness. "I can no more wipe out or cut myself off from yesterday," she writes, "than I can remake the person experience has made of me."

When she's done writing, she slowly slides down out of her chair until her stockings touch the carpet and she's kneeling. It's a position she's found oddly comforting recently. A woman on her knees, alone in America. As if in prayer.

PART 1

South

. 1 .

HER MOTHER WAS BORN IN 1856 in Charleston, South Carolina. She was, therefore and presumably, an American, though there was no law at the time explicitly saying so.[1]

A year later, the US Supreme Court ruled that a "negro"—whether slave or free, born in America or elsewhere—couldn't be an American, didn't have the same rights.[2]

Three years after that, South Carolina became the first state to break from the Union. Her mother became, therefore and presumably, no longer an American.[3]

The stated reason for the break was equality under the law: the "negro" question. Northern states had "denounced as sinful the institution of Slavery," were encouraging enslaved people to escape, were refusing to return those who did. Southern slave-owning states saw that as not only a breach of Constitutional law but a challenge to fundamental business and property rights.[4]

Three months after secession, on April 12, 1861, Confederate batteries attacked Fort Sumter in Charleston Harbor. It was the first major military action of the Civil War. The next day, her mother, four years old, hurried down to the shore with her parents and older brothers.[5] She would have seen what others in the crowd saw. "I had a splendid view of the harbor with the naked eye," wrote a young Charleston woman in her diary. "We could distinctly see flames amidst the smoke. All the barracks were on fire . . . [W]ith the telescope I saw the shots as they struck the fort and saw the masonry crumbling."[6]

By eight o'clock in the morning, the fire had spread. The crowd on shore cheered. At one o'clock, the US flag was shot down, then pulled back up. By evening, the fort had received some three thousand shells. Though the Union soldiers had sustained no injuries, they were overwhelmed. A white flag appeared.[7] It was the first Confederate victory in a war the grown-ups seemed to think would be a short and victorious one.

Some four years and 620,000 deaths later, the war was over, and the little girl, now eight, became an American once again. But decades later, an old woman, she would sit in a straight-backed chair in Minnesota and curse the Yankees, telling her grandchildren about that first Confederate triumph and the long siege of Charleston that followed. She was still proud of the rebellion, the secession, and still felt—in her own way—separate. As if she did not, and maybe didn't want to, belong.

Mother was the child of immigrants.

Her father was from a village of one hundred near the town of Strakonice in southern Bohemia. Strakonice, with a population of four hundred, was a textile town, known for its tanners, hatters, and cutters.[8] Many of them lived near the river in a neighborhood known as Jew Town.

Mother was the child of Jews.

To understand what that might mean was to go back and piece together centuries of history. Jews had been "invited" into Germany in the Middle Ages "to provide needed financial and commercial services that were considered inappropriate for Germans to perform."[9] Outsiders, they could travel between the Christian and Islamic empires, accepted by neither, able to barter with both.[10] Starting in the late tenth century, Bohemian state records mention them as slavetraders.[11] They also went from town to town as peddlers, making deals and lending money. These were "inappropriate" occupations. Germans were farmers, soldiers, members of trade guilds—not middlemen. Jews were, in that sense, not Germans.

In times of peace, the majority population may have seen the Ashkenazim or German-speaking Jews as merely different, but the First Crusade in 1096 brought a massacre of Bohemia's Jews. There was another in the Prague ghetto on Easter of 1369.[12] In the early sixteenth century, the predominantly Roman Catholic city of Pilsen, near Strakonice, passed an ordinance requiring Jewish women to attach yellow and white ribbons to their veils and Jewish males to wear certain coats to "be distinguished from other people." The year after the law took effect, all Jews were driven out of Pilsen—as they were driven out of most cities in Bohemia. They retreated to small villages like Strakonice.[13]

In 1509, two Jews living in Strakonice were accused of murdering a gentile boy, then hanging him upside down to collect his blood. It was the ancient "blood accusation": that Jews killed Christians for mysterious, ritual purposes. The two Strakonice Jews were burned to death.[14]

Gradually, Bohemia's Jews were allowed back into the cities. By the end of the seventeenth century, Prague was home to ten thousand, with another twenty to thirty thousand scattered in small towns.[15] In 1727, the Hapsburg monarchy introduced more specific prohibitions: Jews were forbidden to own land, had to pay a special tax, were restricted in what they could read, write, and talk about.[16] Still, over time, many Bohemian Jews had come to think of themselves as loyal citizens of the empire.[17]

In 1741, Jews in Prague celebrated the birth of Prince Joseph II with a parade. A Jewish postal worker led, followed by schoolteachers and their students, then furriers, butchers, tailors, buttonmakers, lacemakers, cobblers.[18] The parade was a show of nationalism, of prosperity, of something like assimilation.

But three years later, Prince Joseph's mother, the Empress Maria Therese, issued an edict stating that "no Jew is to be within the royal city of Prague" and that within six months, "all Jews shall leave the entire kingdom of Bohemia. . . ."[19] Christian mobs smashed the entry to the Jewish quarter, gutting temples and schools. The lacemakers and butchers fled.

Eventually there was a reprieve, but the authorities set out to limit the Jewish population. An immigration cap restricted the number allowed to come into the region. And laws called *familianten Gesetz* determined who could marry and start a family: a male Jew could only apply for a marriage permit if he was at least twenty-four and had enough money saved to pay three years of taxes.[20] One modern author has called the *familianten Gesetz* "reminiscent of the bans placed on American black slaves. . . ."[21] The methods differed—America had the auction block, whippings, rape—but the goal was similar: suppression and control.

While Jews were eventually allowed back into Pilsen, they couldn't own a house; they could only pass through as traders.[22] Some managed to accumulate enough wealth to run small stores, but they were still restricted to separate schools and separate housing. They prayed, married, and got buried differently, and they spoke a different language: a "low German" mixed with Hebrew that came to be known as Yiddish.[23]

The great-grandfather of the woman keeping a diary in Minnesota was born in Bohemia, "devoting his attention to mercantile interests."[24] As Europe began to industrialize, this kind of mercantile, middleman work—the kind that Germans saw as "morally degrading"—became more central to the economy.[25] Soon, "[t]he commercial and manufacturing interests of the land [Bohemia] were almost exclusively in the hands of Jews. . . ."[26] According to the official town history of Strakonice, Jews played a major role in the nineteenth-century clothing industry.[27]

Under Joseph II's Toleration Edict of 1782, Bohemian Jews could open factories, no longer needed to wear identifying clothing, could send their children to university. The goal was to "maximize the Jewish contribution to large-scale commerce."[28] But Jews still were prohibited from entering craft guilds, the Jewish Tax remained, and the population was still limited: no more than 8,600 Jewish families could live in Bohemia at any one time.[29] And when Joseph II died in 1792, Jews had to live under a reactionary "reversal."[30]

Her grandfather was born in 1817. The year he became a teenager, an observer in Bohemia reported: "In the country, the Jew lives off the peasants, he trades, haggles, buys, and sells. He is the supplier of the country people, their adviser, treasurer, in short, their factotum. . . . Trade," the report goes on, "is the real element of the Jews, not because it is a comfortable way of supporting oneself, but because all the other means have generally been closed to him. . . ."[31]

Jewish children like her grandfather could attend cheder, elementary school.[32] For the most part, boys studied in Hebrew, focusing on Talmudic studies, but there were also classes in German; those who were considered gifted could go on to yeshiva after their bar mitzvah. Girls had to end their formal education at puberty.[33] Her grandfather must have done well; he managed to get enough schooling to qualify as a teacher.

But he wasn't the firstborn. That meant he wouldn't have an inheritance, couldn't get married. And it was difficult to find work. So, after graduation, he left his family and Bohemia for a small town in northwestern Poland. With a population of under two thousand, it had fewer than seventy-five Jews—not enough to support a synagogue or a qualified religious instructor.[34] He tried to make a living as a teacher and a bookkeeper, doing some tutoring to make ends meet.

Greater Germany's population of Jews remained a tiny minority of about 1 percent, but the raw numbers would grow through the nineteenth century from around 150,000 at the start to 587,000 by 1900.[35] Rabbi Isaac Mayer Wise (1819–1900) noted that in the rural Bohemia where he was born, "the former isolation of Jewish religious life was breaking down. . . ."[36] Still, Jews were looked on as temporary residents who would one day go back to wherever they came from.[37] One writer of the era called them "a special Semitic nation that happens to live among us. . . . The bond that binds them to one another is much stronger than the one that binds them to the country they inhabit."[38] To a Jewish poet, this prevailing view was the source of "[the] great anguish / Of loving one's country, yet being a stranger!"[39] It was a partly voluntary, partly enforced isolation: a kind of manufactured loneliness.

By the time her grandfather turned twenty-one, more and more Jews were deciding that the best option was to leave. In Bavaria, for example, the first fifty years of the nineteenth century saw the Jewish population drop by half.[40] Crowds of emigrants became a common sight as they marched across Europe toward its port cities.[41] "One might take it," wrote one observer, "for a convoy of wounded."[42] By 1839, according to a German paper, the docks were milling with Jews, "many more single people than families . . . motivated not by greed but by the conviction that . . . they will not be able to settle and find a family."[43]

Some of it was push. "Whatever you and many others may say about America," a contemporary of her grandfather wrote, "you do not know European slavery, German oppression, and Hessian taxes."[44] But there was also pull. According to a popular song of the time, America was a place "Where a man is a man if he's willing to toil / And the humblest may gather the fruits of the soil."[45] In the more prosaic words of a Jewish woman writing from Virginia in 1791, "One can make a good living here, and all live at peace. Anyone can do what he [*sic*] wants . . . Jews and Gentiles are as one."[46]

That was the American promise: not just freedom but equality. According to South Carolina's Charles Pinkney, in his state it only took "a very moderate share of property" for a freeman to have "all the honors and privileges the public can bestow." True, Pinkney qualified this promise: "Every member of Society, almost, will enjoy an equal power. . . ." But America had "a greater equality," he proclaimed, "then is to be found among the people of any country, and an equality which is more likely to continue. . . ."[47]

In 1839, age twenty-two, her grandfather left the little Polish village, said good-bye to family and friends, found his way to a port, and boarded a ship bound for New York.[48] With him, he must have carried some of that manufactured loneliness, that "great anguish" that had left him without a real homeland.

The trip usually took between two and three months, the ships often stuffed with over five hundred emigrants.[49] There's no evidence her grandfather kept a journal of the trip, but one young Bohemian Jew, on a "fast-sailing vessel" out of Hamburg, did. People "of every class and faith" were packed in "the hell of the between-decks. . . ." "The food is so bad, that in Bohemia the pigs would not consider it a delicacy; hardly palatable."[50] The supply of bread, rice, potatoes ran out; water grew scarce; disease spread. Most ships lost 10 percent of their passengers.[51] Those who survived spent days and weeks staring at the swell of the Atlantic, trying to measure invisible progress. "Boredom reigns here, and we must accept it . . . Still I keep in mind and remember again: America will make amends for everything. . . ."

When the ship finally reached New York harbor, the relief and the sense of possibility overwhelmed. "I have seen America, my wishes are fulfilled. . . ." There wasn't a Statue of Liberty; no Mother of Exiles yearning for "the wretched refuse of your teeming shore."[52] And the immigration center on Ellis Island hadn't been built, either. Her grandfather's ship tied up at the Battery on the southernmost tip of Manhattan, one of forty or so that docked each day.[53]

At the other end of the gangplank was a huge and mostly empty land. More accurately, an emptied land, thanks in part to the Indian Removal Act of a decade earlier. Tribes from Alabama, Mississippi, and Tennessee had been marched off on what came to be known as the Trail of Tears. "[T]he Indian," as one observer put it, "is hewn out of rock. . . . He will not learn the arts of civilization, and he and his forest must perish together. . . ."[54] In this new country, then, to be native was to be a noncitizen. Only settlers—which meant only immigrants—were recognized as Americans.

All that empty land was a key part of the new country's appeal. When her grandfather arrived, the whole continent had only seventeen million residents. In comparison, Germany—just twice the size of New York State—had thirty million.[55] There was land for the taking, and the "appropriate" American occupation was farming. "Those who labor in the earth," wrote Thomas Jefferson, "are the chosen people of God if ever he had a chosen people. . . ."[56] By the early nineteenth century, the United States was "really and truly *a country of farmers*."[57]

For many, that left New York, Philadelphia, Charleston as mere embarkation points. In 1810, the nation only had ten urban centers with more than ten thousand people.[58] A large percentage of immigrants passed through them quickly, eager to stake their claims on the frontier. And the nation was eager to have them. So, anyway, George Washington had told Irish immigrants in 1783: "The bosom of America is open to receive not only the opulent and respectable stranger, but the oppressed and persecuted of all nations and religions. [We] shall welcome [them] to participate in all of our rights and privileges if," Washington went on, "by decency and propriety of conduct they appear to merit the employment."[59]

There were other "ifs."

If they were White (however that was defined). The first Naturalization Act of 1790 limited citizenship to "any alien, being a free white person."[60] Blacks in the South couldn't vote, and while international slave trading had been abolished in 1807, since then New York, New Jersey, Connecticut, and Pennsylvania had all rescinded Blacks' right to vote.[61]

If they were male; women in the United States couldn't vote or own property.

If they supported the United States. The Alien and Sedition Act of 1798 allowed for the deportation of those who spoke or wrote against the new government.[62]

Finally, when the Constitution was ratified, most states only allowed Americans the right to vote if they were landowners or tax payers.[63] Apprentices and tenant farmers couldn't vote. As James Madison put it, "those who hold, and those who are without property, have ever formed distinct interests in society. . . ."[64] Her grandfather was in the latter group: those without.

These "ifs" rose partly from the feeling that America's bosom really shouldn't be open to just anyone. A couple decades before Washington welcomed the Irish, Benjamin Franklin had worried that German immigrants—"boors," he called them—had begun to "swarm into our Settlements. Why should Pennsylvania," he asked in 1751, "funded by the English, become a colony of *Aliens,* who will shortly be so numerous as to Germanize us instead of us Anglifying them, and will never adopt our Language or Customs, any more than they can acquire our Complexion?"[65]

Here, before the nation was even formed, was a summation of its great fear: fear of different complexions, different customs, different languages, of the other.

America might become a nation of immigrants, but it didn't intend to become a nation of *Aliens*.

A solution was proposed as early as 1782: the melting pot. In *Letters from an American Farmer*, J. Hector St. John de Crèvecoeur described the process of becoming an American as alchemical, "individuals of all nations are melted into a new race of men." Faith, custom, language were thrown into the pot and out came "a new man, who acts upon new principles . . . new ideas . . . new opinions. . . ."[66] An American was created by "leaving behind him all his ancient prejudices and manners. . . ." That didn't mean the new man ended up without prejudices. "[He] receives new ones from the new mode of life he has embraced, the government he obeys, and the new rank he holds."[67] But they'd be shared prejudices, American prejudices. As if to signal the change, many took on or were given new names, names without history, American names.[68]

Her grandfather was among the first Bohemian Jews to make it to New York.[69] He arrived with little to no money, about to enter a city—a nation—where he didn't speak the language, didn't know the customs, didn't share the prevailing religion. He had no job or family waiting. It was an immigrant's loneliness that was added on to the "great anguish / Of . . . being a stranger" in the land he'd come from.

Wouldn't most of those arriving have felt something similar: the loneliness of the vast empty land before them, the loneliness they were trying to escape behind them? Here, anyway, at the end of the gangplank, was a nation that proclaimed the "self-evident" truth "that all men are created equal . . . endowed by their Creator by certain inalienable rights. . . ."[70] With some hard work and luck, he might cast off the loneliness, melt into a new race, become an American.

. 2 .

SHE NEVER KNEW HER grandfather; he died a year before she was born. He was more legend than fact, more the personification of what had happened to the family, that hazy, undated moment when they had stepped away from the Old World and entered the New. It was her grandfather who had walked down the gangplank into a city of 391,000.

It didn't look like the America America had promised. It wasn't the wide open, emptied land. That was beyond—and beyond her grandfather's interest. He had no experience in farming; his New World was here, in the midst of the burgeoning industrial age.[1] Textile mills and other factories had sprung up, dependent on cheap domestic and imported labor. The building of the Erie Canal and the development of a railroad system had connected east and (middle) west. In two decades, by the start of the Civil War, the nation would have sixty respectably sized cities.[2]

New York was the largest. Eighty percent of its residents lived in Manhattan, packed into the area from the Battery, where his ship docked, to about 14th Street.[3] When he arrived, this maze of downtown allies and streets was in the midst of a cholera epidemic that was killing forty residents a day.[4] The disease was a product of overcrowding, dirty water and food, lack of sanitation, substandard housing: a disease of the poor.[5] According to a report on the epidemic, "for the most part, the temperate, the moral, the well-conditioned escaped."[6]

Meanwhile, the amoral (by these standards), the intemperate, the "wretched refuse" kept arriving: 600,000 people came to the States during the 1830s. Over the next two decades more than 3.5 million would pass through New York City: a third Irish, a third German.[7] Some—more and more—didn't continue on to be farmers but stayed. The surge of *Aliens* made for a city and nation in flux.

Six years earlier, up in the Boston area, the backlash against Irish newcomers had led to Protestant Americans burning a Convent school.[8] A year later, during the summer of 1834, the working class "New York Irish" had rioted. Egged on by the city's Tammany Hall machine, convinced the abolitionist movement was a British plot to have freed slaves take Irish jobs, the mobs began by attacking "Negroes . . . holding religious services." Over four days, they sacked and burned churches, destroyed a Bowery theater, looted abolitionist-owned stores and homes. The mayor had to call out the National Guard. Half a dozen Blacks were "mutilated."[9]

For safety, for comfort, to combat loneliness, immigrants often bunched together in ethnic and religious neighborhoods. Integration was dangerous. The "original American melting pot" was the Five Points neighborhood below Canal Street, which was also (or therefore) referred to as a "slum" and "modern Sodom."[10] Fresh off the boat, her grandfather would have found his way to "his people:" up from the docks through Five Points and the maze of streets along the East River. The first Jewish neighborhood was south of Houston Street. It was mostly made up of old wooden housing: one- and two-story structures subdivided to handle the flood of newcomers.

Farther north, a stretch of marshland had recently been turned into Tompkins Square Park. Around it, three- to five-story apartment buildings were going up to house mostly German immigrants, both Christian and Jewish. The typical tenement in *Kleindeutchland,* or Little Germany, had twenty-four two-bedroom apartments housing some 150 new arrivals.[11] In all, New York was home to some 12,000 Jews, which amounted to a little over 2 percent of its population and a quarter of all the Jews in the country.[12]

The city's jobs, like its housing, tended to be divided up among ethnic groups. The German Catholics in *Kleindeutchland* were mostly carpenters and bricklayers, tanners and cigarmakers. Many of the Irish left their neighborhoods to do construction or work the docks; they were sometimes referred to as "niggers turned inside out."[13] Nearby, but living in their own enclaves, were the converse: "smoked Irish."

There's no reason to think her grandfather had ever seen a person of color before. New York State had officially abolished slavery in 1827; three years later, New York City was home to nearly 13,000 free Blacks.[14] These descendants of Africa, involuntary immigrants, couldn't ride on city streetcars or serve on juries and were largely banned from the skilled trades.[15] By 1860, the city would still have only 300 eligible Black voters.[16] One escapee from slavery, arriving in the city the fall before her grandfather, found his excitement quickly shifting to "a feeling of great insecurity and loneliness. . . . I was in the midst of thousands," wrote Frederick Douglass, "and yet a perfect stranger. . . ."[17]

Immigrants competed to get work, to fit in. The year before her grandfather landed, New York's *Colored American* reported on how the newest immigrant Irish were changing the workforce. "Along the wharves where the colored man once done the whole business of shipping, unshipping . . . in stores where his services were once rendered, and in families where the chief places were filled by him, in all these situations there are substituted foreigners or White Americans."[18]

If the national promise was equality, these immigrant neighborhoods—
Jewish, Black, German, Irish—seemed to be incubating the opposite. Sixty years
after independence, the nation was setting up what felt like permanent social
strata. In Boston, a committee reported on "a downward movement of the poorest
classes [which] must sooner or later lead to a condition like that of the Old World
where the separation of the rich and the poor is so complete."[19] Had her grandfather left one set of social restrictions only to enter another, similar one? Or was
this land of opportunity going to "make amends" for Old World inequities?

New York Jews congregated on the Lower East Side, plying the trades many
already knew: peddling, selling used clothes, lending money.[20] Downtown's Chatham and Baxter streets were lined with tailor shops. Men hawked garments of
all kinds; general stores carried whatever could be bought cheap and sold for a
profit.[21] With tenants packed into tiny rooms, with new arrivals every day, with
the population slanted toward young single men out to make their fortunes, the
community was both close-knit and competitive. "The whole city appeared to me,"
wrote one Bohemian Jew, "like a large shop where everyone buys or sells, cheats
or is cheated. . . . I had never witnessed anywhere such rushing, hurrying, chasing,
running."[22]

The explosive, expanding city was full of people trying to make it, to become
Americans, to melt. The way a popular novel of 1845 put it: "Everything is fleeting,
and nothing stable, everything shifting and changing, and nothing substantial! A
bundle of hopes and fears, deceits and confidences, joys and miseries, strapped
to a fellow's back like Pedlar's [sic] wares."[23] For her grandfather, that bundle was
real. As he described it in a letter to family back in the Old Country, he began his
American life "as every immigrant," peddling.

In 1839, as he started his new life, peddling was what almost half of all Jewish
males did; in five years, that would jump to 70 percent.[24] Storekeepers and manufacturers needed peddlers. A manufacturer could try to draw buyers to the factory
or to a centralized market, and there was some distribution through consignment,
placing product in country stores. But with America still largely rural—isolated
farms and settlers constantly moving west—a sizable part of the population remained out of reach.

Back in the early nineteenth century, Connecticut clockmakers started mass-
producing more watches than their small New England towns could buy, so the
owners would temporarily close their factories, pack their goods on a mule or
horse, and go out peddling, "bringing to each farmer's door those small necessities which it would have been troublesome and expensive to have procured
otherwise."[25] These Yankee peddlers—strangers from the big city, ambassadors of
industrialization—were quickly labeled seductive and "tricky." They carried not

only the latest manufactured products but urban values that rural America often saw as corrupting.[26]

Soon, manufacturers were hiring immigrants to do the peddling. Jewish storeowners enlisted eager young men, fresh off the boat.[27] "Accordingly a basket is hastily fixed up, and he is hurried into the country."[28] The basket might have clothing, shoes, tinware, jewelry, eyeglasses, linen, and samples of other goods. It was a way not only to up sales but also to boost the store's reputation: the peddler doubled as a sort of walking advertisement.

It was an odd, specific way to get to know a country. The work was solitary, lonely. A peddler would be sent out into hard-to-reach areas where "the country merchants . . . receive them coolly and oppose them step by step."[29] Still learning the language, never mind the customs, a peddler—her grandfather—had to be able to knock on a farmer's door and in the few moments it was cracked open (usually by the woman of the house) establish trust. He had to persuade, bargain, strike a deal, and leave with the customer satisfied enough to welcome him back the next time he passed through.[30]

By the 1840s, the peddler was most likely a foreigner wearing strange clothes, speaking broken English in a strange accent. He became widely known as a "black magician," a "modern trickster," a "confidence man."[31] The stereotype became "the shrewd peddler selling trinkets at outrageous prices to the lonely farm wife while her husband labored unknowingly in a distant field."[32] To some degree, immigrants came to embrace that image. A peddler's job, after all, was to sell America what it might not necessarily need. As a comedian from the 1840s put it, "It's good to be shifty in a new country."[33]

Her grandfather went from being a teacher/tutor/bookkeeper in a familiar society to a day-to-day hustler in a foreign world. According to a Bohemian Jewish observer, "[There were] a number of young fellow-countrymen of culture transformed into factory hands, cigarmakers, and peddlers."[34] Many came to regret departing for the New World. "O, how very much have I sacrificed," wrote one Bohemian Jew, ". . . torn myself from my brother and sister, renounced the home of Cohn; all that in order to suffer in America and to go peddling . . . [to] cry 'Do you want to buy?' sweat and carry my basket."[35]

It was hard work for small profit, made that much harder because her grandfather arrived during the economic depression that ran from 1839 to 1843.[36] A heady period of speculation had led to the panic of 1837. The price of cotton dropped from 20 cents a pound to 10; banks failed; land sales fell. When the farmer's door cracked open, the farmer's wife had little money and more reason to hold onto it. "O misguided fools," wrote one Jewish peddler in his diary. "You have left your friends and acquaintances, your relatives and your parents, your home and your fatherland, your language and your customs, your faith and your religion—only to sell your wares in the wild places of America, in isolated farmhouses and tiny hamlets . . ."[37]

Her grandfather probably started not in tiny hamlets but on the streets of New York, selling locally, gradually moving to established routes upstate and out in New Jersey. Typically, a Jewish peddler left on Sunday and sold all week, coming back to home base on Friday for the Sabbath.[38] There were longer circuits north into New England and west over the Alleghenies toward the frontier. Eventually, her grandfather may have gone south, following the commercial network that stretched down the East Coast past Washington, DC, and Virginia into the Carolinas. The South was particularly ripe territory since it manufactured very little itself. Many isolated Southern communities depended on—and mistrusted—Jewish peddlers.[39]

It was entry-level work. The idea was to peddle until you'd put away some savings, established a line of credit. First came a regular route and a good reputation among customers and wholesalers. Then someone like her grandfather might graduate to owning a horse, maybe even a horse and wagon, letting him carry more goods per trip. He'd still be shouting, "Do you want to buy?," still knocking on strangers' doors, but he'd be on his way to the next step: owning a store. That was the peddler's dream. It turned him into a businessman, a resident, maybe even an American.[40]

The work kept him on the road for days, weeks at a time. In a sense, his network of customers, manufacturers, fellow peddlers was as close as he came to an American family. It was a family founded on business, on turning a profit. When he returned to New York—in the brief interim before going out with a new bundle of goods—he lived among his own. And in the changing city, he and his neighbors tried to remake some semblance of what they'd left behind.

Two decades before he'd arrived, Jews from Germany, Poland, and Holland had established a New York synagogue called Anshe Chesed, "People of Kindness." It was too small and poor to hire a rabbi, but they rented a room on Grand Street, the first Jewish congregation on the Lower East Side.[41] A decade later, they'd graduated to renting a hall over the New York Dispensary at White and Centre Streets; that's where Anshe Chesed was meeting when her grandfather arrived. By then, it had become the largest Jewish congregation in the States. In 1842, three years after his boat docked, the congregation was successful enough to justify buying and converting an old Quaker meetinghouse way east on Henry Street.[42]

Anshe Chesed kept traditional temple. To the outside observer, it seemed like chaos. The cantor, or *hazan,* stood in the middle of a milling crowd of men. While he read from the Torah or sang, the (male) believers recited their prayers, rocked quietly with their heads covered, talked among themselves, sang. Women were seated separately: second-class citizens with no role in the service and no say in temple business. While it might strike some as unruly, to an immigrant Anshe Chesed offered a reassuring scene: a piece of the Old World brought to the New. If the words recited and sung were sometimes lost in the hubbub—one observer in New York City claimed that the "majority of Israelites" didn't understand the prayers—there was meaning in the familiar, in the ritual and repetition.[43]

Four years passed in New York. Her grandfather went from a newly arrived twenty-two-year-old to a young man known in the community, with connections among merchants and wholesalers. And amid the long days of travel and selling, he managed to learn a trade: he became a house and sign painter as well as "a skilled glazier."

It wasn't the peddler's dream—he didn't own a store—but it must have felt like proof of the American promise. Back in Europe, painters' guilds only let in approved apprentices, and the master craftsmen were inevitably Christian. In Bohemia, the painters' guild banned Jews altogether. Even if they had the skills, local laws often prevented them from working.[44] But in America, he could find—probably right in Little Germany—both a painter to teach him the techniques and a supplier to provide the basic tools of the trade.[45] The early city directories listed hundreds of painters and at least one paint manufacturer in the Jewish part of town.

Working as a housepainter might feel like a comedown for an educated man, but it was a step up from peddling. It promised a trade, a career, a chance to prosper, to be equal. One contemporary of her grandfather's, John W. Masury, arrived from New England to be a clerk in a Brooklyn paint store. Masury was a Gentile, not a Jew, but he still illustrated the possibilities. From clerk, he'd go on to become a manufacturer, an inventor, and a key figure in America's ongoing industrial revolution.[46]

The problem, as her grandfather saw it, was that the New York market was too "crowded." An ambitious young man could do better in a smaller city. Through his new family—the network of Jewish merchants and peddlers—he had connections in Charleston, South Carolina. Charleston had an established Jewish population; its synagogue was linked to Anshe Chesed; it welcomed immigrants. Compared to the ethnic slums in the North, the South offered an *Alien* an almost instant way to become an American, to shed at least some of his loneliness.

. 3 .

WHEN HER GRANDFATHER ARRIVED, Charleston was the tenth largest city in the United States with some thirty thousand residents.[1] An engraving of around that time shows an elegant red-brick seaside town, its protected but relatively shallow harbor dotted with marshy islands. Schooners, paddleboats, rowboats pass under a sky crowned by tropical storm clouds.[2]

More leisurely and less crassly commercial than New York, Charleston savored the difference. As one resident put it in 1831, its White population cultivated a "deep rooted hostility to everything northern [and] a reckless opposition to the General government. . . ."[3] While the North was industrializing, the South had stuck with cotton and rice. Some of Charleston's leading citizens established a rail line early, but others banned steam engines: machinery might mean progress, but it disturbed their peace and quiet.[4] An historian describes Charleston as "the city that had forced time to stand still."[5]

Her grandfather liked the city immediately. "The climate in Charleston," he wrote, "is only insignificantly warmer than in New York. The winter is almost meaningless."[6] One of Charleston's primary functions was to serve as a seasonal home for the region's well-off plantation owners.[7] Spring in the humid coastal Lowcountry was for planting, and during the oppressive summers, those who could afford it decamped to the inland mountains, returning to the plantation for fall harvesting. It was the fallow months—January to March—that were Charleston's high season. Then the city maintained "a frantic round of balls, horse races, concerts, and theatergoing."[8] Race Week in February featured an opening grand ball on Tuesday, followed by a Jockey Club Dinner on Wednesday, culminating in the "coming out" ball Friday night. That's where the wealthiest plantation owners presented their marriageable daughters to society, an Old World ritual that proudly emphasized their New World status.[9]

Charleston's elite counted themselves among the nation's wealthiest 1 percent.[10] Where the mean value of a typical worker was about $80, for plantation owners it was nearer $54,000.[11] The contrast was stark. The majority of the city consisted of "rude, ill-shaped neglected structures [on] narrow streets."[12] The city didn't have the kind of sprawling immigrant neighborhoods found in New York.[13] Only some 20 percent of its residents were foreign-born (compared to nearly half of New York City's).[14] There was a largely immigrant and working class section in the north of town called the Neck, but much of the White population lived in ethnically and economically mixed neighborhoods.[15]

And then there were the prestigious blocks lined with plantation owners' "imposing, detached houses." Many were in the ornate Greek Revival style with massive exterior columns and, on each floor, a "great verandah" balcony laced with black ironwork. Inside, the high-ceilinged airy rooms were heavily decorated.[16] The city as a whole was in decline.[17] The port had begun to fade as early as 1820, unable to compete with the growth of New Orleans and Mobile, the opening of the Erie Canal, improved steamship service out of New York and Boston.[18] But the wealthy planters maintained their lifestyle, serviced by local merchants, many of them Jewish.[19]

South Carolina had been home to Jews since 1695. Around 1800, it had more than any other state: of the 2,500 Jews in America at the time, 500 lived in South Carolina compared to 400 in New York.[20] Unlike Maryland, where Jews weren't allowed to vote, South Carolina promised something like equality.[21] Any religion (except the Roman Catholics) could establish a church in the state; any White man (who owned fifty acres) could go to the polls.[22]

Jews made up 5 percent of Charleston's White population, participating in the Chamber of Commerce, the Board of Health, and serving as commissioners of public schools and directors of major insurance companies.[23] Judah P. Benjamin, a nonobservant Jew, went from his father's dry goods store on King Street to Yale University and, eventually, the US Senate.[24] In this comparatively democratic arrangement, her grandfather quickly found work as a "sign, room, and glass painter." He specialized in what he called Rouleaux: roller painting.

A painter's job in the 1840s was comprehensive. The chemistry for ready-mixed paint hadn't been worked out, so a painter made his own colors by hand. The base or "hiding" pigment was typically white lead; in addition to bringing out the color, it prevented mold and mildew.[25] Using a paint mill, or an old-fashioned mulling stone, he ground the chosen pigments to a fine dust, then mixed them with linseed oil and the white lead to make a paste.[26]

Every painter had his own formulas, and each color was an individual concoction. The paste was thinned with more oil or turpentine until it was liquid enough to be picked up by a brush (or roller) and applied.[27] There were tricks to this as well. Even with the best grinding, paint still tended to have its lumps and to spread unevenly. To get a smooth final surface, you loaded your hog hairbrush with color, went with the grain of the wood, then sanded with rotten stone or pumice, and reapplied, building up five to ten layers.

American painters had to learn the techniques kept secret within the European guilds. How to paint pine molding, for example, to make it look like English oak.[28] "To imitate with colors, the veins and grains and figures in a piece of fancy wood," a painter's handbook explained, "requires the same faculties, the same development of perceptive powers, the same care and skill and talent, as are required to portray the lineament of the human face. Not in the same degree, perhaps, but in the same direction."[29]

Skilled painters were in demand. In the plantation owners' fine city homes, the entryway floors were often painted to look like tiles or Turkish carpets. Stairwells tended to be more somber: a stone gray or maybe a *faux* marble. Drawing rooms, on the other hand, were meant to be "gay:" a grayish-pink called "ashes-of-rose" or various shades of green, like a spring bower. Libraries were tinted yellowish-brown, and dining rooms were often wall-papered (another skill the enterprising immigrant needed to know) with a painted trim to pick up the pattern. Upstairs bedrooms, which got more natural light, could be a rich yellow or a dark green.[30]

Painting tended to be slow, painstaking work and had its occupational hazards. "When a house painter mixes oil and turpentine with the dry pigment, its lead is released in fumes which the man must breathe. Or this free lead also enters through the skin. It eats up the painter's stomach and nerves and poisons his bones."[31] But it was less exhausting and more dependable than peddling. Rebounding from the panic of 1837, the mid-1840s marked the beginning of a national period of "great industrial prosperity."[32] Northern textile mills demanded more cotton, which meant plantation owners were seeing more profit and could afford more luxuries. Her grandfather had been right: "The business," he wrote after some time in Charleston, "is much better than in New York, since it is not as crowded as there."

Within a few years of moving to Charleston, her grandfather decided to take the monumental step from painter-for-hire to store owner: the peddler's dream. The shop he opened was a comprehensive one, selling, as he wrote, "everything they need in my line." That included pigments, turpentine, brushes, "various oils," ground stone, stencils. The connections he'd made in New York proved key, and shipments with his name on them came in almost monthly on the New York steamships. As he bragged, "I know how to get these goods from far better sources than all of the other merchants here, and therefore am able to sell them at a significantly cheaper price."

He prospered, pleased with both himself and his adopted city. In a letter, he described Charleston as "an important port, very good developed commerce, and it is the most intelligent city of the United States. There are many Jews here from countries all over the world." The city's Beth Elohim synagogue boasted one of the nation's largest and wealthiest Jewish congregations. A visiting rabbi from New

York described Charleston's Jews as "people of culture and refinement . . . American aristocrats." They included "influential merchants, bankers, lawyers, physicians, authors, politicians, political officials, most of them rich and descended from the old Portuguese families."[33]

That lineage made them Sephardic Jews, dating back to the so-called golden age of Portugal and Spain. As Columbus helped "open" the New World to Europeans, his sponsors King Ferdinand and Queen Isabella were closing their kingdom to Jews.[34] By the time Beth Elohim was founded, Sephardic rites had traveled around the world, and the descendants of the old families considered themselves a class above German-speaking Ashkenazi like her grandfather.

Beth Elohim, affiliated with an Orthodox synagogue in London, conducted services in Spanish and English.[35] Its impressive building didn't fit in with the rest of Charleston. Built in the "typical Sephardic style," its two stories had a minaret on top, the main assembly room on the east/west axis, with balconies for the women and children along each side, and the ark containing the Torah scrolls on the east wall so that worshippers facing it were facing toward the holy city of Jerusalem.[36] It was a structure that looked elsewhere, overseas, for inspiration.

The temple's three-hour weekly service of readings and responses was traditional: each worshipper praying a different prayer, chanting a different song, rocking in place. Its 1820 constitution welcomed all as members—as long as "he, she, or they are not people of color."[37] But as early as 1824, a splinter group had started lobbying for change. The reformers were mostly young men in their thirties and forties.[38] English-speaking, more assimilated than the Sephardic traditionalists, many of them born in the United States, they'd grown restless with their temple's Old-World style.[39] They began agitating for a Judaism that was more democratic, more American.

They didn't ask to get rid of tradition altogether. "We wish not to overthrow, but to rebuild."[40] They wanted to keep "such ceremonies as are considered landmarks to distinguish the JEW from Gentile . . . [and] to preserve and perpetuate the principles of Judaism in their utmost vigor and purity."[41] But they advocated for "a system of rational religion; of substance, not form." They believed a practical approach was more suited "to the age and country in which we live, to the feelings, sentiments and opinions of Americans."[42]

Their demands were relatively simple but fundamental. They wanted more liturgy spoken in English. They wanted the service to be organized and shortened. They wanted to be able to include instrumental music and to worship without the prescribed head coverings. They wanted women to have more standing. And they didn't want to be told the Messiah was coming, that the dead would be resurrected, that Jews would inevitably return to Palestine.[43] Their lives were here and now, in America, and they wanted their religion to reflect that.

The ruling board of Beth Elohim turned them down. So, in 1825 some fifty members broke off to start the "Reformed Society of Israelites." They met in the city's Masonic Hall and would go on to worship separately for almost a decade, making Charleston the American birthplace of Reform Judaism.[44]

Five years before her grandfather's arrival in 1843, fire destroyed Beth Elohim's first synagogue. The blaze began in a nearby paint shop (an occupational hazard for a business that relied on oils and turpentine) and burnt its way down the city's main commercial thoroughfare, north King Street. Beth Elohim promptly put up a larger, grander, brownstone synagogue. It traded in Sephardic design for the more fashionable—and more "American"—Greek Revival, complete with grand entrance columns and a front portico. (The Lincoln Memorial, built twenty years later, would share many of the new temple's features.)[45] Nearly fifty feet high, the temple had a sixty-foot diameter dome centered by an ornate chandelier.[46] It cost $40,000 and ended up looking a little like a plantation owner's house. "Behold, O Mighty Architect" wrote a female poet and member of the congregation, "What love for Thee has wrought; / This Fane arising from the wrecked, / Beauty from ashes brought."[47]

The congregation had become more liberal and agreed on installing a pipe organ, but Beth Elohim's traditionalists opposed any further change, including more recognition for women.[48] Females had organized a Sunday school, only the second in the nation, and did most of the teaching. They also contributed to the service, with sixty of the seventy-four hymns in the new hymnal written by Penina Moïse. That made her among the first females to shape American Jewish ritual. Moïse's hymns championed unity over "dread estrangement," proclaiming: "How beautiful it is to see, / Brethren unite harmoniously!"[49]

But Beth Elohim couldn't find harmony. The reformers and the conservatives fought for three years in court.[50] One commentator called it "the battle for the hearts and minds of American Jews."[51] This time the reformers were the majority. The Sephardic orthodox left, and a more progressive congregation took over the new temple.[52]

Her grandfather—young, educated, forward-thinking—sided with the reformers. They wanted what he wanted: to be more American. For the next five years, he built his new life as an up-and-coming businessman, a respected member of society, an active participant in his temple. After almost a decade in the New World, he could see America's promise coming true.

But with all that, a major reason he'd emigrated was to be able to start a family. In his early thirties, he was still single, still—in that sense—alone.

. 4 .

THE CHARLESTON PAINT STORE WAS a kind of outpost, a distribution center. Her grandfather depended on his northern connections for pigments, turpentine, and the new items he was branching out into: glass, window blinds. The thirty-three-year-old made regular trips back to New York City to see friends and maintain contacts with his extended business family.

It was on a visit in 1850—seven years after moving south—that he met a woman from his native Bohemia. "She tended to come to my lodging house for a beer . . ." he wrote later. "The first time she came in and stood before the front door, the sight of her, her grace and her purity, affected me so much that I couldn't speak enough of her to my fellow lodgers."

Back in Bohemia, women traditionally stayed home: bearing and raising children, keeping house, cooking, taking care of the livestock. If their husband managed to start a store, they might help run it but only while he was away peddling. Their marriages were often arranged through a *shadkahn* or marriage broker, who negotiated a dowry between the two sets of parents. It's been described as a kind of "economic and political transaction. . . . Marriage had as much to do with getting good in-laws and increasing one's family labor force as it did with finding a lifetime companion and raising beloved children." These arrangements were how "[a] propertied family consolidated wealth" and how the poor tried to get by.[1]

That tradition had already begun to disintegrate in Bohemia. Under the restriction that only the eldest Jewish son could marry, many young women—even those pledged to fiancés—waited years before they could wed.[2] As emigration fever took hold, the Bohemian villages emptied of eligible men. That left young women stranded, unable to marry, forbidden from most jobs, resigned to taking care of their aging parents. And their religion offered few consolations. It made an early nineteenth-century Bohemian Jew wonder if women enjoyed "fewer favors from God, had "fewer hopes of eternal bliss? . . . Why should the female sex come away empty-handed?"[3]

Without much hope at home, one obvious answer was to leave. And one obvious destination was America, even though the New World promise of equality didn't exactly apply to women. They couldn't vote or own land in America, and it was next to impossible to get an equal education.[4] Still, the young woman her grandfather saw standing at the door of the inn had left home at eighteen and crossed the Atlantic alone. It was an act of desperation and bravery.[5] It was also a declaration of independence.

The year her ship docked, 250 women convened in Seneca Falls, New York, to declare: "We hold these truths to be self-evident, that men *and women* are created equal."[6] They went on to say that "the history of mankind is a history of repeated injuries and usurpations on the part of men toward women."[7] In the end, the convention resolved that "woman is man's equal," that laws stating otherwise "are contrary to the great precept of Nature, and therefore of no force or authority," and that women should have the right to vote.[8] Decades of struggle would follow.

By 1850, the population of the United States was increasing by more than a third every ten years. (Its twenty-three million included 50,000 Jews, a number that would triple in the coming decades.)[9] As a country in constant mix—nearly 10 percent foreign-born and many of the rest only a generation removed from the Old World—it was still defining itself, finding its voice.[10] According to Ralph Waldo Emerson, America was "a country of the future . . . a country of beginnings, of projects, of vast designs and expectations. It has no past. . . ."[11]

In that "country of the future," the idea of who was an American was being redefined. Herman Melville called his fellow Americans "the peculiar chosen people—the Israel of our time . . . God has predestined, mankind expects, great things from our race."[12] Not just a new nation, but a new race, the end product of the melting pot. Based on the majority who had "equal rights," the new race self-defined as White, male, Anglo-Saxon, respectable. So, in the North, with the emerging demands of factory work, immigrants were urged to be punctual, clean, disciplined; that's what it meant to be an American. In the South, those values were less important than the overwhelming requirement to not be Black.[13]

Some women questioned the paternalism built into this definition. "If Absolute Sovereignty be not necessary in a State," one wrote, "how comes it to be so in a family?"[14] Frederick Douglass challenged the racial distinctions. To him, the nation did indeed have a past it needed to acknowledge and rectify. In 1850 he helped organize a convention at which fugitive slaves voted to abolish slavery and claim their rights as full-fledged citizens.[15] And immigrants bridled at the accusation that the country's "deterioration," as one poverty agency put it, was due to "the immense influx of foreigners, many of them being of the most thriftless, degraded class."[16]

The woman her grandfather saw drinking beer at the inn was arguably a member of that degraded class. She'd landed with a contact in the New World—an uncle in Philadelphia—but the teenager had stayed with him only three months. She'd left his care, it was explained, "because there was not the slightest trace of the Jewish religion there." That may have been a sign of how seriously she took her faith—or a way to explain her subsequent travels. She'd left Philadelphia for New York City, where she'd come under the protection of a man from Prague, "from whom—after half a year—she got away with much difficulty." This time, no explanation was given, either for the difficulty or the escape.

By the time the Charleston paint store owner saw her at the inn, she appears to have been on her own in New York for over a year. She must have had a job, though there's no indication what it was. In the decade she arrived, only 10 percent of American females were in the official labor force. Former farm girls ran the looms of the huge New England mills, typically receiving half what men were paid. And there was domestic work: cooks, maids, cleaning women.[17] But most American women were "homemakers."[18]

It's not surprising that the paint store owner saw the young Bohemian woman at an inn. In mid-nineteenth-century New York, boardinghouses were common meeting places. The city's Jewish newspapers featured ads for subdued, respectable establishments. "Mrs. Weill's Private Boarding House" solicited "the friends of a delicious and *kosher* table." Widows rented out spare rooms, and the better inns were endorsed by leading rabbis.[19] But the Brooklyn preacher Henry Ward Beecher admonished his parishioners, "Abhor Sodom and Gomorrah—or boardinghouses!"[20] The inns and taverns along Bowery and Chatham streets, amidst the Jewish neighborhood, were famous for their entertainments. Magicians, dancers, ventriloquists, women singers, circus acts, various kinds of musicians helped draw customers. P. T. Barnum built his reputation in this neighborhood, his curio and variety show highlighting everything from jugglers to gypsies. The decade the teenage girl arrived from Bohemia, a new trend was emerging: blackface performers who put on burnt cork to mock, mimic, and pay tribute to African American stylings.[21] The audience watched as their nation forged its culture.

After that first sighting, the paint store owner inquired about the woman among his fellow lodgers, then arranged for a proper introduction. It was a bow to Old World courtship traditions, but theirs was an American meeting. By the time they got together, both the twenty-one-year-old woman and the thirty-three-year-old man had managed to survive in the New World essentially on their own. Part of their new life, of the American promise, was that young people could meet by chance at a public inn—and a first impression might lead anywhere.

The courtship bloomed and quickly led to a proposal. Rather than having the marriage in Charleston—which meant, as he explained to her parents, escorting a single woman on a two- or three-day ocean voyage—they decided to have the ceremony at Anshe Chesed in front of friends and business associates.

In some ways, the ceremony was their "presentational ball": an announcement that they'd come out as Americans. The New York synagogue had grown and changed since he'd been away. Like the young couple, it had assimilated. The year he'd left the city, the congregation had hired a new young rabbi: Dr. Max Lilienthal. A graduate of the University of Munich "with a brilliant reputation established abroad," Lilienthal quickly became one of the city's prominent orthodox leaders.[22]

At first, the new rabbi had left things much as they'd been. An observer in 1846 thought the worshippers were "as ill-behaved as in Germany," going on in an "intolerable sing-song"while the cantor "trilled like a nightingale and leaped out like a hooked fish."[23] But soon the not quite thirty-year-old Lilienthal convinced the temple elders to ban side conversations. He wanted to deliver formal sermons and expected his attendees to listen. It was the first step toward reform. The year of her grandparents' wedding, Lilienthal had begun talking about "this epoch of Jewish science," lobbying to have Anshe Chesed eliminate traditional elements "that cannot stand the trial before the forum of science, knowledge and common sense."[24]

What Lilienthal was proposing—what had already started in Charleston—was a kind of fundamentalism. It coincided with the back-to-basics, born-again Christian revival known as the Second Great Awakening. Jewish reformers argued that although the Bible was divine, subsequent rabbinic laws—including the commentaries of the Talmud, dress codes, and certain rituals of diet, prayer, and mourning—were not. They saw these as late additions: foreign elements picked up during the Jewish diaspora, contributing to "materialism and an indifference to spiritual ideals"[25] To get to the essence of Judaism, they needed to be eliminated. "[O]ur creed will only then shine," Lilienthal proclaimed, "with the eternal light of the Heavenly truth, when all these foreign elements will be removed, and we again will stand upon the solid rock of the Mosaic law!!"[26]

The spring before the wedding, Anshe Chesed had left the old Quaker meetinghouse; by June, they'd finished construction on a massive new three-story red-brick temple on the Lower East Side's Norfolk Street. The Moorish-looking structure was built to reflect Anshe Chesed's new profile as a reform temple. Like in Charleston, the congregation had added a pipe organ.[27] Instead of the traditional depiction of the Ten Commandments, the new temple displayed them in "controversial" stained-glass windows that lined and lit the dark interior: a modern touch, almost a kind of advertising.[28]

The couple's decision to be married there—and have the ceremony performed by Dr. Lilienthal—sealed their commitment to the new Judaism and their new country. For the young bride, it was a split from her distant family's Old World traditions, the start of a new life. For the groom, it must have confirmed his transformation into an American merchant. He'd left the city a peddler, returned a businessman. The elaborate service asserted that he was now part of a freshly minted middle class, which some estimated included a quarter of New York City's immigrant Jews.[29]

In a letter back to Bohemia, the groom boasted that the ceremony was "one of the most beautiful in New York." The two stood in the spanking new vaulted interior, the dark carved wood highlighted by gold paint, light streaming in through the stained glass. The ark was on the east wall in a raised nave; there was seating for some twelve hundred people, including women's balconies rising two stories on both sides. The temple, according to the groom, was "fuller than it had ever been for a wedding."

With family back in the Old Country, the bride's cousin and a New York friend escorted the couple. According to the groom, his bride "truly looked more like an angel than a human." Where in orthodox ceremonies the rabbi often stood in the middle of the congregation, at Anshe Chesed Dr. Lilienthal addressed the celebrants from the top of a set of stairs in front, more like a Christian church. He delivered, the groom reported, a "very beautiful sermon." Then with the couple standing under the wedding canopy, the ring was presented, the wine tasted, the wedding contract signed. The seven blessings were recited over a second glass of wine; then a glass was placed on the floor. When the groom smashed it, it served as the traditional symbol of the scattering of Jews after the destruction of the Temple in Jerusalem: Jews as perpetual immigrants.

Later, the groom wrote that his bride "wept a great deal" at the beauty and solemnity of the occasion and "[at] being so far away from her loved ones on such an important day." The paint store owner had arranged for a dinner to follow, attended by some forty people including "the most outstanding representatives of the Bohemian Community . . . The richest and most sophisticated. . . ." Then the married couple observed the traditional seven days of receiving guests and gifts before returning to Charleston by steamboat.

In a letter home to his new bride's parents, the paint store owner made sure to describe Charleston and the religious community their daughter would be entering. Beth Elohim now had about forty members, whom he described as English and Sephardic Jews.[30] "[T]hey keep only one holiday. They go through the Torah reading in three years. They have a choir of women accompanying an organ." The scant details were enough to let his Bohemian in-laws know that while some traditions were preserved, this was New World Reform Judaism. In fact, some considered Beth Elohim "the most advanced reform congregation in America."[31]

It remained controversial. The newlyweds hadn't been settled more than a few months when there was a furious public debate. An orthodox leader publicly grilled the reformers: "Do you believe in the personal Messiah? Do you believe in the bodily resurrection?" To which the defiant crowd responded with a loud, "No!"[32] The congregation wasn't waiting for a savior; their rebirth was here in

America. As a reform leader put it at the dedication of Beth Elohim's new building: "This synagogue is our *temple,* this city is our *Jerusalem,* this happy land our *Palestine.*"[33]

Her grandfather's paint store, one of at least a half-dozen in the city, was at 30 Beaufain Street, just south of the College of Charleston. That put it a block and a half off King Street, the main north-south thoroughfare on Charleston's peninsula and "the emotional if not the geographical center of the city for Jews."[34] King Street was the primary route plantation owners took into the city. As they rode down it in fine horse-drawn carriages, driven by uniformed Black drivers, they passed by fabric shops, furniture shops, paint shops: businesses founded to cater to their needs. 30 Beaufain fit into a neighborhood of closely packed buildings where store owners often lived above their ground-floor shops.[35] That the young couple resided in a separate residence at 24 St. Philip Street signaled their prosperity and success.

It also seemed to signal the defeat of loneliness. A store, a home, a family: here was America's promise fulfilled. If the goal had never really been equality (an impossible idea?) but simply the chance to get ahead, to fit in, Charleston might well have been the new Jerusalem.

Except that it ran on darkness.

.5.

SOUTH CAROLINA'S FIRST EUROPEAN settlers believed that if the Lowcountry—the coastal tidal swamps that stretched some forty miles inland—could be "cleared, opened, and sweetened by culture, [they would] yield plentiful crops of rice."[1] The trouble was that the area was all but impenetrable. Workers trying to drain and terrace the marshes died of snakebite, yellow fever, exhaustion. The landowners soon came up with a solution. As early as 1680, an observer in the area wrote: "Since people have found out the convenience and cheapness of slave labor, they no longer keep white men, who formerly did the work on Plantations."[2]

Indentured European immigrants gave way to forced African immigrants— especially West Africans, who had developed cultivation skills in their own wetlands on what was known as Africa's Rice Coast.[3] They knew how to plant, irrigate, harvest—and were thought to be less susceptible to local diseases. Plus, they were expendable; those who died turning swamps into rice paddies were quickly replaced. They were, after all, not citizens but commodities.

By 1698, the colony was successfully exporting ten thousand pounds of rice a year, and within a decade of that, South Carolina's enslaved Africans outnumbered its free Whites.[4] This formula—the slave formula—made the economy. And that, in turn, made Charleston. The American ideal of the independent farmer on a self-sufficient family farm made no sense for rice; the scale was too large for that, the acreage necessary to turn a profit demanded at least thirty workers.[5] By 1730, these big plantations were producing twenty million pounds of "Carolina gold" a year, and by the beginning of the 1800s, 40,000 acres of rice land had been cleared and 780 miles of irrigation and flood-control canals dug.[6] Slaves maintained the complicated system, sowed in the spring, cropped and shored the canals in the heat of summer, harvested in the early fall, then winnowed and threshed the rice for market before winter set in.

The brutality of the work helped make early nineteenth-century South Carolina one of the few states where slave mortality exceeded birth rate. But its economy hummed. As the rice-laden ships pulled out of Charleston harbor, others pulled in carrying human cargo to replace the dead and dying. Before the slave trade was banned in 1807, the city was the port of entry for somewhere between 40 and 60 percent of all Africans brought to North America.[7]

In one way or another, the whole city took part in this system and that included Charleston's Jews. One set of data from 1797 found that out of seventy-three heads of Jewish households, thirty-four owned slaves.[8] By 1830, about 90 percent of Charleston's Whites kept other human beings in bondage—and at 83 percent, the city's Jews weren't far behind.[9] Plus, Charleston's relative lack of anti-Semitism meant Jews helped enforce the slavery laws as constables, jailers, deputy sheriffs, detectives.[10]

The overseas slave trade was closed three decades before the newlyweds arrived, but the formula didn't work without fresh slaves replacing old stock. The solution was breeding. Slave families were begun on the plantation, then brought into the city to be split up and sold: another kind of harvest.[11] The city's largest slave auctions were held behind the Customs House near the docks where the newlyweds stepped off their ship from New York. There were smaller "brokerages" —over thirty—scattered throughout the city.[12] The business of slavery was everywhere. "Almost daily," one observer noted, "large troops [of slaves] in faded, dirty clothes were seen shuffling along in loose, irregular file, in the dusty streets."[13]

By the time he returned with his young bride, her grandfather had lived in Charleston almost eight years. He'd adjusted to the racial status quo. To walk the streets of Charleston was to walk a majority Black city. The percentage of South Carolina's African Americans (although they weren't, officially, Americans) had been increasing rapidly since the turn of the century. The year the newlyweds settled on St. Philip's Street, slaves made up nearly 60 percent of the state's population.[14] Within Charleston, there were some twenty thousand Whites to about the same number of slaves.[15] For White residents of the city, slavery was, as the British ambassador observed, "the very blood of their veins."[16]

One result was a social hierarchy as complex and strict as any city in the New or Old World.[17] Distinctions were made not only between Black and White but within those groups. There was, for example, the ruling class of Whites— politicians, plantation owners, professionals—two-thirds of whom could boast of being born in America. They served as the city's landed gentry, with old money and ties back to Great Britain.[18] In contrast, two-thirds of the "petty proprietors" —the grocers, restauranteurs, paint store owners—were foreign-born.[19] "The mercantile and planting classes," as one city resident put it, "were on the best of terms."[20] But social distinctions remained, echoing Thomas Jefferson's belief that a "corruption of morals" came to those who "depend on the casualties and caprices of customers."[21]

There were also distinctions drawn among so-called Blacks. Charleston was home to 3,500 free persons of color, three-quarters of whom were mulatto, "the free brown elite."[22] They were the descendants of slaveowners, who regularly forced sex on their property. It was an open secret that Black nursemaids and playmates assigned to White children were often half-brothers and sisters. "[T]he mulattos one sees in every family," wrote a female South Carolina diarist, "exactly resemble the white children—and every lady tells you who is the father."[23]

Over 80 percent of these free people of color had a skilled trade—butchers, tailors, coopers, painters—and according to one report, an astonishing 99 percent could either read or write, well above the rate in Savannah, New Orleans, or Washington.[24] They had their own Brown Fellowship Society that served as bank and charity organization.[25] Many were property owners; some ran their own businesses; and by 1860, more than 130 free Blacks owned slaves.[26]

Her grandfather tried to explain this system to his in-laws back in Bohemia. "The way someone at home occasionally buys a few cattle . . . here, they buy slaves. . . . Every Tuesday there is a slave market. The slaves are brought in from the country and auctioned off on the square. Like cows, they are examined thoroughly by eager buyers . . . Often an entire family is put up for sale, from which the father is sold to one person, the mother to another, and every child to someone else."

In Bohemia, the goal had been to control and cap the number of Jews. Here, as the huge cotton operations out west demanded more and more slaves, coastal states like South Carolina became breeding grounds, shipping humans to Mississippi, Georgia, Louisiana. But in both places, the key was the family. For the system to work—for the rice to be harvested, money made, the elegant houses paid for and kept up—slaves could only have one stable structure: slavery itself. Black families, with their network of support and safety, had to be constantly broken.[27]

"It is usual," her grandfather explained, "to rent negroes for work." Slaves were a kind of currency: you could trade them for land or loan them out. "The price of a slave," he continued, "depends on the age and health of the slave. They are between one hundred to a thousand dollars, children draw a smaller price, and older people for still less. Between 18 and 40 years [the prime age for labor and breeding] the price is the highest. A good craftsman who is also moderate and full of character is worth more than one who is merely good for day labor." On the plantations, her grandfather noted, "Some cotton growers have about three hundred slaves."

In Charleston, slavery was more domestic. The city had no need for harvest crews or factory hands; the largest Black working force was probably on the docks, loading the rice and cotton, unloading the manufactured goods that came back in return. Still, most of the plantation owners stocked their city houses with nurse maids, gardeners, coachmen, stable boys. In the airy, richly painted dining rooms, Black waiters served lavish meals prepared by Black cooks. All told, the average in Charleston was two slaves per owner.[28]

"Anyone in the city who has a bit of wealth," her grandfather wrote, "has a few slaves to do the work, because the whites (especially the women) don't do anything." He was exaggerating—or maybe just narrowing the definition of White. By 1850, slaveownership had dropped: only about three thousand of the city's twenty thousand non-Black occupants owned slaves.[29] But those were the people of consequence: plantation and business owners. In Charleston, to be a successful American was to own slaves.

The paint store owner overestimated the city's percentage of Blacks, saying they outnumbered Whites five to one. But he may have been talking about how it felt: the crush of Black bodies on the streets and docks, the few Whites who maintained order. That White minority defended the slave formula by arguing against basic equality. "[M]en are not born physically, morally, or intellectually equal," therefore it was the responsibility of those God had endowed with superior qualities (White people) to take care of those without (Black people). Hence, slavery.[30]

Built into this formula was the great fear of the other. The city's White minority was constantly aware that their human currency might turn on them. Something like that had happened in Charleston's recent memory. Denmark Vesey bought his own freedom around 1800 and then became a founding member of the city's African Methodist Episcopal Church. There, he began preaching from Exodus "how the children of Israel were delivered out of Egypt from bondage."[31] Vesey expected the same of America, the new Jerusalem. He reportedly masterminded a plan for a South Carolina slave rebellion. When word of the plan leaked in the summer of 1822, Charleston's mayor called out the militia. Vesey and five slaves were hanged as examples; they were followed by thirty others. The city became a kind of police state.[32]

According to Lieutenant William Tecumseh Sherman, stationed in Charleston the year before her grandfather arrived, the city was "policed to perfection and guarded by soldiers, enlisted by the State, who enforce order with the Bayonet. . . ."[33] Another, later visitor was struck by "the martial ceremonies, the frequent parades of militia. . . . [and] numerous armed police."[34] Charleston funded a three hundred man "city guard": uniformed watchmen who patrolled with musket and bayonet.[35]

Her grandfather outlined the city's racial laws. "At nine in the evening, they beat the drum and the slaves must be home. Five in the morning, they beat the drum again and the negroes are allowed to be on the streets." Whites in the city—whether they were members of the elite, store owners, or housepainters—expected Blacks to step off the sidewalk to let them pass. "A negro who raises his hand against a white woman," the paint store owner observed, "gets 10 years in penitentiary." Not far from his store, on Magazine Street, there was an area known as the "workplace" where Blacks were taken to be whipped if they broke curfew or showed any kind of disrespect.[36]

The whole system struck her grandfather as peculiar, but by the time he settled in with his young bride, he seems to have adjusted. As another Southern Jew wrote, "I never questioned the rights or wrongs of slavery. Its existence I regarded as a matter of course, as most other customs or institutions."[37] That fit with the Talmud's advice to itinerant Jews: "The law of the land is the law."[38] In Charleston, where some two thousand slaves were bought and sold each month, seven of the city's auctioneers were Jewish and four of the forty-four slavetraders. An important local merchant, Benjamin Mordecai, once spent $12,000 on slaves in a single sale.[39] "It would seem to be realistic to conclude," wrote historian Bertram Korn, "that any Jew who could afford to own slaves and had need for their services would do so."[40]

Participation in this system, the slave formula, was how immigrants to the South became Americans. It didn't gain them entrance into high society: horse racing and coming-out balls. That was reserved for plantation owners and native-born Christians. But Charleston's fixation on skin color allowed men like her grandfather to achieve relative success and citizenship. Immigrants were welcome, thanks to some simple, brutal math. There were more Blacks than Whites—more owned than owners—and to counter that, *Aliens* were counted on the ruling side of the ledger.

By 1860, the paint store owner was prosperous enough ("White" enough?) to invest in real estate. He owned a building a block west of the paint store that he rented to a single woman. He also owned one a block north; its occupants were listed simply as "Slaves."[41] They may have been someone else's, rented out for city work, temporary residents in her grandfather's building. It's also possible he owned them.

Her grandparents had left the Old World because they'd been denied the right to marry or start a family, to own land, to vote. They'd come to a country that promised to "make amends for everything"—and in some ways it had: they'd successfully entered the Southern merchant class. But part of how they'd become Americans was by denying other people the right to marry or start a family, to own land, to vote.

How to reconcile that? In a letter to his in-laws in Bohemia, her grandfather wrote: "The feelings of the negroes are blunt, indifferent, and don't care for freedom." In Charleston and elsewhere, it helped to treat African Americans as less than human, to draw a line, to maintain a distance. If that separation helped you become an American, it also created a new kind of loneliness.

.6.

DIDN'T THE MEANING OF ASSIMILATION change, depending on where you were, who you were? The deal the immigrant couple seemed to have struck was to accept slavery and, in return, be allowed to melt: to be part of Charleston society, run a business, start a family. They had a son a year after the wedding. The mother was twenty-two. Another followed a couple years later. The children were born in America, therefore and presumably Americans. It was a crucial distinction, especially as divisions in the country deepened, including a resurgent fear of *Aliens*.

In the 1850s, a Protestant fraternal organization called the Order of the Star-Spangled Banner emerged in New York City. Members of the secret society identified as pro-American—anti, that is, immigrants and immigration.[1] They supported a twenty-one year wait before foreigners could become naturalized.[2] Starting with forty-three members, within two years the order would swell to more than a million, evolving into the Know-Nothings or American Party, influential enough to help elect over a hundred congressmen and eight of the nation's thirty-one governors.[3] In 1855, a young Abraham Lincoln wrote a friend: "As a nation, we begin by declaring that 'all men are created equal.' We now practically read it 'all men are created equal, except negroes.' When the Know-Nothings get control, it will read 'all men are created equal, except negroes, and foreigners, and catholics.'"[4]

More newcomers kept arriving. In the 1850s, as the nation's population clicked past 31 million, it added almost 3 million immigrants, some 2 million of whom were German and Irish Catholics.[5] Many now got off the boat and stayed in port cities, the percentage of people living in urban centers nearly doubling in the decade after 1840.[6] Charleston, meanwhile, was "not advancing much in wealth or population."[7] Periodic plagues swept through: smallpox in 1853, the next year a yellow fever that killed some six hundred, and in 1856 another round of yellow fever that took another two hundred and fifty.[8] That was the year the couple's first girl arrived.

She would grow up to be the mother of the woman in Minneapolis, the mother whose death would prompt the writing of the diary.

She was born in the midst of a raging national debate about slavery. That spring of 1856, the question was whether Kansas should be admitted to the union as a free or slave state. In May, Senator Charles Sumner of Massachusetts took the floor in the US Senate and gave a two-day long speech on the issue. In the process, Senator Sumner, an abolitionist, criticized the senator from South Carolina, Andrew Butler: "[H]e has chosen a mistress to whom he has made his vows, and who, though ugly to others, is always lovely to him; though polluted in the sight of the world, is chaste in his sight—I mean the harlot, slavery."[9]

Two days after Sumner's speech, South Carolinia Congressman Preston Brooks confronted him. "[Y]ou have libeled my State and slandered my relative . . . and I deem it my duty to punish you." It was bad enough to have attacked slavery but to do so by mingling the images of harlots and Southern womanhood pushed Brooks a step too far. There on the floor of the Senate chamber, the South Carolina Congressman beat the Massachusetts Senator with a gold-headed cane until Sumner lost consciousness. The Northern press, horrified, treated Sumner as a martyr to the abolitionist cause. But according to a Charleston newspaper, "Sumner was well and elegantly whipped, and he richly deserved it."[10]

Abolitionists framed slavery as a moral debate. Harriet Beecher Stowe's *Uncle Tom's Cabin,* which had appeared the year of the immigrants' New York wedding, made its appeal especially to women, who were seen as the nation's conscience. Howe has a female character declare, "The most dreadful part of slavery, to my mind, is its outrages on the feelings and affections—the separating of families, for example."[11]

The families being separated were Black, but abolitionists argued that slavery also undermined the domestic arrangements of Whites. As a Northern woman, a Jew, wrote in 1820, "One of the curses of slavery is the entire dependence the poor mistress is reduced to when she is rich enough to have all her wants supplied by numerous servants."[12] A Southern woman was not only dependent on slaves to help her with her primary job—"children, home and servants"—but in many cases, the husband fathering mixed-race children. Wives either had to pretend not to notice or admit, as one did, that she was little more than "chief slave of the harem."[13]

There's no evidence the paint store owner's family had these problems. There's also no evidence that they objected to slavery. A few Southern women had begun to, making a connection between owning other human beings and women's rights. As early as 1836, a daughter of Charleston's plantation elite, Angelina Grimké, wrote *An Appeal to the Christian Women of the South.* As she put it, "What then can women do for the slave, when she herself is under the feet of man and shamed into silence?" Two years later, her sister Sarah Grimké produced *Letters on the Equality of the Sexes and the Condition of Women.* The South Carolina diarist Mary

Chesnut believed most White Southern women were "abolitionists in their hearts, and hot ones, too." In Chesnut's view, "There is no slave after all like a wife."[14]

But the economy, North and South, ran on cheap labor, not equality. While some might take a moral stand against slavery, a free Black population meant having to pay people to work, to harvest rice and pick cotton. Prices would go up; the New England textile mills would suffer; American industry would falter. And the trade balance with England, which bought almost 80 percent of the South's cotton, would be threatened with radical change.[15] As an 1850s New York City merchant explained to an abolitionist, "We cannot afford, sir, to let you and your associates endeavor to overthrow slavery. It is not a matter of principle with us. It is a matter of business necessity."[16]

The paint store in Charleston depended on a stable economy and the regular arrival of merchandise from up North. The American financial system was, if anything, becoming more interlocked, more dependent on mass production and transportation networks. Speculators were pouring money into the railroad and other new technologies. Meanwhile, factories continued to grow, helped by the cheap labor of more and more immigrants. While America was still a nation of farmers (who would average, in 1860, about double the three-dollars-a-week female factory workers brought in), the dream was shifting—from forty-acres-and-a-mule to something more like the peddler's dream: own-your-own-business.[17]

Then came the panic of 1857. As in 1837, the bubble of speculation burst. As banks failed, railroads went under, and nearly 400 businesses collapsed in New York City alone. To Southern slaveowners, it seemed like a vindication of their refusal to modernize: while Northern industry staggered, slaves continued to fetch "extraordinarily high prices" even two years into the panic.[18] This human currency served as collateral for Southern planters and merchants, who owed New York firms some $200 million.[19] And slavery was woven—or lashed—into more than just the textile industry. Northern capital directly funded and profited from illegal slavery runs to Africa and Cuba.[20]

Businessmen like her grandfather's suppliers, his extended economic family, often defended the slave trade. According to one New York newspaper, the city's antiabolitionists included the "moneybags of Wall Street . . . great dry goods and commercial houses . . . [and] rich Jews and other money lenders."[21] This financial sector argued that slavery was inevitable and a historical necessity. In a widely acclaimed sermon delivered by New York's "most prominent spiritual leader," Rabbi Morris J. Raphall argued that the Biblical story of Ham proved slavery was "the oldest form of social relationship."[22] How evil could it be if Abraham, Isaac, Jacob, Job, "all these men were slaveholders"?[23]

On the other hand, Baltimore rabbi David Einhorn declared in 1855 that slavery was "the cancer of the union." As he saw it, "the old world is fast crumbling to pieces, and a new world seeks to rise from the ruins."[24] When John Brown raided Harper's Ferry in the fall of 1859, three of the twenty-two men who rode with him were Jews.[25] The action mobilized abolitionists and left Charleston in a state of "uneasiness and even of terror." The city bolstered its militia.[26]

In the midst of this rising tension, her grandparents' day-to-day life went on. A third son was born the year of the financial panic, a second daughter in 1859.[27] By the time her grandmother, the woman at the inn, was thirty-one, she was raising five children: an eight-year-old son, another six years old, their eldest daughter who was four, a three-year-old son, and a baby girl. According to the paint store owner, his wife "takes care of the business while I am busy with the painting." But South Carolina law classified a wife as a "feme covert," a woman legally protected by and dependent on her husband. She had no property rights and couldn't buy or sell in her own name.[28] A woman could make independent business decisions as a "sole trader," but her main responsibility remained childrearing, cooking, cleaning, sewing, supervising her servants/slaves.

Soon, the growing store and family moved, renting a commercial space right on King Street, with an apartment on the second floor. It was north of the College of Charleston, in a more commercial section where White residents outnumbered Black three-to-one. In a majority African American city, this block of Whiteness was accomplished by overlooking religious and ethnic differences. Their family's neighbor in one direction was a Jewish tailor; on the other side was the pastor of the church of St. Patrick.[29] The Irish now formed the city's largest immigrant population, followed by Germans. Jews were counted among the Germans; all were counted as White.

Who did her grandfather's paint store sell to? The most likely answer is whoever walked through the door. Accepted as White, identifying with the plantation owners but remaining *Aliens*, Jews were able to do business across the color line. Historically, "The Jewish peddler in the rural South," writes Hasia R. Diner, "may have been the only individual to enter the homes of Blacks and the homes of whites with the same goal in mind: selling goods to anyone willing to buy."[30] That often carried over to store owners; in the South, writes one historian, "Jewish merchants catered to every need of the African American community."[31] Charleston's 1850 census identified seven German painters, five Irish, thirty-six so-called Native White, and eleven free Black.[32] There were also slave painters (not counted in the census), hired out by their masters.[33]

If her grandparents dealt with all kinds during business hours, their primary social circle remained fellow Jews. Regular attendance at temple cemented connections, maintained tradition, kept loneliness at bay. Beth Elohim had grown to a hundred and five members—forty men and sixty-five women—led by a progressive German-trained lawyer who had "taken an active part" in the 1848 uprisings in the Old Country.[34]

Her grandfather was a loyal member of the congregation and sat on the board of the Hebrew Benevolent Society. In the mid-nineteenth century, there was little governmental help for the poor. The worry, as one Boston agency put it, was that "temporary aid might end in permanent support."[35] Charity was left to private agencies, usually revolving around a church or an ethnic group; the Hebrew Benevolent Society offered help to Jews in need, especially newly arrived Eastern Europeans known as "Polish" Jews.[36] Its motto was "Charity Delivers from Death," its official seal featured a skeleton with a sickle in one hand and an hourglass in the other.[37]

The paint store owner's family apparently fit right into Beth Elohim's mostly prosperous congregation. Their children would have mingled with the sons and daughters of local merchants, although only the boys would have been taught to read and analyze the Torah. Where the parents mostly spoke Yiddish and German and maintained an Old-World strictness, the next generation was exposed to a seductive American freedom. Charleston, after all, was a port, and running through its strict social castes, its racial segregation, its ethnic groupings was an openness that came from streets full of foreign sailors, out-of-towners, vendors.

Still, the city insisted on its social hierarchies. One of the only arenas where her grandfather could have met as an equal with Christians and other "Whites"— "the best example of Jewish participation in life in Charleston," as one historian put it—was a secret society: the Ancient and Accepted Order of Free Masons.[38] Charleston's First Masonic Lodge was established in 1736 and had its first Jewish member by 1753. In 1792, it participated in the dedication of the city's first synagogue.[39] Later, when the lodge started its Supreme Court of Scottish Rite Masonry, four of the eleven founders were Jewish, considered "a stunning example of assimilation."[40]

If it was assimilation, it wasn't exactly melting into America. From the outside, Masonic rituals appeared as foreign as Orthodox Jewish or Roman Catholic customs. Behind the lodge's closed doors, costumed men played out variations on supposedly ancient European rites featuring coffins, skeletons, burning torches, and various reconceived Christian symbols. The woman keeping a diary in Minneapolis wasn't privy to these secrets; women weren't. And she doesn't mention if her grandfather had been a Mason. But she knew the importance of the organization in her family's history, its role in building community, fighting loneliness.

Freemasonry had come out of seventeenth-century European stone mason guilds. Joining these proto-trade unions meant initiation into stone-working skills and other trade secrets. Fellow masons identified each other through special handshakes, passwords, ritual protocols. Over time, membership shifted from educated craftsmen to middle- and upper-class gentlemen.[41] Calling itself "the world's first religion," the organization claimed to transcend economic and religious differences. In Freemasonry, a man might be judged not by his background but his character.[42]

The Ancient Order quickly spread to the American colonies, where it became a testing ground for the concept of equality. New World Masonic lodges functioned as "schools of government." Members—at first drawn largely from the "mercantile elite"—wrote their own constitutions and practiced an early form of democracy.[43] The lodge was their laboratory; they called it a "sacred asylum."[44] Ben Franklin, Paul Revere, George Washington were Masons. By the 1850s, Masonic ritual had been "arranged to suit the American mind."[45]

Ceremonies differed from lodge to lodge, but almost all featured a ritual where the initiate overcame difficulties on a symbolic journey that climaxed with him being "killed" by elders and reborn as a new man.[46] "Who is this that comes into this holy sanctuary?" the elders would ask. And the lawyer or clerk or store owner would answer, "It is a lover of wisdom, and an apostle of liberty, equality and fraternity."[47] "[I]n Freemasonry," writes one historian, "the Jews of South Carolina have always taken a prominent part."[48] Here in the dark of the sacred asylum, Gentiles and Jews could at least act out the melting pot, emerging as brothers and equals.

Meanwhile, out in the real world, racial, ethnic, and political differences were tearing at the Union.

. 7 .

AS SOON AS NEWS OF ABRAHAM Lincoln's presidential election reached Charleston, residents poured out into the streets, demanding secession.[1] Lincoln had run as a moderate, intent on preserving the Union.[2] That included slavery. He'd expressed a "natural disgust [to] an indiscriminate amalgamation of the white and black races" and announced he had "no purpose, directly or indirectly to interfere with the institutions of slavery in the States where it exists."[3] The idea was to calm Southerners and appeal to Northern businessmen who maintained, "We want peace not panic."[4]

But the rumor up North was that a vote for Lincoln was a vote for freed Blacks —who would then come north and take immigrants' jobs.[5] It seemed to have worked in places; Lincoln lost New York City, for example, and New Jersey.[6] All of the deep South voted against Lincoln. Its economy depended on some 400,000 "masters" who owned four million humans worth some $2 billion.[7] At the time of the 1860 election, almost 90 percent of all African Americans were not Americans at all but slaves who, per the Supreme Court's 1857 *Dred Scott* decision, "had no rights which the white man was bound to respect."[8]

When Lincoln won, the *Charleston Mercury* wrote, "The tea has been thrown overboard, the revolution has been initiated." Within days, South Carolina's General Assembly passed a resolution that Lincoln's new administration was "based upon principles of open and avowed hostility to the social organization and peculiar interests of the slave holding states of this Confederacy."[9] In late December, at Charleston's St. Andrew's Hall, South Carolina became the first state to secede from the Union. The signers of the ordinance of secession were primarily planters and lawyers, the "slave-holding elite."[10] They were prepared to go to war—a war, as one historian put it, over "free versus slave labor."[11]

At Charleston's first public reading of the secession ordinance, "loud shouts of joy rent the air . . . Old men went shouting down the streets. Cannon were fired. . . ." The next day, there was a parade.[12] "We are divorced, North and South," wrote diarist Mary Chesnut, "because we have hated each other so."[13] It was like a family breaking apart; eventually, eleven states would side with South Carolina. But for those first few months, Charleston was in a kind of limbo, no longer part of the Union but not officially at war.

Then came the part the little girl would remember and recount: the bombing and capture of Fort Sumter. "[T]he combat," wrote one observer, "drew crowds from the most distant parts of the city to witness the fight, the whole eastern face of the battery lined with anxious spectators, following the ricocheting of the balls, with flashing eyes and excited tones."[14] After Sumter fell, the Union quickly put up a blockade around Charleston.

The plantation owners' wives still peeked out of their elegant carriages. Blacks, free and slave, still stepped off the sidewalks when Whites came by. And there were still services at Beth Elohim. But the docks were quieter. Ships leaving with cotton or rice had to run the blockade, hugging the shoreline, dodging the deep draft Union vessels anchored just off the harbor. A return trip with manufactured goods and other supplies meant the same. Stores that depended on northern products—paint stores, for example—soon saw their stock depleted.

On Charleston's streets, the assumption was that the war would end quickly and victoriously. Still, people began talking about plans to go elsewhere after spring planting. Many went inland to the closest large city, Columbia. Beth Elohim would eventually send its Torah and other valuables there.[15]

In May 1861 Union forces crossed the Potomac in Virginia. There, in June, the two armies skirmished for the first time. In late August, Cape Hatteras, North Carolina, became the first Southern port successfully closed by the Union blockade, and in November, General Robert E. Lee arrived in Charleston to assume command of newly formed coastal defenses.[16]

That month, Union soldiers sunk sixteen whaling ships in the mouth of Charleston Harbor to reinforce the blockade.[17] A diary kept by a German resident described the city as "very dark and gloomy. Our enemies appear to be increasing their forces all around us."[18] On the other hand, to a young Charleston woman from the plantation-owning class, that winter began "very gay. . . . There was no thought of anything but speedy triumph. . . ."[19] The actual fighting stayed far away, and a city store could still advertise stock that included three tons of Zinc paint in "25 lb kegs," three cases of Chrome Yellow, and three cases of Chrome Green.[20]

The worst blow Charleston suffered was eight months after Fort Sumter's fall and was apparently unrelated to the war. On December 11, 1861, a fire broke out near the warehouses at the intersection of East Bay and Hasell Streets. Some said it was caused by the cooking fires of "slave refugees."[21] First noticed around ten o'clock at night, it began small, but a strong northeast wind soon created "a Hurricane of Fire."[22] Since most of the city's regular firemen had become soldiers, only amateurs were left to fight the flames. Plus, the night fire took hold during low tide, limiting how much water was available. The flames raged in a mile-wide swath across the peninsula, consuming some five hundred and forty acres, one-third of the city. The spires of cathedrals toppled, the great meeting halls were gutted.[23] As her grandparents hustled the family toward safety, the glow could be seen by sailors on the Union ships miles out to sea.[24]

In all, some five hundred and seventy-five buildings were destroyed, mostly in the commercial section. (Seventy of them were owned or rented by Jews.)[25] One witness described the aftermath as a "scene of desolation and smoldering ruins."[26] What with the war draining resources and the blockade limiting supplies, few even tried to rebuild. "People are moving in crowds from the city. Carts are passing at all hours filled with furniture. . . ."[27]

Her family stayed—and found itself in a new economy. With virtually all manufactured goods, medicines, and all but the most basic foods snuck in through the blockade, the black market quickly became the only market.

From just before the fire in late 1861 to mid-1863, thirty-six ships managed a total of some 125 trips, an average of a couple a week.[28] At least five new trading companies formed to take advantage. William Bee Importing and Exporting enlisted 245 stockholders, twenty-six of whom were German businessmen, *Aliens* able to move in when old money abandoned the city. Profits for these black-market companies ran to nearly 150 percent.[29]

Charleston became "a center for privateering," with a fleet of privately owned ships. "They are seldom captured," a British observer noted, "and charge an enormous price for passengers and freight."[30] *Isabel,* a steamer that had helped evacuate the Federal troops from Fort Sumter, belonged to Moses Cohen Mordecai, president of Beth Elohim. Mordecai was Charleston's most prominent "shipping tycoon," his prewar fortune made by importing fruit, sugar, tobacco, and slaves. The *Isabel* now went from being the pride of Mordecai's peacetime business to a successful pirate ship.[31]

As the war wore on, the Union grip grew stronger, and by the spring of 1862, shortages were forcing more stores to close. "In these blockade times," wrote the *Charleston Mercury,* ". . . none but the wealthy can indulge in pure coffee. . . ."[32] According to a circular in the local paper, "The stagnation of business, consequent on the blockade, had already greatly diminished the amount of employment open to the laboring classes . . . The greatly enhanced price of provisions has still farther aggravated the evil. . . . The fact stares us in the face. Hundreds of families of our soldiers have not earned, and cannot now earn, the means of purchasing the necessaries of life."[33]

By the summer of 1862, Charleston was surrounded by some six thousand Union troops.[34] They tried to take the city in June but were turned back (with the son of Beth Elohim's rabbi killed in the fighting).[35] The governor of South Carolina issued a public resolution "that Charleston should be defended at any cost of life or property."[36] When General Lee was recalled to Richmond to become military advisor to Confederate President Jefferson Davis, he ordered his successor to defend Charleston "street by street and house by house as long as we have a foot of ground to stand on."[37]

Even if the paint store business had been able to get inventory, it had stopped making economic sense. All the able-bodied painters had either been drafted or fled. And between the fire and the war, there were no houses to paint. By September 1862 an observer noted: "All the furniture, stores, and indeed everything moveable, was sent into the interior . . . Two provision stores only remain. Many of the inhabitants reside about three miles outside the city, in barracks similar to soldiers."[38] This remaining population was placed under martial law.[39]

On New Year's Day, 1863, the Emancipation Proclamation took effect. Lincoln framed it, at least in part, "as a military measure," a way to subvert the slavery-dependent Southern economy.[40] Not long after emancipation, Confederate President Davis wired the mayor of Charleston: "[I]t is very desirable that all the citizens . . . able to bear arms and not subject to enrollment for military service should be promptly organized for local defense."[41] Her grandfather joined Company D of the home guard. It appears to have been the designated Jewish company, led by Andrew Jackson Moses, a prosperous merchant and slaveowner.[42]

Company D's volunteers considered themselves Confederates, as did most of the twenty-five thousand Jews across the South. In Charleston, some hundred-and-eighty Jews joined the rebel army; twenty-five of them would end up dying for the cause.[43] As historian and rabbi Bertram Korn later wrote, "No Jewish political figure of the Old South ever expressed reservations about the justice of slavery, or the rightness of the Southern position."[44]

Burnt-out Charleston had become an armed camp for thirty thousand Confederate troops.[45] In April 1863 the Union's fleet of ironclad ships tried to enter the harbor. Women and children were advised to leave.[46] Her family was among those who remained—her grandmother giving birth to their sixth child, another daughter. By the summer, the Union had increased its siege force by another ten thousand and was shelling Fort Sumter. Schools were closed; so were most churches.[47] A façade of normality was maintained with some groups of young people holding parties and going on excursions, but only four ships passed the blockade between July 1863 and March of 1864. It was hard for most residents to get even basic necessities.[48] "Prices are getting more exorbitant, even at auction" wrote a young member of the city's remaining elite, "the Jews outbidding all others and setting up a quantity of little shops. Toothbrushes at," and she underlined the outrage, "$2 each."[49] That was more than a worker's typical daily wage.

The anger toward war profiteers cut across partisan lines. On the Union side, in December of 1862, General Ulysses S. Grant issued an order expelling "the Jews as a class" from his military district, accusing them of "violating every regulation of trade."[50] A Jewish newspaper protested, asking what the reaction would have been "[if] any general of the United States had issued an order expelling from his command all 'Negroes' . . . ?"[51] On the Confederate side, while the *Charleston Courier* sympathized with consumers facing outrageous prices, it cautioned against blaming any one group of people, standing "earnestly and emphatically against any whole sale denunciation of Germans or Jews, or of German Jews. We have no more and no less opposition to an extortioner who happens to be a German and a Jew . . . let us hear no more abuse of a class as a class."[52]

Was her grandfather one of the "extortioners," part of the black market? Family lore maintained that they'd stayed in Charleston out of loyalty and Confederate patriotism. The South was their America; it had taken them in and made them "White." Her grandfather, the original immigrant, had now lived there for almost two decades. But the mere fact that the family came out of the war in good economic shape strongly suggests involvement in the black market.

Most of the plantation owners had left by now—their fine homes boarded up or blackened by fire—but the thousands of Confederate soldiers offered a customer base for all kinds of contraband. Bacon was already selling at a dollar a pound in the spring of 1863; a year later, it would climb to six dollars a pound. Tea could fetch twenty-five dollars a pound.[53] The "extortioners" bid on whatever items made it to the Charleston docks or commissioned their own blockade runners to come up from Nassau with fruit and clothing. One of the prized items was quinine, the common treatment for malaria. Where quinine sold for ten dollars in Nassau, it fetched five hundred in Charleston.[54]

Her family stayed even after Union guns began shelling the city in mid-August 1863. The Yankees' biggest cannon, the Swamp Angel, lobbed two-hundred-pound incendiary shells from five miles out. It aimed for the steeple of St. Michael's church, located the next street over from King, in the heart of the old downtown. On Christmas Day, 1863, 150 shells fell. It became the longest successful cannon attack in wartime history.[55] In what Herman Melville called "the rush, and the burst, and the havoc," another wave of residents left for outlying towns, and most who decided to stay relocated to the northern part of the city.[56]

Charleston's permanent population had dropped from forty thousand to four thousand.[57] Its remaining six thousand soldiers were surrounded by some twenty-seven thousand Union troops. The Yankees were no longer trying to take the city; the strategy was to keep the Confederate soldiers bottled up while Union General William Tecumseh Sherman began his scorched-earth campaign in Mississippi. Charleston waited, its streets mostly deserted. "The City here," wrote one eyewitness, "is in a very lawless condition, robberies and assaults every night."[58]

That was the landscape her mother grew up in. If prewar family life had been sheltered—a quiet, middle-class combination of Old World and Southern propriety —those routines had long since been broken. There was no school for the six kids, no place outdoors that was safe to play, no getting together with other families in quiet parlors, no temple. Instead, bombs fell; soldiers marched; block after block stood empty. The city's elaborate system of social differences had largely dissolved; now everything was intermingled and temporary. To a seven-year-old girl, it must have felt both terrifying and exciting. The one real constant and the only real safety was in family.

In September 1864, General Sherman captured and burnt Atlanta. In mid-November, he started his march across Georgia to the sea. Many thought Charleston would be his first target. The city called for more troops, but General Lee and the Confederate Army were in Virginia, defending their capitol of Richmond. On December 21, 1864, Sherman took Savannah, a hundred miles south of Charleston, then began advancing up the coast. "The whole army," Sherman wrote, "is crazy to be turned loose in Carolina."[59]

Almost all "affluent townspeople" had now left.[60] As her mother remembered it, years later, the family was on the verge of leaving themselves when, on the night of February 17, 1865, Sherman set fire to Columbia, South Carolina. Two-thirds of it burned.[61] That night, Confederate authorities decided to abandon Charleston. The retreating Confederate troops torched warehouses of rice and cotton, blew up the railroad depot, spiked cannons, sunk gunboats. The fires they lit raged out of control, consuming four square miles. Some 150 civilians died.[62]

The next day, the first Union troops entered the abandoned city. Five years earlier, it had been White Confederates celebrating secession; now, to underline what the war had been fought for, the Union army was led by "colored troops." They marched through town "with the Old Flag above them," as a Northern reporter wrote, "keeping step to freedom's drum beat, up the grass-green street, past the slave shambles. . . ."[63] They marched by deserted planters' houses, windows broken, columns toppled.[64] "The streets looked as if piled with diamonds," wrote one observer, "the glass lay shivered so thick on the ground."[65]

Charleston's liberated Black population greeted the troops with "cheers, blessings, prayers, and songs." They sang "John Brown's Body" and "The Battle Cry of Freedom." "The white population," a Union soldier recalled, "remained within their homes, but curiosity led even them to peep through the blinds at the 'black Yankees.'"[66]

In the coming days, freed slaves occupied some of the elegant homes in a delirium of emancipation and possibility. Black Charleston soon organized a welcoming parade. Four thousand Black families walked alongside representative tradesmen: Black barbers, Black tailors, Black painters. Marchers carried a banner, "We Know No Masters but Ourselves"; at the end of the line came a horse-drawn wagon bearing a coffin with the sign, "Slavery Is Dead."[67]

At Gettysburg, Lincoln had declared that the United States remained dedicated to the proposition that all men are created equal—and that the Civil War was being fought for "a new birth of freedom." The Black population of Charleston drafted a resolution of thanks to the president and the Union Army. But the population behind blinds (wouldn't that have included her family?) saw, as one witness wrote, "a city of ruins, of desolation, of vacant homes, of widowed women, of rotting wharves, of deserted warehouses, of weed-wild gardens, of miles of grass-grown streets, of acres of pitiful and voiceful barrenness."[68]

Both sides agreed the price had been horrendous. "Anyone who is not satisfied with war," said General Sherman, "should go to Charleston, and he will pray louder and deeper than ever that the country may, in its long future, be spared any more war."[69]

. 8 .

CALL IT A WAR OF FREE-VERSUS-SLAVE labor, and free labor appeared to have won. On April 14th, 1865, the Union flag was once again raised over Fort Sumter. That same day, President Lincoln was assassinated.

Up North, Rabbi Lilienthal mourned what he called "the first laborer-President." To Lilienthal, Lincoln's election had revealed "the full meaning of American liberty and equality. . . . [F]ollow his example, and we shall finally, and in fact, establish the equality of mankind."[1] Meanwhile, a Jewish woman in Charleston wrote in her diary: "God grant so may all our foes perish."[2]

Her grandfather was now in his late forties. He and his family had to remake their lives in a ruined city and a new culture: the era of Reconstruction. According to one observer, conquered Charleston consisted of Yankees, freed slaves, and "colored soldiers."[3] Its economy needed to be rebuilt from scratch. "The business district and the handsome residences in the lower half of the city were entirely uninhabited."[4] Local banks had no capital to loan; the railroads had been destroyed; both Blacks and Whites were out of work.[5] Compared to the year war broke out, rice production in the area had dropped by almost 80 percent.[6] And farm values were down over 40 percent.[7] Bertram Korn described the postwar South as "[a] soil returned almost to its primal wilderness . . . troops of childless mothers, widowed wives, and orphaned children."[8]

Most of the Jewish population had deserted the city, many for good. With the congregation of Beth Elohim "disastrously diminished by death, and removals and by the ravages of War . . . ," no services had been held for years.[9] The synagogue was described as "much disfigured by the explosion of shells . . ." windows broken, "[the] ceiling crushed in many places," the whole "dilapidated."[10]

Like other Southern Jews, her family had backed the losing side. They'd tried to assimilate into a society that was now in ruins. Still, the *New York Herald* observed, "It is a noteworthy fact that not an Israelite left with the Yankees."[11] Remaining members of the temple continued to speak in favor of the South's native rights, of "constitutional liberty," and of "vindication." They described themselves as "undismayed by our reverses, unconquered by our defeat."[12]

Her mother spent the second half of her childhood in a transfigured city. With victory, the Union had freed some four hundred thousand South Carolina slaves. Sherman, during his march up the coast, had ordered rice-fields "for thirty miles back from the sea" be used for "the settlement of the Negros now made free."[13] Some former slaves stopped working the Lowcountry rice fields to start their own subsistence farms.[14] Others headed for Charleston. Soon the city was, as one visitor put it, "full of country negroes"—who would help account for most of its modest increase in population, from some 40,500 in 1860 to almost 49,000 ten years later.[15] Where it had long been a majority Black city, now the majority was free Black.

The city's streets became an ongoing celebration, Black women dressing "in King Street style," Black men in bowlers. Whites were horrified. One woman visitor noted, "The colored persons are awful sassy in Charleston. They take the inside of the walk of a white person, and they insult you as quick as they see you, and if you say a word they make faces at you."[16] Another Charleston native remarked, "We very rarely go out, the streets are so niggery and Yankees so numerous."[17] Within a year of war's end, ten new Black churches had gone up.[18]

Charleston's Jockey Club had once been the site of the annual February horse race, a highlight of the plantation owners' social season. During the war, the Confederate Army had used it as a prisoner of war camp and a burying ground. In the first months after surrender, freed Blacks dug up the Union dead, reburied them with proper services, and set up a memorial. To further honor the dead liberators, on May 1, 1865, ten thousand Blacks (and some Whites) paraded through the streets of Charleston. At the front walked three thousand Black children singing "John Brown's Body." To the rear came the colored Union troops who had liberated the city. After the dedication of the cemetery, there was a picnic shared by citizens and soldiers. It was the nation's first Memorial Day.[19]

One resident sketched the city: "The houses were indescribable; the gable was out of one, the chimneys fallen from the next; here a roof was shattered, there a piazza half gone; not a window remained."[20] Rebuilding began, if slowly, which meant people needed supplies, paint and glass. Lee surrendered to Grant in April 1865; by November, the family had their store back up and running at 329 King Street. "Kept constantly on hand," it assured its customers, "a full supply of Paints, Oils, Varnishes, Brushes, Glues," as well as window glass, oil lamps, concentrated lye, and potash.[21] Wherever her family's income had come from during the five years of war, it had ended up with enough capital to restart its business and reconnect to Northern suppliers.

If the store's clientele was still a mix of White and Black painters, their relationship to each other had changed. More than a year after Lee's surrender, on the Fourth of July 1866, Charleston's Black population again celebrated their independence by massing along the Battery. Where the little girl had watched the bombing of Fort Sumter five years earlier, freed Blacks watched fireworks until two o'clock in the morning. A White resident complained, "The Fourth was a dreadful day for us on South Battery. The whole affair was an outrage which would not have been permitted in a civilized community."[22] The implication was that civilization—true civilization, anchored in slavery—had disappeared.

The new equality didn't go down easily. That week of the Fourth saw what was characterized by some as a "race riot." Colored Union troops had been named as the city's provost guards. Not only did White Charleston resent them, but White Union troops rebelled at having to take orders from Blacks.[23] Later in August, per an eyewitness, there were two or three weeks of "serious and bloody riots between White and colored citizens and troops," and incidents continued through the next year.[24] In September 1866, a Union general ordered Charleston's police to turn over their weapons or be arrested.[25]

In what remained of the planters' summer homes, many of the maids and drivers had simply walked off. Wrote one White family member in shock, "We are literally our own servants except for cooking."[26] Another observed how "[t]he owner of two hundred to five hundred slaves, with a princely income, has not only to submit to the most degraded employments, but he frequently cannot obtain them. In some instances, he has to drive a cart, or attend a retail grocery, while he may have to obey the orders of an ignorant and coarse menial." To the once powerful, this new equality was "unnatural" and a form of "social degradation."[27]

South Carolina's reaction was to pass, within months of the Confederacy's defeat, "Black Codes" (later known as Jim Crow Laws) reinstating slavery-like restrictions. If freed Blacks wanted to work as anything but a farmhand or a servant, they had to pay a special tax. They were forbidden to leave a plantation without the owner's permission.[28] By decree of Lincoln's successor, President Andrew Johnson, land appropriated in wartime was returned to White owners. And the Black Codes declared freed slaves couldn't vote. "This is a white man's government," is how South Carolina's governor described the state's 1865 constitution, "and intended for white men only."[29]

Late in 1866, the federal government passed a civil rights act that nullified the Black Codes.[30] President Johnson vetoed it, but a two-thirds majority of both Houses overcame the veto to guarantee all citizens—all male citizens—would have the legal right to vote and own property. The new federal law demanded that former Confederate states rewrite their constitutions. Some change occurred faster than that. In March of 1867, Black residents of Charleston successfully integrated the city's new horse-drawn streetcars—by riding them until resistance faded.[31]

In 1868, South Carolina's Reconstruction government passed a constitution mandating equality. More than half of the writers of the new constitution were

Blacks.[32] One introduced a resolution that "the system of legislation . . . will never be permanent until women are recognized as the equal of men . . ." but it was ignored.[33] The new Charleston would elect nine African Americans to its city council—the first Black aldermen in the city's history—and a White Yankee abolitionist as mayor.[34] At the Republican Party convention in Charleston, delegates supported laws reapportioning land, abolishing corporeal punishment, breaking up large plantations, and improving economic conditions for the small farmer.[35]

In July 1868, a fourteenth amendment was added to the United States Constitution, stating that "all persons born or naturalized in the United States" were therefore (and no longer presumably) citizens. In theory, this new definition of an American would apply to the entire reunited nation of some 35 million, including 150,000 Jews and all immigrants, both voluntary and forced.[36] Six months later, the fifteenth amendment guaranteed the right to vote "shall not be denied or abridged . . . on account of race, color, or previous condition of servitude." Again, in theory.

In September 1868, 94 percent of South Carolina's eligible Blacks registered to vote.[37] Women, however, were still excluded. That rankled abolitionists like Elizabeth Cady Stanton. "Tyranny on a southern plantation," she declared, "is far more easily seen by white men in the North than the ways of women in their own household."[38] She fumed that the vote was now available to "Africans, Chinese and all the ignorant foreigners the moment they touch our shore"—but not females.[39]

The members of Beth Elohim struggled to get back to the old normal. In 1867, one-third of the congregation was stricken from the rolls "for their inability to pay dues." The president of the temple, a wholesale grocer, had to resign due to "business embarrassments." What had once been the largest Reform congregation in the country was no longer big enough to support a rabbi.[40]

In postwar Charleston, Jews were still kept out of the "prestigious cotton and rice trade dominated by old Carolinians." But of the city's fifty dry-goods merchants, one-third were Jewish. As were one-third of its twenty clothing dealers. There were three Jewish druggists in town as well as a handful of German Jewish doctors, lawyers, and bankers.[41] According to a Charleston saying of the time: "The Germans own it, the Irish control it, and the Negroes enjoy it."[42]

Her grandfather became chairman of the reorganized Hebrew Benevolent Society.[43] The war had tested its motto, "Charity Delivers from Death." At the end of 1868, the Society's 112 members noted "an unusual amount of distress and destitution prevailed among a portion of our coreligionists during the past year, and that the Society from its limited means would only partially relieve this suffering."[44] A representative was sent north to raise funds from sympathetic northern Jews in Baltimore, Philadelphia, New York City.[45]

That the paint store owner had been made chairman was a sign of his relative prosperity. Four times a year, the holds of the *Sargossa*, the *Lockwood*, the *Gulfstream* carried merchandise he'd ordered wholesale from New York to be sold retail on King Street.[46] Despite the war, despite Reconstruction and the changing face of Charleston, he'd gone right back to his successful business model. The paint business itself, however, was changing.

One breakthrough came via John W. Masury, the New Englander who'd started clerking in a New York paint store around the same time her grandfather learned the trade. Masury patented a "metallic can" that could be "hermetically" sealed with a "rim or ring of thin brass or other soft metal" and easily opened with a pen knife. It helped make Masury paints a national product: manufactured and packaged in Brooklyn, then shipped by boat or the expanding railway system across the country. The new technology created a new market and helped usher in "enormous growth in the paint industry."[47]

Reacting to changing times, her grandfather's store added a new range of merchandise. He started carrying materials for gilding and architectural "Draughting," as well as wax to make artificial flowers and decal-like images that could be transferred to fabric and pottery.[48] Gauging by his inventory, the leisure plantation class was well on its way to recovery. He was soon doing well enough to invest in a small house, a couple blocks off King Street, that they rented out.[49] And to sit for a formal family photograph.

In the center rests the immigrant mother in a full gown with ribbons. The girl first spotted drinking beer at an inn is now a prim middle-aged matron. She stares straight at the camera, her dark hair parted down the middle, her hands folded on her lap, a look of quiet competence. To her left, her husband is a broad-faced, energetic man with big ears and a wide mouth, slightly uncomfortable in his dark suit, bow tie, stiff collar. Around them are grouped their children: the four boys behind and to their left, dutiful in their best clothes; the two girls to the parents' right, separated by their Old-World grandmother, ancient in her frilly bonnet. The girl who would become the diarist's mother is at the edge of the group. In her white calf-length dress, she looks like she's just run into the frame. She shows the broad, eager features of her father, including big eyes that look a little wild, a little angry.

The children had grown up in a rebel city first under siege, then occupied, then defeated. They'd played in the ruins of what earlier generations had built. Though they might still be Jews first, they weren't exactly *Aliens*. The question was whether they qualified as Americans.

In her diary, the Minneapolis woman retells an old family story. It's simple enough. One day, the boys—her mother's brothers—rowed out to Sullivan's Island, a few miles from Charleston's docks. Sullivan's Island had once been the port of entry and quarantine station for the region's slaves; now, like the rest of the city, it had been bombed to rubble: a perfect place for kids to explore. The day the brothers rowed out, a "terrific storm" sprang up. Hours passed. At home, their mother panicked, sure her children had drowned. It's true, the diary notes, "their boat almost capsized," but the story ends with their walking in the door, late for dinner but safe.

That's all there is to it. Yet the story got told and retold. Maybe their childhood was so regulated, so supervised, that this one adventure stood out. Or maybe there was something about the contrast between the immigrant's panic and the boys' calm, the Old-World mother fretting at home compared to her children out exploring the city, unafraid and on their own. Like American kids.

The girls in the family—twelve, nine, and six—weren't allowed this kind of adventure. They were being raised to be proper young ladies. A Charleston etiquette guide detailed what that meant. Where men could be "bold, arrogant, and self-willed," women were supposed to be "timid, confiding, and submissive." Where men went out to "court the bustle of the world and its loud praises," women were to "limit their wishes to the precincts of home, to the innocent prattle of 'little ones.'"[50]

In the latter half of the nineteenth century, women would go from being a tenth to a quarter of the national workforce. But in Charleston, a respectable girl was expected to stay at home, leading "a sheltered life, empty of worldly experience." When she married—usually in her teens—her husband became "the paramount Lord of her heart and her treasure."[51]

While the boys explored Sullivan's Island, the girls dressed in crinolines and lace that didn't allow for boating adventures or, for that matter, much outdoor activity. Taught to model themselves on "Southern women of the genteel class," they learned how to embroider and play an instrument, how to entertain guests and manage a household. When it came to the kitchen, they didn't so much study cooking as study how to direct others to cook. Her mother, the wild child at the edge of the family portrait, was supposed to forget the wartime world—the disruptions and the glimpses of a different kind of freedom—and prepare for a life limited to "the domestic circle, the school, the hospital, and the bed of suffering."[52] This was the female version of Southern "Whiteness."

Beth Elohim encouraged this return to the old normal. For all its reforms, it still believed "the primary responsibility of women was to attend to the needs of the family." Females were "exempted from all positive religious observations like communal prayer."[53] Though women could sing in the choir and teach Sunday school, temple decisions were still made and services still conducted by men.

Charleston had elected as their new mayor the northern abolitionist Gilbert Peabody, but the sitting mayor challenged "the validity of the election" in a controversy that went on for months.[54] The White ruling class continued to resist change. It looked in horror, for example, at the integration of public schools. As one resident put it, "the little nigger race shall be prepared to enter college, whilst our poorer white children are growing up in Ignorance and vice."[55] Many home-schooled or enrolled their children in all-White private institutions.

On the Black side of the ledger, workers tested the new equality by rallying for equal pay. In postwar Charleston, nearly 30 percent of the Black population worked as skilled laborers.[56] One author calls them "the avant garde of political activism in Charleston."[57] In January 1867, the dock workers struck, demonstrating on the steps of Charleston's central post office. With the support of other workers, this "Radical Union League" succeeded in getting a raise.[58] A year later, they did it again, this time calling for $2.50 a day and the right to overtime pay. Refusing to load rice, cotton, manufactured goods (like paint supplies), they won on both counts—though they got nowhere on their demand for an eight-hour day.[59]

Despite victories like these, postwar American wealth was increasingly concentrated in larger businesses. You could see the pattern in the paint industry. The new Masury cans meant product could be shipped farther, faster, and more cheaply. A readily available, more standardized national brand meant painters no longer needed to mix their own colors. As less skilled workers were hired, wages fell.[60] Industrialization was having a similar effect across the country, and people had begun talking about "wage slavery" and "white slavery."[61] At the same time, so-called common laborers realized that the fight for decent pay, reasonable hours, greater job safety didn't have to be waged one person or even one trade at a time.[62] In the decade after the Civil War, twenty-six national trade unions sprang up, including railroad engineers, iron molders, machinists, miners.[63]

In Charleston, in the fall of 1869, there was a "remarkable and heretofore unprecedented outcropping" of strikes, from the longshoremen to ships carpenters to tailors.[64] Soon, the city's "journeyman" painters were contemplating their own. The percentage of Black painters had climbed in the postwar city, even as the percentage of immigrants had dropped.[65] Crews were segregated, with skilled White housepainters getting the same as dockworkers had won, $2.50 a day, while journeymen White painters got $2. Meanwhile, the highest daily pay for Black painters was $1.75. The strike would call for a standard pay scale of $2.50 a day for "first-class" painters and $2 for journeymen—no matter their skin color.[66]

On Monday, October 25, 1869, Charleston's painters didn't show for work.[67] It was a rare example, in the South or North, of a biracial labor action. If the strike succeeded, Whites were liable to get more work (they wouldn't be underbid as often by "colored" painters), Blacks would get higher pay. In some ways, it would unify, if not integrate, the workforce, promising a new version of equality: if workers stuck together, they might all gain.

Soon, there were only "about eight white and six colored painters" still working. The strike was "orderly," according to one paper, and looked like it might succeed.[68] After all, the postwar rebuilding of Charleston was producing enough demand for workers to gain some leverage. The two weeks that the painters stayed out must have severely cut profits at the family store. According to the *Charleston Daily News,* the strike was "an attack by labor upon the proprietor just when he needs every favorable circumstance for the reestablishment of a business on which, not his support only, but that of his hands depends. . . . We are just beginning to live"; the paper went on, "capital is not abundant. . . ."[69]

As the family store sat idle, crew bosses waited to see if they would be entering a new era. In the end, the old ways were too strong. The White painters settled for raising journeymen's pay to $2.50 a day. That meant a kid just entering the trade had a chance to make a decent salary. With that, they went back to work. But once their White allies settled, Charleston's Black painters lost their bargaining power. They, too, returned to work—at the same wages.[70] For them, the brief moment of solidarity had gone for nothing, except maybe to show how hard real change would be.

.9.

HER GRANDFATHER SEEMS TO HAVE stayed out of the painters' strike. He'd worked hard not to swing a brush, to be a "proprietor," and his standing in Charleston society was based on maintaining a certain distance not only from Blacks but from workers, White or Black. As Reconstruction tried to alter the old social alignments, the family acted as if it could return to normal, as if the America that had accepted them still remained.

The small house over on Anson Street brought in some rent money, but the store was the main source of income. With its expansion, it was doing well enough not only to support the nine of them but to make it possible to host relatives, including the wife's seventy-five-year-old mother (brought from Bohemia), a twenty-two-year-old woman from Austria (to help with the kids?), plus an eighteen-year-old White servant girl. Then word came that the paint store owner's brother back in Bohemia was in failing health; could he send over his eighteen-year-old son? The Charleston merchant had become the extended family's connection in the New World, the immigrant who'd made it. His nephew arrived by steamer on February 2, 1869.

South Carolina welcomed the teenager for the same reason it had other immigrants, including the paint store owner. In 1870, the state had 416,000 Blacks compared to 290,000 Whites.[1] It was actively recruiting Germans and other Europeans to counter the newly enfranchised Black vote. The head of the state's immigration commission, a former Confederate General, declared South Carolina needed "men and women of her own blood and kindred." A local newspaper backed the call for "industrious, thrifty, enterprising white settlers." The hope was that within a couple of decades, the newcomers would help "throw the negroes into the shade."[2]

The arriving teenager had been born in Bohemia the year his aunt and uncle met at the inn in New York. As they were establishing themselves in Charleston, he was doing well enough in elementary school to qualify for further study. He never talked much about his childhood. There were memories of village May Pole dances, of how delicious the local peaches were, and of how "the peasants all loved the emperor, Franz Joseph." That last hinted at his politics. Franz Joseph became Emperor during the uprisings of 1848 and reigned under a new constitution which conceded "civic and political rights" were "not dependent on religion."[3] By 1860, Bohemian Jews were allowed to marry, to choose where they lived, to buy land.[4] Anti-Semitic riots had followed the reforms, but many Jews believed Franz Joseph's liberal benevolence had protected them from even worse.[5] For the rest of his life, the young immigrant had "a warm spot for the Germans."

According to the Minnesota diary, he never spoke of "the anti-Semitism or the injustice rampant in the German bureaucracy about which we read in the novels of Franz Kafka, [his] contemporary co-patriot." Kafka, born more than thirty years later, wasn't exactly his contemporary. And where Kafka's family were relatively well-off Bohemian Jews—he'd go to an elite high school in Prague, for example—the nephew of the paint store owner had to leave his village to further his studies in the nearest large city of Budweiss. With a population of around fifteen thousand, Budweiss was already famous for its beer—and its prejudice. Jews hadn't been allowed to live in the city for three hundred years. Though that changed with Franz Joseph, when the nephew arrived, the city was home to fewer than a thousand Jews and had no formal Hebraic schools.[6] Compared to Kafka, who lived at home in a cosmopolitan society, the nephew spent his adolescence mostly on his own: three years studying in a smallish city, probably boarding with relatives or at the home of his tutor.

Where Kafka went on to study chemistry and eventually got a law degree at the University of Prague, the nephew's possibility for higher education ended in 1866 as Germany declared war on Austria. The sixteen-year-old left Budweiss and found work for a year in a button factory in Teplice, northern Bohemia. There, laborers stripped and shaped mussel shells and ran machines that punched holes in pearls.[7] The teenager lasted about a year. In 1868, he sailed for the United States, hoping to leave behind the world Kafka would chronicle, a world of random justice, of mindless work, and nameless victims.

The teenager who stepped off the boat in Charleston was slight, with distinctive gray eyes, dark hair kept neatly parted, the beginnings of a moustache. His aunt and uncle were determined he'd avoid the immigrant loneliness they'd felt. They welcomed him, brought him home to meet his seven cousins, and immediately gave him work as a clerk in the family store. Not long afterward, when his father died in the Old Country, he effectively became the paint store owner's ward.

Of Charleston's nearly 49,000 residents, 12,000—roughly a quarter—were unemployed in 1870.[8] One visitor wrote that it was "a city, first, of idle ragged negroes . . . with no visible means of support." Almost as prominent were the carpetbaggers: "political adventurers from the North . . . fattening on the humiliation of the

South." And then there were the "Jews and Massachusetts merchants doing well on the semi-legal and negro custom."[9]

It's hard to tell if her grandfather was one of those—if his income came from the "semi-legal and negro"—but he was doing well. On top of some $3,000 in cash (about $66,000 in 2022 dollars), he owned real estate worth $18,000 (nearly $400,000 in 2022 values). That was far more than his immediate neighbors: a hardware store manager, a tailor, a locksmith.[10] His forty-year-old wife oversaw a household of a dozen people in their home in Charleston's Fourth ward.

In this crowded, welcoming atmosphere, the teenage immigrant learned English and the paint business at the same time. He was a polite young man said to have a "quiet, unassuming way [that] radiated an influence of cheer and friendliness and a wholesome spirit of reverence." He attended temple with his new family and clerked in the family store with his cousin, the owner's eldest son. The two might have been twins—about the same age and sharing the same name—except one was born in America, one wasn't.

A couple years after the cousin arrived, the family enrolled their eldest daughter, fourteen by then, in a newly organized private school, Miss Kelly's Academy for Young Ladies. Henriette Aiken Kelly had first tried to get the College of Charleston to admit females. When it refused, she'd started the Charleston Female Seminary for White Christian girls. The emphasis, it turned out, was more on "White" than "Christian." With many of the elite families still not reestablished, and tuitions hard to come by, Miss Kelly's accepted students from any respectable enough, non-Black family. That included Jews.

In the South before the war, only about 40 percent of the boys and 35 percent of the girls had some schooling; that was half the percentages in the North.[11] South Carolina had been the only Southern state without any public education system. Slaves were forbidden to learn to read or write, and though Charleston did eventually improve on the state's "pauper schools" for poor White children, it wasn't until after the war that Northern abolitionists set up and ran what were called freedmen schools.[12] When the 1868 constitution opened education to all races, a local paper made the point: " . . . with [Blacks] going to school . . . white people, if they wished their children educated at all, have been compelled to send them to private schools at much expense."[13]

Miss Kelly founded her academy "to establish a school for young ladies that should equal the best schools at the North."[14] Before women's colleges like Wellesley and Radcliffe, this was as high as higher education went for most "ladies." Miss Kelly's was one of Charleston's "fashionable schools for planters' daughters," designed to introduce them to the right families and groom them for their domestic duties.[15] But it also aspired to more, to "intellectual and artistic satisfaction."[16]

The year before it opened, Susan B. Anthony and Elizabeth Cady Stanton started the National Woman's Suffrage Association, supporting a Congressional "Equal Rights" amendment for women. Miss Kelly's was a Southern variation on this postwar feminist movement.

It opened in 1870 in a room in the founder's home. Within two years, the funds had been raised to construct a two-story building set back off a street opposite the College of Charleston, not far from the paint store owner's house. The classroom walls were lined with blackboards, while the girls' desks were designed to fold up so the space could be opened for calisthenics. The school's motto was *mens sana in corpore sano*: a sound mind in a sound body. The number of students in the four-year program quickly grew to a hundred and forty. It employed ten full-time instructors and a lecturer.[17]

Her mother, the eldest daughter, was the only one in her family to get this kind of schooling. It was impressive, first, that her parents had the money—then that they chose to spend it on education—and finally that the education was for a girl. From then on, her siblings "looked up to her as an intellectual," according to the diary, and she "never tired of talking" about those years at Miss Kelly's, especially the friends she made, "some of them descendants of the original Huguenots who had settled in Charleston a century earlier."

Wasn't this, then, the American promise fulfilled? The daughter of immigrant Jews getting her education alongside the children of Charleston's oldest and finest. True, Miss Kelly's was segregated and exclusive. But if the promise was less about equality than the chance to get ahead, Miss Kelly's stood as proof—for the girl student, for her parents—that this young second-generation American had been accepted.

As the fourteen-year-old started at Miss Kelly's, the immigrant cousin entered his own version of finishing school. In Charleston, he'd listed himself as being "in the mercantile business," but for a young immigrant who wanted to get ahead, the defeated southern city was history. By 1870, it had dropped to twenty-sixth on the list of America's largest, sandwiched between New Haven, Connecticut, and Indianapolis, Indiana.[18] A "minor seaport of little commercial significance," it had half the population of Louisville, Kentucky; New York City was almost twenty times bigger.[19] Staying in the paint business in Charleston meant either working for his uncle or competing against him. So, the cousin furthered his (business) education by heading to New York.

Three decades had passed since her grandfather had originally stepped off the boat. Many Jews were still housed in the two-story, wood frame buildings from Rivington to 14th Street on the Lower East Side, but New York was now home to 1.3 million people. Two-thirds of the city's 60,000 Jews identified as German or were the children of German-born parents, but that was changing as more Eastern Europeans were starting to arrive.[20]

Since her grandfather's day, New York's *Alien* neighborhoods had become even more established. According to an 1868 study, "[the immigrants] no longer as formerly melt away . . . they no longer conform to our habits, opinions and manner, but, in the contrary, create for themselves distinct communities, almost as imperious to American sentiments and influences as are the inhabitants of Dublin or of Hamburg."[21] There were vast Irish settlements, for example, where the residents led cramped, working-class lives, five times as likely to be without trade skills as the city's Germans.[22]

These distinct communities battled each other, as in the 1863 draft riots when New York had been the scene of a four-day "all out race and class war." Mobs of enraged White workers had targeted both the rich and the "colored."[23] The *New York Times* called the protestors not "white men [but] barbarians . . . every whit as ferocious in their instincts as the Minnesota savages. . . ."[24] 450 were arrested, 119 left dead in this "grimy slur on the Republic's faith. . . ."[25]

But the postwar economy depended on these barbarians. In 1870, one-third of the workers in manufacturing and mechanical industries were foreign-born, a percentage that would hold until 1920.[26] The worry was that industrialism was cutting back against the American promise, creating a "well-marked and persistent class," the working poor.[27]

At the other end of the economic spectrum, some *Aliens* were becoming successful to an almost unimaginable degree. For many Jews, the route was retail. The early peddlers had carried sacks organized into "departments"; later, when they established brick-and-mortar structures, they called them department stores. By the 1840s, there were almost 58,000 across the country. Since then, competition had led to expansion; the Mom-and-Pop operation grew into an all-purpose retailer carrying a vast array of manufactured goods, the so-called "Department Store Octopus."[28]

Macy's, "the largest store in the world," had the Straus family as key partners: Bavarian Jews, they'd immigrated to Georgia in the mid-1850s, then come up to New York after the Civil War.[29] Another Bavarian Jewish family, the Bloomingdales, came directly to the city, where their two sons started selling hoop skirts in 1861. By the late 1880s, their ladies shop employed some thousand people.[30] Stern's, Gimbel's, Abraham and Strauss, these family-owned operations ballooned into major businesses. It was happening outside New York as well. In Columbus, Ohio, Simon Lazarus, rabbi of Temple Israel, grew his 20' × 50' shop into F&R Lazarus and Company, occupying thirty-two acres of floorspace. The giant emporiums drew customers with advertised come-ons: "It Fits or You Don't Pay." Some offered a shoeshine with every pair of shoes sold, while others developed the concept of free home delivery.[31]

To make investing in this postwar expansion easier, legislatures eased the laws restricting joint stock companies. Banks floated notes to finance railroad lines to carry both manufactured goods and bumper crops of western wheat and corn.[32] New York emerged as the overheated economy's financial center, and there were soon major Jewish-run investment firms like Kuhn, Loeb, and Goldman, Sachs.[33]

So, the immigrant cousin arrived in a city where, as one observer put it, "Prosperity was written all over the face of things. Manufacturers were busy, workmen in demand; streets and shops were crowded, and everywhere new buildings going up . . . Prices of commodities were high, demand pretty good. Everybody seemed to be making money."[34] Riding this version of the American dream, successful merchants were moving uptown between 50th and 90th streets, some as far north as Harlem. Here, they built grand homes in newly created neighborhoods. The congregation of Anshe Chesed would abandon their relatively new temple on Norfolk Street for a modern synagogue on fashionable Lexington Avenue and 63rd Street.[35]

One observer of late-nineteenth-century New York City claimed, "the social line between the laborer and the capitalist is here very faintly drawn."[36] But if the cousin had come to the city to cross that line—to move from store clerk to store owner—it doesn't seem to have worked. In his two years in New York, he may have made business connections, but he never hit it big. And if he'd come north to strike out on his own, he didn't do that, either.

But maybe those were never his intentions. Maybe his future had already been decided, and these "finishing school" years in New York were simply so he could experience the big city and mature. Maybe he knew all along that his route to becoming an American was to return to the South and, at age twenty-three, open a branch of the family business. And marry the boss's daughter.

. 10 .

THE IMMIGRANT NEPHEW LEFT New York to open a paint store in St. Augustine, Florida.

In some ways, his move was like the original immigrant's, leaving the big city for a less competitive market. Except this was thirty years later in a rapidly changing nation; there was support from the parent store in South Carolina; and the nephew didn't do it alone, didn't carry the same loneliness. He went into business in partnership with his closest "twin" cousin—two twenty-three-year-olds heading into the wilderness together.

Plus, St. Augustine wasn't Charleston. The total population of the slow-moving coastal town was barely seventeen hundred people.[1] There was no train, and the mail was brought by a stagecoach that made three stops a week. The main way into town, a bridge, had been burned during the war. Now, you crossed the harbor and entered town on a beat-up scow pulled by ropes.[2] The streets were narrow, the old houses dilapidated, and one of the few landmarks was the downtown slave mart, abandoned.

While some optimistically called St. Augustine "the Newport of Florida," a visitor in 1870 claimed, "It looks as if it had fallen asleep when vacated by the Spaniards and had hardly yet begun to wake up."[3] It was a throwback to preindustrial America. Though their paint store might not face much competition, it would have trouble finding customers.

It didn't help that in the fall of 1873, as the cousins arrived in Florida, the overheated national economy blew. The credit that had powered New York's financial district blazed out; expansions and mergers ceased. In mid-September, the empire of Jay Cooke—investment banker, railroad tycoon, financier of Union war bonds—collapsed, followed by the New York banking house of Fisk and Hatch. Less spectacular, equally drastic, was what happened to more typical men and women. "The working people of this country," one observer wrote, " . . . suddenly find capital as rigid as an absolute monarchy."[4] The panic of 1873 began six years of economic depression.

It affected both the victorious North and the recovering South. In Charleston, some thirty-eight businesses failed, and three of its four banks couldn't make their payments.[5] In St. Augustine, the newly opened paint store closed. But instead of giving up all together, the young cousins moved their operation forty miles north to Jacksonville. Maybe a different location could counter the national economy.

Jacksonville, a sixteenth-century Spanish fort town, had become American in the 1820s. It was named after Andrew Jackson, the territory's first military governor, who had "opened" the land by driving the Indigenous people west on the Trail of Tears. In their place came speculators and settlers. One was Moses Levy, a Sephardic Jew, who snapped up fifty thousand acres to build a new Jerusalem.

Levy believed assimilation was a pipe dream. In his view, "Barbary, Turkey, Poland, the wilds of Prussia . . . [Jews have] tried them all, and everywhere found an enemy in man."[6] Born in Morocco, Levy had made his fortune in Caribbean lumber and shipping and now wanted to build "an agricultural refuge for persecuted Jews throughout the world."[7] The United States, Levy decided, was "the only place that Jews can look for an asylum"—not as citizens (a Jew who thought he or she was "Dutch, French or any other patriot . . . [was a] liar . . .")—but as permanently separate *Aliens*.[8]

The rich soil and mild climate around Jacksonville seemed ideal. With determination and plenty of capital, Levy established a series of communal farms based on "the spirit of neighborly consideration." Levy's so-called "Sacred Cause . . . reintroduced sugarcane as a viable crop; organized the first Florida development corporation; [and] was instrumental in establishing the territory's earliest free public school . . ." open to both boys and girls.[9]

By 1830, Levy's settlement had a hundred residents, about the same size as Jacksonville at the time. But there were fundamental problems.[10] "It is not easy to transform old clothing men or stock brokers into practical farmers."[11] To be viable, the agricultural paradise needed people who knew something about working the land. Levy's solution was the traditional one: to bring in slaves. So much for equality. The new Zion had disbanded by 1836.

When Florida entered the union in 1845, almost half its population consisted of slaves.[12] Moses Levy's son, David, became the state's first senator and the nation's first Jewish senator, though he changed his name to the less Jewish-sounding Yulee. A Jacksonian Democrat, Senator Yulee opposed his father's "religious socialism," opting for the more American ideal of individual achievement and the "cult of the common man."[13] Known as the "Florida Fire-Eater," he supported big landowners, bankers, and slavery, helping push his developing state into the Confederacy.[14]

In the decade before the Civil War, "North and west of the town was a forest of tall pines . . . [and to] the east as well as the south, there was a thick grove of oaks."[15] The St. Johns River connected the deep-water port to the interior, and the city became the center of the northern Florida lumber industry: live oak mostly, dragged to the wharves, much of it used to build ships.[16] By the time the first gas, telegraph, and railroad lines were put in, Jacksonville's population had doubled to a little over two thousand.[17] "The streets, straight and laid out at right angles, were of deep, grayish sand . . . ," the ones downtown "lined with splendid, moss-draped oaks."[18]

During the Civil War, Union gunboats laid siege to Jacksonville on four separate occasions. Mills, wharves, and many of the houses were destroyed. By the time the Confederacy surrendered, the city had become "a melancholy sight" filled with "the old ruins of burned buildings . . . [and] the dingy appearance of once neatly painted dwellings."[19]

If Charleston was the Old South, Jacksonville wanted to be the New: a projected vacation land of beaches and tropical jungles. Northern visitors were fascinated by Florida's tall, white-blossomed magnolia trees, stretches of dark pine, and understory of pink azalea, blue wisteria, sharp palmetto. But the standard of living—compared to Charleston or New York—was still primitive. "Prepare yourself," wrote one resident who lived not far from Jacksonville, "for to see a great deal that looks rough and desolate and coarse."[20] While there were orange trees and roses year-round, winters often brought a killing frost, and from July through September, the heat was "excessive."[21]

The success of the cousins' store depended on reconstruction, both the era of Reconstruction and reconstruction of the city's housing stock. A provisional governor told the "colored" population to return to their plantations and "call your old Master—'Master.'"[22] But in 1868, Florida, too, was forced to pass a new constitution which banned Jim Crow laws and gave the vote to Black males. This led to the election of the state's first Republican governor, who then appointed Florida's first Black Secretary of State. The paint store—and its owners—had to adjust to this new, enlarged definition of what it meant to be an American.

For many Floridians, it was too much. Especially those who believed that a true American was a White American. There were a couple of attempts to remove the Republican governor from office. When those failed, a new form of resistance sprang up. It was a society with some similarities to the Masons: secret handshakes and greetings, strange rituals and apparel, a hierarchy of leaders designated by exotic foreign-sounding names. The new society began with a group of Confederate veterans in Tennessee on Christmas Eve, 1865, and soon controlled much of rural Florida. Its goal: to reestablish the supremacy of the White race. It called itself the Ku Klux Klan.

By the fall of 1869, the Klan had killed nine people in the Jacksonville area, seven Blacks and two Whites. The number would eventually reach "at least 170 persons," ten times the figures in neighboring counties.[23] One target was a Jewish merchant known to be "generous in extending credits to Blacks farming their own land." The KKK told him to leave. "I would rather die than leave" was his response, claiming it would cost him $20,000 to abandon his business. Ridden across the Georgia border, he tried to walk back and was murdered in broad daylight.[24]

In the midst of this bloodshed, residents promoted Jacksonville as "a potential metropolis."[25] Boosters talked of the curative powers of year-round sunlight. Invalids and consumptives trekked from the North, as did investors. With the addition of freed slaves, the city's population rose by almost 13 percent in the decade after 1860.[26] Harriet Beecher Stowe—known as "the little woman who started the Civil War"—bought a plantation some fifteen miles outside Jacksonville. Looking for "a refuge from the [New England] March horrors," she was one of many snowbirds.[27] "[A]ll the north," she wrote, "seemed moving down on the South. . . ."[28]

Abolitionists like Stowe saw Reconstruction as the dawn of a new era. "We need to know, all of us, that, from the moment of the death of Slavery, we parted finally from the régime and control of all the old ideas forced under the old oppressive systems of society, and came upon a new plane of life."[29] But it was hard to conjure that new plane from Jacksonville's day-to-day reality. Stowe described the postwar city as attracting "the *debris* of slavery, washed together in the tide of emancipation."[30] Northerners investing in hotels and winter homes hired those ex-slaves for the toughest manual labor, and Stowe claimed that only made sense. She quoted a local White landowner, "The negro constitution allowed them to undergo with less suffering and damage the severe exposure and toils." According to Stowe, it was not only the freedpeople's "gayety and good nature" that made them excellent workers, but "their docility, and perfect subjection to discipline."[31] It was an argument not much different from the KKK's and, two hundred years earlier, the first owners of rice plantations.

Jacksonville had started calling itself "The Winter City in a Summer Land."[32] Its waterfront was crowded with schooners, paddle wheelers, and steamships with regular routes to Savannah, Charleston, New York. The cousins hoped its boom was just beginning. Their store opened during a period when, as one economist put it, "The middleman came to be the dominant figure in industry." As manufacturers turned out more product, wholesale jobbers stocked the shelves in new markets like Florida. During the 1873 panic and the depression that followed, retail stores remained a key link in the distribution chain.[33]

Around the cousins' paint store, Jacksonville grew to over seven thousand, with plans for more elegant homes and hotels.[34] All those new buildings needed painting. And painters. A good deal of the work was done by skilled Blacks, trained as slaves and now functioning as free men of color. "When I was a child," wrote Black writer and activist, James Weldon Johnson, a native of Jacksonville, "I didn't know that there existed such a thing as a white carpenter or bricklayer or painter or plasterer or tinner."[35] Like the parent store in Charleston, it seems likely the cousins' business prospered thanks in part to its Black clientele.

Jacksonville's Jewish community was too small for a synagogue, but it established a cemetery, which meant the ceremonies for the dead could be conducted locally.[36] By 1871, the city had eighteen Jewish families, the most in the state of Florida at the time. The small but established society of Prussian and German Jews was prosperous enough to organize its own Benevolent Society to collect funds "to assist sick and needy visitors."[37] The young bachelor cousins became members of this community: business owners, fellow believers, part of the rebuilding process.

Back in Charleston, the store owner's eldest daughter graduated Miss Kelly's at age seventeen. She must have known from the start that she wasn't like her classmates, the daughters of landed gentry. Side by side, they had learned the same lessons, the same domestic skills, the same distancing that came with privilege. But her classmates had had their "debuts" when they were around fifteen. At grand balls in places like the Jockey Club, they'd been presented to society—which is to say, presented to eligible male suitors. Parental negotiations followed to guarantee suitable matches. In the nineteenth century, the age of consent for most American women was between ten and twelve. Well-off White women like the graduates of Miss Kelly's were typically married by seventeen, often to men twenty years older, men who had amassed or inherited enough wealth to "bid" on the young brides.[38]

For the Jewish daughter of a paint store owner, the end of school could only mean returning to her own, separate society. Instead of "coming out" with her classmates, she stayed in—in the small pool of Charleston's suitable Jewish bachelors. After graduation, her parents arranged her engagement to a twenty-three-year-old Bohemian Jew, an immigrant who'd only been in America four years but was part owner of a viable business. Her parents were confident he was a solid citizen from a good family.

He was, after all, their nephew, her cousin.

Cousins marrying was fairly common in nineteenth-century America. In isolated communities, there were only so many viable partners. In larger towns and cities, self-defined groups excluded outsiders—by religion, by skin color, by ethnic background, by income. The goal might be to melt into an American, but in the meantime, you stuck to your own. The free Black citizens of Charleston, for example, weren't permitted to marry Whites and often disdained marriage with enslaved people. As a result, the small community "was extremely inbred."[39] People knew the practice might contribute to mental illness, depression.[40] But the standards for a "suitable match" could become so limiting that only relatives passed the test. Thomas Jefferson, John Adams senior and junior, Martin Van Buren, Robert E. Lee all married cousins.[41]

The diary doesn't provide any details of the courtship. There's no meeting at an inn, no tremendous first impression. The couple-to-be lived in the same house for two years—she barely a teenager, he just entering his twenties. Maybe the attraction began then. Maybe they were considered too young. A couple years of separation followed, and nothing appears to have been formalized until after his successful launching of the Jacksonville store and her graduation.

Or maybe there was no romantic courtship. Maybe this in-family, paint-store-business marriage was a practical matter. He'd opened a new store in a relatively new city in a relatively new state. Compared to Charleston or New York, it was frontier living, where success would depend on the East Coast network of merchants, the smaller circle of Jews from the South, and, most important, the family business in Charleston. For him, the marriage offered a way of strengthening those ties. For her, it promised stability and security; she was marrying in.

It seems likely her parents had approved the plan when they helped set him up in Florida, maybe even back when they'd trained him in the paint business. For that matter, marriage might have been a consideration when they agreed to host him in the first place.

If their daughter had already been promised to her cousin when she enrolled at Miss Kelly's, her time with Charleston's elite was just a fling before she returned to her own, to her family. No wonder she reminisced about those few years for the rest of her life. In retrospect, they must have stood out as a period of something like equality—a chance to be, for a brief time, a different kind of American.

. 11 .

AS IF TO REINFORCE FAMILY TIES, they planned a double wedding. The daughter would marry her immigrant cousin, while her brother—the "twin" partner in the Florida store—would marry a Bohemian girl from upstate New York.

The ceremony should have been in Charleston. After all, one bride and two grooms were from there (and the Bohemian bride appeared to have no American relatives). But South Carolina law prohibited it. "No man shall marry his mother, grandmother," began the state's revised statutes of 1873, and went on through "brother's daughter, sister's daughter, father's sister, or mother's sister."[1] The alternative was a ceremony in Jacksonville, but the local Jewish community didn't have a formal congregation or a synagogue. So, they settled instead on a point halfway between. Savannah, Georgia, was an overnight steamer trip from both Jacksonville and Charleston. Home to a hundred-year-old Jewish community, it had a respectable brick temple and a new reform-minded rabbi.[2] The double-wedding took place there on November 1, 1874.[3]

Decades later, in her diary, the woman in Minnesota remembered her mother and father as a close but mismatched couple. She describes the immigrant as "a man of few words, of deliberate judgement, who often took my mother and all of us to task for letting our imagination run away with us. . . ." He had grown into a cautious businessman, a believer in facts and moderation, who worried about what might go wrong. "He always avoided being too sure of anything."

Her mother, on the other hand, was "very articulate and out-going—also impulsive, especially in her earlier years." She was the intellectual, raised in relative privilege, shaped and in some ways set free by the war years. According to the diary, "[she] never stopped living in Charleston." That formal society, the values of the old Southern aristocracy (as taught at Miss Kelly's), the way of life based on slavery, stayed with her. But if the deliberate groom and impulsive bride seemed like an odd match, the couple shared religious values and a passion for "things of the mind," for education and the written word. And both believed in a close-knit, loyal family.

After the ceremony in Savannah, the two young couples headed back to Jacksonville. To the conservative businessman husband, it was returning to a job half-finished: establishing the store, making his fortune, becoming an American. To his lively, American-born wife, it meant trading the polish of Charleston society for the relative isolation of a raw, emerging city.

With its customs house and US federal courts, Jacksonville was Florida's main port of entry.[4] While it boasted eighteen places of worship, a Masonic lodge, and a number of temperance societies, the business center was only a couple of blocks on Bay Street, which "turned its back on the St. John's River . . . [where] several rickety wharves jutted out into the magnificent stream."[5]

Commerce was fed by imports. The mayor had a store that sold imported buggies, carriages, harnesses and whips; he was also the agent for the Tennessee Improved Farm Wagon. Nearby was a pharmacy that stocked drugs, medicines, "fancy and toilet articles," brandies, Kentucky whiskey, and "the celebrated Florida Pine Tar syrup." There was a boot and shoe shop, a home-furnishings store that stocked everything from glassware to cooking stoves to kerosene lamps, and a farm store for fertilizer, grains, hay feed, and garden seeds in bulk. Jacksonville was too small for the phenomenon of the Department Store Octopus, but these one-man (or one-family) operations were little monopolies. The only viable alternative to buying a harness at the mayor's store was to have one shipped in by special order at considerable expense.

The 1878 Jacksonville directory would list twenty-three house and sign painters and one portrait painter; the cousins' place was the only paint supply store. Advertising as "Importers of and Dealers in Paints, Oils, Varnishes . . ." they also carried: "Glues, Brushes, Axle Grease, Window Glass, Doors, Sashes and Blinds, Sand and Emory Paper, Gold and Metal Leaf, Bronze, Pumice Stone, Artists' Materials, Rope, Twine, Kerosene Lamps, etc."[6] Their logo was a drawing of paint brushes and cans, but a historian of Jacksonville's early days notes that they also dealt in "Johnson's prepared Kalsomine [a white-wash manufactured in Brooklyn], whale oil soap and paraffin oil for orange trees [an insecticide]."[7]

The paint business continued to evolve. America's early New England exteriors had been mostly dark colors; lead-based Indian red was a favorite. Since then, there had been a move toward white and yellow (which especially made sense under the sharp Florida sun).[8] In Brooklyn, John W. Masury had come up with another innovation. After patenting the easy-open metal paint can, he devised a water-cooled mill, a "technology breakthrough in paint manufacturing" that produced a variety of quick-drying products and helped open up a whole new range of colors.[9]

Masury's (which would eventually occupy a full city block) manufactured its paints in a central factory, then transported them to wholesale outlets that distributed them to stores as far away as West Bay Street in Jacksonville. Green was the first reliably reproduced color, but soon there was a wide spectrum to choose from—and the colors were uniform, not dependent on the formulas of the individual painter.[10] A home or business owner now had options. And with less expertise required, the trade became more democratic: more people could afford paint, and it was easier to apply. The age of the Old-World craftsman, of guilds and trade secrets, had ended.

From Bay Street, a resident recalled, "the town extended back eight or ten blocks and straggled out on three sides."[11] The two pairs of newlyweds shared a house on West Adams, a residential street two blocks inland from the store.[12] They were active in Jacksonville's Jewish community, which grew from twenty-three people in 1870 to a hundred-and-thirty by 1880.[13] In late 1877, the Charleston "twin" became treasurer of the local chapter of B'nai B'rith. At the same time, his sister—the graduate of Miss Kelly's—was authorized "to receive donations for erecting a synagogue."[14] In the three years it took before the building was dedicated, the socially minded young bride helped lead the fundraising.

But the point of marriage was children. The accepted middle-class division of responsibilities was: males in charge of "worldly aggrandizement," females in charge of education, religion, family.[15] About a year after the double wedding, the Charleston "twin" and his Bohemian wife had a son. But there's no record of the immigrant and his Charleston bride having a child. It was as if they'd missed a cycle. When they did have a daughter, three years later, their business partners were having their second child, a son.

As the two interrelated couples raised their babies, they were joined by the next youngest Charleston daughter, who married Jacksonville's leading liquor merchant.[16] It was as if the center of the family was shifting to the Florida city, where the population would increase by over 10 percent during the 1870s.[17] Maybe it was easier to fit in, to become an American, as part of a growing middle class in a growing city. Jacksonville now boasted a half-dozen dentists and a dance academy; it noted with pride as more of its narrow wooden boardwalks were converted into proper brick sidewalks.[18]

The local economy depended on tourists: 14,000 visitors in 1870, 100,000 by 1885.[19] Northerners came down on the promise of a "curative" climate, investors for the cheap land. "One of the principal features of the city," its 1878 guidebook claimed, "is the hotels, of which there are many."[20] The fanciest was the St. James, with its ornate dining room, shady verandas, and a trained, uniformed staff of Blacks to wait on the guests.[21] Outside of town, wetlands were turned into orange groves, and John W. Masury himself would take some of the profits from his Brooklyn paint factory and buy 1,500 acres just across the border in Georgia.[22]

According to James Weldon Johnson, "Jacksonville was known far and wide as a good town for Negroes." In 1865, a speaker had reminded his audience that "the bone and sinew of the colored man" had built the city, giving them "equal title to enjoy and govern it."[23] Reconstruction saw Black policemen, Black members of the city council, Black justices of the peace.[24] "The negro children," according to Harriet Beecher Stowe, "are bright; they can be taught anything."[25] She lamented that just outside her Jacksonville home were "forty colored children without any means of instruction."[26] But her goals for them remained limited. "[Education is] all that is wanted to supply the South with a set of the most desirable skilled laborers."[27]

The South continued to fight Reconstruction and change in general. Charleston had elected an immigrant mayor in 1871, but he was a conservative German who believed in the old Confederate values. Those trying to alter those values—especially Northern abolitionists—were, as a Charleston paper put it, "[r]adicals not only demanding social equality—a doctrine repudiated by all the world beside—but [. . .] surreptitiously, yet effectually establishing Communism—the equality of goods. . . ."[28]

By this formula, equality was radical, un-American. And that belief extended beyond the South. The postwar Supreme Court ruled that Blacks could be Americans—did, that is, have the constitutional right to vote. But in the same year, it declared that women couldn't; that was a step too far.[29] And the presidential election of 1876 seemed to confirm that "all the world" repudiated social equality. The nominee of the Democrats, Samuel J. Tilden, pledged to end "the rapacity of carpetbag tyrannies in the South."[30] Opposing him, the nominee of the party of Lincoln, Rutherford B. Hayes, also supported the South's right to "the blessings of honest and capable local self-government"—an easily decipherable code for a hands-off policy on racial issues.[31] During the campaign, some Southerners tried to keep Blacks from voting. In South Carolina, a still-uncounted number of freedmen were killed; in Florida, Republicans nominated an all-White slate of candidates, and opposition voters were harassed, their ballots "lost" or disqualified.[32]

In the end, Tilden and the Democrats ended up with a huge majority of the popular vote, but Hayes eked out a one-vote Electoral College win, thanks to controversial counts in Florida, South Carolina, and Louisiana. A trainload of Republicans, sent to count ballots in Florida, was "ku-kluxed" along the way; twelve companies of federal troops had to be sent to the state capital to maintain the peace.[33] In South Carolina, armed White militia, known as Red Shirts, intimidated voters and stuffed ballot boxes.[34] Finally, in a secretly negotiated compromise, Hayes was awarded the presidency. In return, he agreed to remove federal troops from the South. As one observer put it, "Carpetbaggers to the rear, and niggers take care of themselves."[35]

To W. E. B. Du Bois, it was the end of "seven mystic years [when] a majority of thinking Americans in the North believed in the equal manhood of black folk." Florida's Republican governor left office in January 1877; the position would be held by Democrats from then until 1967. While Jacksonville was one of two Florida cities that still had Black political officials, with federal troops withdrawn, the experiment called Reconstruction—the idea of racial equality—became, as Du Bois put it, "nearly inconceivable."[36]

Only a dozen years after "free labor" had won the Civil War, this question of equality was also roiling workers. The panic of 1873 had left three million unemployed; by 1877, that had grown to five million.[37] Fortunes were being made in railroad monopolies, while the average brakeman and fireman took home thirty dollars a month, ten dollars less that the average unskilled worker.[38] On July 16th, 1877, when owners tried to cut wages another 10 percent, railroad workers struck—first in West Virginia and Maryland, two days later in Ohio, then Pennsylvania.[39] The protestors derailed trains and blocked freight deliveries. It was a wildcat action without formal leadership or an organizing union.

In less than a week, what's been called the Great Upheaval spread from 80,000 striking railroad workers to some 500,000 in other fields—all demanding better pay and shorter hours.[40] "The singular part of the disturbances," the *Baltimore Sun* noted, "is the very active part taken by the women. . . . Better to starve outright, they say, then to die by slow starvation."[41] The target became ownership in general and "the extremes of wealth and poverty," as the *Chicago Tribune* put it, " . . . a fact to tempt disorder."[42] The *New York Herald* blamed the Upheaval "on immigrants, "men [sic] incapable of understanding our ideas and principles."[43] Meanwhile, prolabor journals compared the Industrial Age's "combined power of capital, protected by monopolies" to the Old World's "regal power and its proud aristocracy."[44] At a mass strike meeting in New York, a speaker railed against the bosses and proclaimed, "Hereafter, there shall be no north, no south, no east, no west, only one land of labor."[45]

The Governor of Pennsylvania wrote President Hayes that the disturbances had "assumed the character of a general insurrection" and asked for federal troops to quell it.[46] The President—who had gotten into office, in part, by promising to pull soldiers enforcing civil rights in the South—now deployed them to stop the strikes. Six protestors were shot and killed in Scranton, eighteen in Chicago, twenty in Pittsburgh.[47] Within days, the Great Upheaval had been put down—at a cost of over a hundred lives.[48] But the insurrection had revealed a new toughness among industrial workers. And raised the specter that America, the "Great Republic of the West," was turning into a "European country, with its castes and fixed hierarchies."[49]

To the young couples in Florida, it must have seemed possible to avoid these larger issues by staying within the buffer of the family, the paint business, Jacksonville's relative prosperity. If that contributed to a certain isolation, a loneliness, maybe that was part of the price of progress. Jacksonville was looking to the future. There was talk of dredging the St. John's River, of hundred-and-twenty-foot steamboats that could carry fifteen hundred passengers, of connections to new railroad lines, of telephone service. The partners in the store donated paint to the construction of the city's new St. Luke's Hospital.[50] Six years after setting up shop on Bay Street, they could see an even more prosperous day coming.

Then, just before the winter of 1880, one of the couples decided to leave.

It doesn't seem to have been because of any sudden decline in the paint business; it would continue, run by the remaining partner. And it doesn't seem to have been because of the changing political situation. They'd arrived in Jacksonville during the so-called radical phase of Reconstruction, had established a successful business as the city's African Americans were gaining equal rights, and had recently adjusted to the return of Jim Crow. Yet just as the city they'd helped build was about to take a major leap forward, the immigrant and his Charleston wife decided to abandon it for the North.

He was twenty-nine; she was twenty-four and pregnant, again. According to the diary, he "was influenced by some salesman travelling around the country who told him the prosperous future of America was in the upper Northwest." That may have been. Even with Jacksonville's growth, it was still a relatively small city, and a paint store there could only be so profitable. New brick sidewalks, new telephone service, a new synagogue were fine things, but with the six-year depression that had started in 1873 finally ending, there was a giddy national sense of opportunity. So, it could have been the lure of expansion, a basic tenet of the American economic system.

What the diary says is: "They left their first child in the South and then came North to Minneapolis with two children."

A first child?

Did that explain the three-and-a-half-year gap between their marriage and the birth of their daughter? If so, the diary doesn't say whether it was a boy or a girl, say when it was born, or give a name. There's no record of it in the census. And there appears to be no gravestone in Jacksonville's Jewish cemetery (where the liquor merchant and his wife erected a marker when they lost their two-year-old).[51]

Maybe this first child isn't in Jacksonville records because it was born in Charleston? That's where the mother had returned to deliver their daughter. But there's no record of it there, either. The only evidence that the child ever existed is the sentence in the diary: "They left their first child in the South and then came North. . . ."

Active members of the Jacksonville community, the couple had been making a life—a family—in partnership with brother and sister, all three couples raising young children in the same city. They seemed to be accepted, on their way to becoming Americans. And then they moved. Was it because they'd had a first child, lost it sometime around 1879, and then decided they couldn't bear to stay in the same house, the same job, the same city?

"They left their first child in the South. . . ." There's no measuring the loneliness in that phrase.

Husband and pregnant wife depart Jacksonville, their two-year-old in tow, leaving the Florida business in the hands of their partner. They head to her parents on King Street in Charleston, where she delivers a son. Before continuing on, the travelers add the mother's twenty-six-year-old brother. He's been helping their father—now sixty-three—with the "Paint-Oil Business" and now passed those duties on to the third son, twenty-three. That's how business—how family—worked: everyone helping, all connected, the operation extending relative by relative. By the time they left Charleston, they were a party of six: father, mother, child and newborn, the mother's brother, and the immigrant's thirty-year-old sister, brought from Bohemia, most likely to help with childcare.

You could say they headed toward industrialism, toward the Gilded Age. The nation's manufacturing and distribution network was creating unprecedented wealth and a new business class. Some were aghast at the change; her mother, for one, continued to hold Charleston's sophisticated, almost European society as the model of real civilization. But for her father, the move north was a leap into the future. Forty years later, he would praise his northern "adopted city" and describe himself as "thoroughly American in spirit and interests. . . ."

In some ways, he'd always be a Bohemian and a Jew. But in the North, the past—including slavery, the KKK, the child left behind—all could be allowed to fade. In a nation of immigrants, of cultural and economic differences, maybe this was the key to becoming "thoroughly American." You go West (and, in their case, North) toward the frontier. You start over. You forget.

PART 2

North

. 12 .

THEY MOVED NORTH AS A FAMILY, as if the family was a kind of container, a protection. As if there was no such thing as loneliness.

They carried cherished furniture, their silver set, china, pictures, and other reminders of the South. But the North they came to was young, a place to start over.

Their destination, Minneapolis, shared certain similarities with Jacksonville. A decade earlier, both had been about the same size. But where Jacksonville had grown to nearly eight thousand people, Minneapolis was now over forty-eight thousand. And where Florida's expansion was pumped by tourist dollars, Minneapolis was driven first by lumber, then agriculture and commerce. Along with its twin city of St. Paul, it was positioned to be a hub of what was then called the Northwestern economy.

Nothing underlined the difference like weather. Minneapolis winters routinely saw temperatures below zero, with average snowfall almost four feet a year. They rented a place downtown on Fifth Street north of Hennepin Avenue, and their memory was of "snow covering much of their two-storied house . . . with, for heat, only a woodstove in the kitchen and a large stove in the 'Parlor.'"

Minneapolis was about to turn forty-five. The first settlers from the east had come around the time her grandmother arrived from Bohemia. They found immense forests crowned by white pine two hundred feet tall.[1] In 1849—the year before her grandparents met at the inn—the territory of about 166,000 square miles only had some 4,500 "Euro-Americans," roughly one-third of these of "mixed Indian and European ancestry." There were also an estimated 25,000 Dakota, Ojibwe, Winnebago, though Native Americans didn't count as Americans.[2] Soon, the last tribe had ceded the last of its native land, and the government began parceling off the wilderness at $1.25 an acre. What followed has been called "an era of speculation"; millions of acres were snapped up.[3]

An example was Nininger City, twenty-five miles south of St. Paul. The settlement began as a single log cabin occupied by a French-Canadian and his "Indian wife." By 1852, a few farmers had established themselves nearby. Then came the speculation. John Nininger, a Philadelphia businessman, bought the lakefront setting and proclaimed it a future transportation/industrial hub. The man he hired to persuade settlers of that—to move west, to start over—was one Ignatius Donnelly.

Donnelly was the son of an immigrant Irish peddler and an Irish American mother who ran a pawnshop in Philadelphia.[4] Donnelly headed west because, as one commentator put it, "Fortunes seemed to be dropping out of the skies, and those who would not gather them were but stupids or sluggards."[5] He and Nininger peddled real estate through a national advertising campaign. They took space in East Coast papers to describe the "large Commercial Town" their site was sure to become; they printed a journal that was handed out on steamboats; business cards were left in barber shops and hotels.[6] The job was to sell America on a new America, a new version of equal opportunity.

It worked at first. Nininger City's building lots, which had originally gone for $6 each, were soon retailing for as much as $200.[7] By late 1856, the town claimed a hundred buildings and a thousand residents. A similar, territory-wide boom pushed the area's White population to over 150,000, with the city of Minneapolis incorporating in 1856.[8] But between then and Minnesota becoming a state two years later fell the panic of 1857.[9] By the start of the Civil War, the only occupied house in Nininger City was occupied by Donnelly and his family. The national economic failure didn't blunt his faith in a new America, but it altered it. He would emerge as an antislavery progressive, no longer peddling building lots but the Homestead Act, "land for the landless."[10]

As the Civil War raged, the new state continued to grow. By 1862, it had 250,000 inhabitants.[11] An improved railroad system opened Minnesota's north woods to a new scale of logging. By the end of the war, lumberjacks and sawmills had deforested some 600,000 acres.[12] More than 89 million feet of timber a year was floated down the Mississippi in huge log rafts; one lumber company was filling over a hundred-and-forty railcars a week.[13] Between the displacement of native tribes and the disappearance of the white pine forests, the Northwest was "opened."

Farmers moved in. The cleared forests and plowed prairies were soon dedicated to a monocrop: "almost the sole occupation" of its farmers was planting and harvesting wheat.[14] As grain prices rose, the railroads expanded, farm machinery improved. The new state served as a breadbasket for the post–Civil War nation.

Wheat was to Minnesota what rice had been to South Carolina. But instead of forced African immigrants, speculators looked to Europe for workers. There, they handed out pamphlets praising the region's rich soil, its unlimited possibilities, its equality. German political insecurity, crop failures in Norway, and the growth of commercial agriculture in Sweden helped push immigrants toward Minnesota. By the time her family arrived from Florida, almost three-quarters of the state's 781,000 residents were either first- or second-generation Europeans.[15] And by the twentieth century, Minneapolis would be able to brag that it was the second largest Scandinavian city in the world.[16]

St. Paul, on the east side of the Mississippi, was the older, more respectable town. In comparison, Minneapolis was industrial, modern, business oriented.[17] In 1858, a canal was dug so that water from above St. Anthony's Falls could turn turbines on up-to-date milling machinery.[18] The milled flour was then loaded onto barges or railroad cars and shipped south and east.[19] The year the family arrived from Jacksonville, Charles A. Pillsbury (a relative of Gilbert Pillsbury, abolitionist mayor of Charleston) built a seven-story stone structure on the east side of the Mississippi River: the largest flour mill in the world.[20] Minneapolis became known as "Mill City."[21]

Together, the twin cities formed the financial center of the northern Midwest. The region's "empire builders"—the bankers, major merchants, political leaders— were largely White males from New England, the country's old guard moving west to assume power on the new frontier. As one writer described it, "Minneapolis is a New England town on the upper Mississippi . . . Yankees, straight from Down East, settled the town, and their New England spirit predominates."[22] They occupied the equivalent social position as plantation owners in Charleston.

Minnesota's farmers, on the other hand—as well as its miners, lumberjacks, railroad men, millworkers—all tended to be immigrants.[23] As early as the 1850s, St. Paul's working-class neighborhood of Lowertown was described as a "potpourri of merging ethnic boundaries and residential life," a mini-version of New York's Five Points. The mix included Irish, Germans, Norwegians, Swedes, Jews and Blacks. Here was the melting pot. Except these "foreign-born laborers," as one social analyst wrote, "were less likely to achieve higher occupational status" than "native-born" Americans. They were "locked into this class structure. . . ."[24]

Between the New England bosses and the immigrant workers, the region soon developed a merchant class. Many of these—founders of the clothing, dry good, furniture stores—were German Jews.[25] At first, they headed for the more established St. Paul, where, by 1858, there were enough to found a temple.[26] In comparison, nearly a decade later, Minneapolis still had only two Jewish residents (both running clothing stores). By 1872, there were nine Jewish families and a scattering of single men and women. In 1877, three years before her family came from Jacksonville, the Jewish population of Minneapolis was still only 172.[27] This in a city of 47,000.[28] Though St. Paul had two synagogues by then, there were only about a thousand Jews in the whole state.[29]

So, her family arrived in an established city, with a going economy and fixed social classes. And they were established, too. "These early Jewish settlers," as one historian writes, "had first lived in other sections of the United States, and most arrived with some accumulated capital."[30] Her family came with money from the

Jacksonville business and probably some from the in-laws in Charleston. Her father already had a reputation as a retailer as well as connections to East Coast manufacturers. He could start over without having to peddle door-to-door.

With his brother-in-law, he set up the first paint store in Minneapolis. They took space in a building on Hennepin Avenue. Once an Indian trail, "hardly more than a muddy lane," Hennepin was by now a major thorough fare, soon to become a primary office district with new stone sidewalks, the city's first luxury hotel, and "the finest theater in the northwest," the four-story Academy of Music.[31]

The store's only competition seemed to be a local drug store that carried "Masury's celebrated railroad colors."[32] But her family established a larger, commercial operation. It started as an "oil house" selling "Machine, Lubricating, Kerosene," but soon became a "Paint and Oil house."[33] That first year, they took out a half-page in the city directory. Claiming the partners were brothers (it sounded better than in-laws?), the ad proclaimed in varying, attention-getting typeface: "Wholesale and Retail Dealers in White Lead, Paints, OILS, GLASS, VARNISHES, BRUSHES, ETC. ETC." It added in bold letters: "MIXED PAINTS A SPECIALTY." A local paper welcomed them: "The young men composing the firm are active, energetic, shrewd business men and will succeed."[34]

By this time, the paint business was about convenience, efficiency, choice. In 1870, Henry Sherwin and Edward Williams had started a manufacturing company in Cleveland. Two years later, they had over $400,000 in annual sales. In the next five years, they got their patent on the first resealable tin paint can and began printing their own labels and promotional materials. Sherwin-Williams' first successful ready-mix paint arrived the year her family moved North. It came with a money-back guarantee: "[T]his paint, when properly used, will not crack, flake or chalk off, and will cover more surface, work better, wear longer, and permanently look better, than other paints."[35]

According to a later biographical sketch, her father arrived from Florida "fully abreast of his times, as is attested by the leading position he held in his own business sphere. Yet he was big enough to be 'old-fashioned' in straight-forwardness, piety, and loyalty to the ideals of his youth."[36] The Gilded Age, with its robber barons and newly popular joint stock companies, concentrated wealth.[37] In the paint business, as elsewhere, mass production and a corporate business model were slowly enabling national companies to pick off smaller competitors. Her father's goal was to keep the "old-fashioned" quality of personal connections—with customers, suppliers, wholesalers—and at the same time take advantage of mass-produced, easily used product. It would be a modern, Northern store.

The family lived in the main Jewish neighborhood, within ten blocks of their synagogue.[38] Like the community that had gathered around Anshe Chesed on

New York's Lower East Side, the Jews in Minneapolis found comfort in their closeness. The year her family moved in, the orthodox congregation of Sharai Tov ("Gates of Goodness") put up its first building, a pale wooden multistoried building with minarets and oval windows. It looked foreign, vaguely Moorish, exotic. The community dedicated the building by carrying their Torah scrolls five blocks from their old meeting place. A choir sang, and the first three verses of Genesis were read.[39]

Despite the orthodox look of its synagogue, Sharai Tov soon joined the national Reform movement, eventually changing its name to Temple Israel. It had been sixty years since Charleston's congregation broke from Orthodox practices, and by now more than 90 percent of the synagogues in the United States followed reform practices.[40] According to a publication of the Minnesota Historical Society, a late nineteenth century Reform Jew tended to see him or herself not so much as a Jew who lived in America but as "an American of the Jewish faith."[41]

Her father became treasurer of the Jewish welfare society, donating to it regularly. Her mother became an officer in the Temple Sisterhood, which did much of the organizing for social events, Sunday school, fundraising.

The German-Jewish community in Minneapolis was small, close-knit, both part of the city and separate from it. Jews belonged to trade organizations, joined the city's booster clubs, supported the local schools and cultural institutions. But they were forbidden from joining organizations like Kiwanis, Rotary, the Lions Club.[42] "In those days," her diary recalled, "Jewish people didn't have a great deal to do in the general community life." They stuck to their own and, even more narrowly, to the family.

That changed radically in a single day. On the 4th of July, 1882, a train pulled into St. Paul carrying two hundred ill-clothed, ill-fed Russian Jews.[43] "[H]ere were not immigrants in the usual sense—Minnesota was well used to immigrants— here," as one historian put it, "were people in flight who still had the marks of persecution on their bodies."[44] They were fleeing pogroms that had begun after the assassination of Tsar Alexander the year before.[45] In a day, the Jewish community in the Twin Cities grew by 40 percent.[46] Over the next four decades, displaced Eastern Europeans made up "the largest stream of immigration in the history of the United States"—over 10 percent of all arrivals in America—and helped increase the nation's total number of Jews from 250,000 to some four million.[47]

To the already established German Jews, the Eastern Europeans were a reminder of a past many were trying to forget. A lot of these new immigrants followed the old path, starting out as peddlers. But unlike the German Jews before them, they didn't seem interested in assimilation, in melting. They were Jews first, Jews in exile; they didn't try to become American. The men could be identified by their beards, long coats, and broad black hats, the women by their wigs. They mostly spoke Yiddish and stuck to their own communities. In Minneapolis, the Russian, Polish and Lithuanian immigrants lived on the north side, the Rumanians more to the south.[48] They were clearly, proudly *Aliens.* They served as a not always welcome reminder that this was still an immigrant nation, that in some ways even the assimilated were passing.

While Minneapolis's population quadrupled between 1880 and 1900, the number of Jews would double to 5,000.[49] Temple Israel's German Jews had begun to move west and south, away from the city center and into what amounted to suburbs within the city limits. Some bought homes in an area called Sunnyside, where a marsh was dredged to make the recreational Lake of the Isles.[50] Her family bought a quarter of a block on Chicago Avenue and Fifteenth Street, near some farmland that would soon become Elliot Park. There, they had two structures built: a single home on the corner for the cousin/brother/partner in the store and a larger two-family for themselves; they'd live in one half, rent out the other.

Three years after the Floridians moved north, the Charleston grandparents followed. The original immigrant was now sixty-five, his wife fifty-three, and after forty years in the business, they passed the King Street store over to the oldest son remaining in South Carolina.[51] As a sign of their achieved status in America, the immigrant husband and wife each had oil portraits made. His—dark, serious— showed a black-haired man in a black suit and formal bowtie. With his carefully trimmed goatee, he looks less like a house painter, or even a store owner, than a scholar. To emphasize his respect for the written word, in his left hand, he holds a small brown book. The Talmud? An accounts ledger? The equally impressive companion portrait of his wife—the woman he'd met at the inn—shows a matron with strong nose and jaw, her dark hair neatly pulled back. In a high-necked, dark green velvet dress, she stares straight out with a no-nonsense gaze. Where her husband holds a book, under her left hand she keeps a piece of writing paper. Letter? Business note? Diary entry? The two of them make a somber couple: educated, serious, prosperous.

But they don't look like Americans. No matter how much they may have adjusted to the New World, these are portraits that might as well have been from the Old Country. There's no sign in the dark clothes, the books, the faces themselves, of this new race that was supposed to be the end product of the melting pot.

Their move to Minneapolis was not only to be close to their children and grandchildren but to take part in the region's astonishing economic boom. In just a few years, home and land sales in the area rose from $4.5 million to $27.5 million.[52] The aged grandparents bought a series of investment properties. They lived to see another grandson arrive in December 1883, the first born in the north. A year later, the Bohemian peddler—become painter, become store owner, become family patriarch—died. He was buried in Minneapolis, and his widow, who stayed on in the city, inherited his estate, including building lots in Minneapolis and adjoining towns.

The new *de facto* family patriarch was the immigrant nephew. After fifteen years in the New World and four major moves—South Carolina to New York to Florida to Minnesota—he ran the most successful of the family businesses. In 1885, he moved it a couple blocks down Hennepin to a larger building on South Fourth Street. Here, on the city's bustling newspaper row, near the new marble arcade and red brick façade of the *Minneapolis Tribune,* the family store advertised itself as an all-purpose jobbing house, providing local contractors and house painters with paint, stains, washes, brushes.[53]

It was a rapidly changing business. Premixed paints had become the industry standard; within a decade of the family's move north, two-thirds of all US paints would be ready-made.[54] Down in Chicago, Sherwin-Williams set up a major plant and distribution center. Soon another company—Benjamin Moore—was experimenting with an interior paint that came in the cheaper-to-ship powder form: all you had to do was add water.[55] Minneapolis was a gateway for moving these new products west.

While there were still the other family paint businesses in Charleston and Jacksonville, Minneapolis was the largest and most prosperous. Its success would be described as "a monument to [the founder's] industry, ability and business acumen," but the founder gave credit to his adopted country, "the land of opportunity." Maybe all men weren't created equal, but if you worked hard and treated people fairly, you'd be rewarded. He saw himself as living proof of the American promise.

In their prosperity, the couple discussed bringing over his aging mother from Bohemia. Typical of their different personalities, "[Mother] talked much about it, enthusiastically picturing details of the trip, an adventure. As always," the diary goes on, "[Father] believed in waiting till he was sure." Before they could reach agreement, the woman died. But they did take in the youngest of his wife's brothers. Ten years her junior, he'd started working at the Charleston store when he was sixteen, then spent three years at a paint store in Chattanooga, Tennessee. He arrived in Minneapolis when he was twenty, and moved into the new family home, where he would live for the next dozen years.

The extended family was part of a neighborhood, a religious community, a regional and national story, but the focus stayed closer to home. When their fourth child, a daughter, was born in 1886, she was given a combined name that honored her two recently deceased grandparents: the patriarch from Charleston and the grandmother who never left Bohemia. She was identified, that is, by family. And would grow up in that protected world, cushioned by prosperity, defined by her history, part of America but kept at a safe distance. A half-century later, she would be the prematurely gray-haired woman writing in her diary: "Are all souls alone like me?"

. 13 .

IF MOTHER GREW UP DURING the Civil War, you could argue that her daughter, born in Minneapolis in 1886, came of age during the Labor Wars.

Part of what the Confederacy had rebelled against was the industrial future. In 1860, the nation had more slaves than factory workers.[1] There'd been little to no industry in the cities where the family had lived: Charleston, St. Augustine, Jacksonville. The role of the Southern merchant was like what it had been in the Old World: an accepted but tainted go-between. Real Southerners—real Americans?—worked the land. Or, better, owned land that others worked.

But that side, the anti-industrial side, had lost the war. Her family had decided to move toward the future, to Mill City, whose wealth was created through transportation centers and refining operations that employed thousands. During the 1880s alone, the Pillsbury Company added six mills equipped with state-of-the-art machinery.[2] The city's booming economy brought profit to its kings of industry and, via trickle-down, its merchants. An *Alien* paint store owner might be no more welcome among the city's old established Yankees than he'd been with Charleston's aristocracy, but at least business itself was respected. It was the lifeblood of the city and of Gilded Age America.

Industrialism brought new strains. A late nineteenth century study of Chicago's Jewish ghetto, for example, concluded "it is almost impossible to maintain the old family life in the environment of the factory system, dependent as it is on the surrender of the individual to the division of labor, with its long hours and employment of women."[3] Her family wasn't in the factory system and could afford to maintain a certain level of tradition, but it was different for those working the city's milling machines, unloading goods, driving delivery wagons, painting houses. They could feel the Gilded Age turning against them. "The people," as one Minneapolis observer wrote, "did not reap anything but disaster from the great bonanza. . . ."[4]

House painters might seem like holdovers from the old handicraft economy, but as painting became less of a skilled trade—as the family store sold more premixed paints and mass-produced brushes—painters became more interchangeable, like millworkers. Barrel makers, a similar semiskilled trade, supplied Pillsbury and other mills, but such an "expert workman who has regular employment" was finding his wages "insufficient to support [his family]."[5] The same squeeze that had caused the Charleston painters' strike of 1869 and the Great Upheaval of 1877 had grown more acute.

Over in St. Paul, trade unionism had taken root early, but in Minneapolis, businessmen, government officials, and law enforcement officers opposed any kind of workers' organization. From their perspective, a union was the opposite of the American promise: an impediment to the free market, restricting who could work where and for how much. Hadn't the nation grown great through individual achievement? Didn't a man who owned a business (and it was almost always a man) get to determine wages, hours, safety standards? Wasn't that what freedom meant, why people had come to this country in the first place? The leaders of Minneapolis prided themselves on a city where anyone could find a job, claim their place, start over. Their city, they proclaimed, was an "open shop."

In this new civil war of workers against management (or was it a continuation of the old Civil War for free labor?), most Jewish store owners were, as one commentator put it, "bourgeois to the core. . . . They saw themselves as businessmen on the way up the economic and social ladder."[6] The owner of a paint store, for example, treated his employees decently—with a kind of Old-World courtesy— and expected loyalty in return. Workers organizing, forming what they called a "brotherhood," could only interfere with business. Owners needed the "open shop" (others called it "right to work") to guarantee a profit that would, in turn, benefit all.

But as more immigrants arrived, as the labor force ballooned, wages dropped; safety was brushed aside; job security disappeared. There was always another warm body stepping off a boat or a train. Laws were passed to ban contractors from importing temporary workers, but tensions escalated.[7] In 1885, when the family's Paint and Oil House was five years old, Minneapolis's painters, decorators, and wallpaper hangers decided they needed to form a local "assembly." To organize more effectively, they joined a national organization called the Knights of Labor.[8]

Like the Masons, the Knights began as a secret fraternal organization. At its start in 1869, the Noble Order of the Knights of Labor was more social than political: a workers club. They adopted grand titles, elaborate uniforms, private codes. A Knight recognized another Knight by wiping the right side of his (it was, at first, an all-male organization) forehead, answered by the other wiping his left side.[9] But beneath the trappings of a secret club, the Knights emerged as a kind of national union. One of its founders spoke of the way capital "crushes the manly hopes of labor and tramples poor humanity into the dust."[10] After the Great Upheaval of 1877, the Knights' growing membership demanded more concrete action from their club. It decided to go above ground. "So long as a pernicious system leaves one man at the mercy of another," the Knights declared, "so long will labor and capital be at war." The solution? "Abolish the wage system."[11]

The Knights became "the most imposing labor organization this country has ever known."[12] It established its own, separate assembly of women workers, though the link between workers' rights and women's rights was still hard for many to make. As one female organizer put it, women had "the habit of submission and acceptance;" to change that, they needed to focus on "constant agitation and education."[13] In 1885, the Knights won a national strike against one of the leaders of the new industrialism, robber baron Jay Gould. The brotherhood's victory over Gould's railroad lines helped increase membership from 71,000 in 1884 to almost 730,000 two years later, when the Minneapolis painters joined.[14]

The local Knights' assembly of painters, decorators, and wallpaper hangers won their action, increasing their pay from twenty-five to thirty cents an hour and reducing the workday from ten hours to nine.[15] More importantly, they challenged the economic status quo, showing the city's open shop might be susceptible to union organizing. Businessmen, predictably, were horrified. As one city machinist dead-panned, "The employer was very much opposed to employees being members of the Knights of Labor."[16]

Strikes like this were part of a national call to action, a potential rebirth of the principle of equality. As Mark Twain declared in 1886: "When all the bricklayers, and all the machinists, and all the miners, and blacksmiths, and printers, and hod-carriers, and stevedores, and housepainters, and brakemen, and engineers and factory hands, and all the shopgirls, and all the sewing machine women, and all the telegraph operators, in a word, all the myriads of toilers in whom is slumbering the reality of that thing which you call Power . . . when these rise, call the vast spectacle by any deluding name that will please your ear, but the fact remains that a Nation has risen."[17]

Twain's list of workers left out farmers, but in Minnesota, they, too, were organizing. The wheat farmer had long believed he was being "systematically exploited by the railroads which hauled his produce, by the manufacturers who sold him necessaries, and by the bankers who granted him loans."[18] Around the same time the Knights of Labor began, a former Minnesota farmer and Mason was struck by how soldiers from the Union and Confederate armies had put down their differences in a Masonic lodge. He decided farmers needed an organization like that and helped charter the order of the Patrons of Husbandry, better known as the Grange.

The Grange brought isolated farmers together for education, debate, dances. As one Minnesotan described it, they gathered to hear "orators in barns, at huge picnics when whole families and villages came in buckboards, the women setting out a rich feast and singing 'The Farmer is the Man that Feeds Us All,' 'The Battle Hymn of the Republic' . . ." That sense of community, of common goals, left the farmers' families "shaking like aspens in the thunder of history."[19] The Grange organized cooperative buying and selling to compete against the big money interests and gave women full rights as members. By the mid-1870s, there were 25,000 chapters across the country, involving three-quarters of a million people.[20]

When, in the early 1880s, the Grange decided to back off electoral politics, Minnesota's farmers formed the Northwestern Farmers Alliance. Again, it started mostly as a social club, but in 1884, when wheat prices fell to their lowest in almost two decades, the Farmers Alliance became more political.[21] It met with the Knights of Labor, and the two groups issued a mutual statement of grievances and demands. Farmers and city workers weren't natural allies: the farmers, especially Scandinavian immigrants, tended to vote Republican, while the city's Irish immigrants backed Democrats. They were brought together by a coalition builder, Ignatius Donnelly.

Donnelly had emerged from his boomtown real estate fiasco as a self-employed author, lecturer, and populist politician referred to as the "Sage of Nininger." An antislavery Republican, he'd written letters to newspaper editors arguing that "any German who came to America in the spirit of the Revolution of 1848 should certainly understand that slavery was immoral."[22] After the Civil War, he lobbied for reconciliation: "We should cease to regard the South as a foreign country inhabited by our enemies."[23] He saw a new postwar America that would either unite, or fall into the evils of corporate industrialism. Donnelly's novel, *Caesar's Column,* depicted the distant year of 1988, when New York was an out-of-control financial center and the nation was run by a corporate oligarchy challenged by desperate workers.[24] Speaking at a Farmers Alliance rally in Minneapolis, he proclaimed, "There are really but two parties in this state today—the people and their plunderers."[25]

Donnelly became a key liaison between the Farmers Alliance and the Knights. He helped to hammer out shared demands for reform: to regulate railroads, to ban child labor, to establish industrial safety standards. He saw both traditional Democrats and Republicans as "plunderers" and became state leader of a third party, the Anti-Monopolists. "Wherever amid the fullness of the earth a human stomach goes empty," he thundered, "or a human brain remains darkened in ignorance, there is wrong and crime and fraud somewhere."[26] He lobbied against big business and for a more democratic government where "the state was supreme over all corporations."[27] Donnelly believed Minnesota could be the proving ground for this alternative vision of American equality.

The two established political parties responded by boxing the Alliance/Knights coalition out of the 1886 gubernatorial race. The Democrats simply dismissed its demands. The Republicans wrote them into their platform, but their nominee for governor made it clear that he supported big business. Still, when the votes were counted, the majority of Minnesota's newly elected legislators were Farmer/Labor candidates. While that didn't end the wage system or wrest all power from the old guard, it served notice that change had begun.[28]

"Open shop" supporters fought to maintain control. They broke the painters' union, for one, and wages were frozen or cut.[29] By the spring of 1890, one report estimated "probably four or five hundred painters in Minneapolis; they work nine hours and wages range from 15 to 25 cents per hour." According to a local paper, the reason the union hadn't achieved more was that "[the trade] literally swarms with unskilled men [so caught] in the blind, senseless competition for work, cheapness has almost become the prevalent rule."[30]

The threat of immigrants, of unskilled "lawless hordes," was used to squelch organizing. When an 1886 labor rally in Chicago's Haymarket Square ended with bomb-throwing and eight dead, business interests blamed "the communistic and revolutionary races" overrunning "the master races."[31] Looking back on this era, political theorist Hannah Arendt saw an almost religious quest. True Americans— patriotic Americans—believed in a "Christian and industrial civilization which embodies all that history has achieved" and saw "guarding vested rights as sacred." Progress itself was Christian; it was entwined with industrialism; what it had achieved should be considered sacrosanct. As each wave of immigrants arrived, "the law had to be confirmed anew against the lawlessness inherent in all uprooted people."[32]

In 1891, the federal government established a Bureau of Immigration to oversee the new *Aliens:* Eastern European Jews, Southern European Italians, Poles. But the Bureau was also empowered to monitor the 16 million "foreigners" already living in America who had come to consider themselves, therefore and presumably, full citizens.[33] In the heightened tensions of the Labor Wars, people began to question if residency was enough.

The painters of Minneapolis tried again. They joined a new union, the International Brotherhood of Painters and Decorators, founded in 1887. In 1890, having enlisted "almost every journeyman in the city," they composed a letter to the city's "master painters," the crew bosses who did the hiring and bought supplies from stores like her family's." We believe that a large majority of the boss painters in this city are disgusted with the way they are compelled to do work and the cheap grade of material they have to use, as well as the small wages they have to pay, on account of the low price they get for their work. How is it that in all the cities of the East they do far better work, use good materials and pay better wages and the bosses make more money than they do here? We claim that it is done through organization."[34]

It was an attempt to convince crew bosses that their interests lay with their crew, not big business. Joining with workers in a single unit would mean more profit for all: better pay, better materials, bigger budgets. It was like Charleston's post–Civil War painters' strike trying to get Black and White workers to overlook their differences for common concerns. And like the coalition of Black and Whites that, with the help of the Knights of Labor, had briefly taken over the city government back in Jacksonville.[35]

In theory, the plea to the crew bosses could also apply to a paint store owner. It was a call to take sides, to band together against corporate control, and a Mom-and-Pop storeowner might join the union side. Wasn't that, after all, how the store had been built? From the original immigrant in Charleston through the various brothers and sisters and cousins, they'd established a network of shared connections. The International Brotherhood of Painters and Decorators was proposing something similar: a union that functioned like a big family." Why can we not work together in harmony for the good of our trade?"[36] In theory, the harmony could include the workers, the crew bosses, even the store owners: the people against the plunderers.

"[T]he fruits of the toils of millions," Ignatius Donnelly proclaimed, "are boldly stolen to build up colossal fortunes for a few. . . ."[37] The painters' union and others like it were trying to reverse that. But what would happen to a small business if organized labor became a reality and succeeded in having a say in, or even abolishing, the wage system? For a family that owned a paint store—"bourgeois to the core"—moving toward economic equality seemed to threaten their "sacred vested rights" as Americans.

If Americans were, indeed, what they'd become.

As these issues swirled outside, safely within the walls of their home, their daughter learned to crawl, walk, speak.

. 14 .

IN HER DIARY, SHE DESCRIBED her childhood as a "time of gold."

An early photo of her shows a gray-eyed, big-eared girl with short fine hair. She began life on her family's side of the big, new, double house. There was her father—the cautious, precise immigrant who went off to work each day—her exuberant dark-haired Southern mother, her sister eight years older, two brothers six and two years older, and her uncle. All were supported and protected by the family business and beyond that, by the tight society of German Jews, which, for all the competition, gossip, and petty feuds, acted as a kind of buffer from the larger world outside.

When she was about a year old, her eldest brother died, age seven. Unlike the child "left in the South," he had a marked grave in the local temple's cemetery. While the infant death rate was declining by 1890, it was still around 15 percent for White children.[1] Thirty-one, her mother focused on her three surviving children and, two years later, had another baby girl.

The paint store became more dependent on large corporations. An advertisement from the spring of 1888 announced it was now a dealer for John W. Masury's national brand. "Every painter and consumer of paints knows that Masury's paints are the best in the market . . . [T]his is the only place in the city, where a full assortment is kept."[2] As it became easier for local distributors to get the "best" national products, competition got stiffer.

The antidote the family came up with was to produce its own. In one building, they continued jobbing, providing Masury's paints and other supplies. But now they took another space where the cousin/partner began manufacturing "Atlas" paint, specially designed to survive Minnesota's brutal winters.[3] "PAINT YOUR BUILDINGS WITH ATLAS Paint . . . the Best and the Cheapest . . . Can match any color at an hour's notice."[4] The idea was to jump from middle-men to producers. If the plan worked, they'd be less dependent on suppliers and might eventually become another Masury, Sherwin-Williams, or Benjamin Moore.

As well as the paint business, her father continued to take advantage of the real estate boom. He invested in building lots in a new residential subdivision and took part in land deals in southern Minnesota. His partner/cousin did the same. The cousin also became a founding member of a cultural organization, the Apollo Club. Built around its male choir, the Apollo Club promised to provide its members with "literary, social, musical, and other like entertainments."[5] The investments, the participation in cultural events, all served as signs that the business owners were Americans—and Americans who were coming up in the world.

In 1892, her parents had their last children, twins. Only one, a boy, survived. In all, her mother had given birth to eight children over seventeen years. Five would reach adulthood: the older sister and brother, the middle child who would grow up to keep a diary, and a younger sister and brother. With her child-bearing years over, the energetic thirty-six-year-old mother could see the day when she'd be free to do more of the charity work she enjoyed.

Her freedom would be bought. Part of her training since Charleston had been how to manage the help: slaves or servants when she was a little girl, freed Black domestics after Emancipation. Here in the North, with five children under the age of fourteen, she hired Scandinavian farm girls to help cook, clean, watch the children. Two-thirds of the Twin Cities' Swedish women worked as domestics.[6] They moved in from the country and, in their *Alien* Whiteness, kept the dark houses and prepared the heavy meals. "[I] finally taught [the maid] to call the girls 'Miss,'" the mother would write, "although for a long time she could not see the use of it." The use of it was to establish who was in charge; the result was to free up the mother to do other things.

She'd been involved in social organizations at least since raising funds for the Jacksonville synagogue. Now, following the path of many women of the era, she funneled her energy and education into what was known as the "club movement." America's democratic vastness seemed to encourage mini-communities—ways to connect, to share, to contain loneliness. Businessmen had the Masons, the Elks, the Odd Fellows; workers had their unions and the Knights of Labor; farmers had the Grange. As well as the Apollo Club, the city's German-Jews had formed their own "literary and social" organization, the Phoenix Club, whose fifty-five members gathered on Hennepin Avenue for entertainment—balls complete with embossed dance cards and live orchestras, whist parties, vaudeville shows.[7]

Post–Civil War, women created even more of their own organizations. By the late 1880s, there were thousands: the Woman's Christian Temperance Union, the National American Women's Suffrage Association, the National Women's Trade Union League, the General Federation of Women's Clubs, and scores of local variants from church groups to book and garden clubs.[8] The same way Freemasonry got discounted as an excuse for a Saturday night beer, the joke was that women's groups were just coffee klatches and gossip mills. But clubs offered one of the few ways for women to get out, to exchange ideas, to share hopes and worries. They provided a place to discuss the issues of the day, "a form of higher education" as one commentator put it.[9] In the 1890s, only a third of all college students were female, but there were now more girls than boys in high school, and the number of female teachers had risen from 90,000 in 1870 to 250,000 by 1890.[10] In connecting women, clubs helped create a national reform network focused on improving public education, libraries, factory conditions, tenement housing, child labor laws, the environment.

When their youngest child, the surviving twin, was two, her mother co-founded the Minneapolis chapter of the National Council of Jewish Women.[11] Its motto—"Service to faith and humanity"—sounded a little like the (Christian) Ladies Benevolent Society back in Charleston. But the Council's service went beyond charity.

It was born out of the 1893 World's Fair and a challenge by feminist and suffragist Susan B. Anthony. "[W]omen have been taught always to work for something else than their own personal freedom," Anthony told the World's Congress of Representative Women, "and the hardest thing in the world is to organize women for the one purpose of securing their political liberty and political equality. It is easy to congregate thousands and hundreds of thousands of women to try to stay the tide of intemperance; to try to elevate the morals of a community; to try to educate the masses of people; to try to relieve the poverty of the miserable; but it is a very difficult thing to make the masses of women, any more than the masses of men, congregate in great numbers to study the cause of all the ills of which they complain, and to organize for the removal of that cause; to organize for the establishment of great principles that will be sure to bring about the results which they so much desire. . . ."[12]

The National Council of Jewish Women was one response to that challenge. Though one of the more left-wing women's groups and "intensely prosuffrage," the Council declared a woman was "first and foremost a devoted mother."[13] According to one historian, Council was "a way to Americanize without sacrificing Jewish identify . . . to acculturate without . . . challenging the limited definitions of gender role. . . ."[14] Excluded from Christian women's clubs, with "Judeophobia" rising in the nation and attendance at synagogues dropping, her mother and other organizers envisaged a group that "devoted itself to the self-education of Jewish women," that took a stand against anti-Semitism, and that could help Jews in need.[15] As suffragette Maud Nathan put it, "Political equality appeals to the imagination of the descendants of Miriam, Deborah, and Esther."[16]

Three years after it was founded, the Council was in fifty cities in twenty-two states.[17] It mainly attracted well-off German Jews. "These were genteel ladies," one commentator notes, "with enough family income to allow them the leisure time and means to perform unpaid club work."[18] Her mother—graduate of Miss

Kelly's, the "intellectual of the family"—saw a way of getting out and into the world, of putting ideas into action. The middle daughter—seven when her mother helped found the organization—would remark: "I heard 'Council' morning, noon, and night."

The Minnesota chapter started with thirty-nine members. It was formed in the midst of a backlash against "foreigners." An organization called the Immigration Restriction League began lobbying to have all in-coming *Aliens* take a literacy test, a way of separating and barring those it called "historically down-trodden, atavistic and stagnant."[19] That included Italians, Poles, Hungarians. The National Council of Jewish Women, in contrast, supported "unrestricted immigration," helped organize settlement houses, provided job training, and sponsored leaflets to be handed to young Jewish women just off the boat.[20] "Beware," they read in English, German, and Hebrew, "of those who give you addresses, offer you well-paid, easy work, or even marriage. There are many evil men and women who have, in this way, led girls to destruction." Her mother was a signatory.[21]

An 1890s guide for immigrant Jews urged: "Forget your past, your customs, and your ideals . . . do not take a moment's rest. Run, do, work, and keep your own good in mind." It was, by now, an established formula for becoming an American: forget your past, start over. But even as Council members like her mother became more American, they worried that in forgetting the past, in melting, they would also forget their religion. In an 1892 US Supreme Court case, the court declared America legally and officially "a Christian nation."[22] Against that current, the Minnesota chapter of the Council initially spent much of its time conducting study groups so women could go home and educate their families about Judaism.[23]

As Mother devoted herself to Council, the middle daughter spent time with their boarder, her young uncle. In his early twenties, he worked as a traveling salesman for the family's business. "His room," she remembered, "was up on the third floor, next to the maid's room. He was very fond of me. I was his favorite. He would come home weekends and tell us of his experiences in the Dakotas held over by snowstorms." Young, exuberant, he was "demonstrative and perhaps did some things for effect." Sweeping the little girl up in his arms, he'd tell wild stories of an outside world that seemed impossibly far from their careful, protected community of German Jews.

When she was around ten, her uncle, now thirty-one, got married. After a dozen years as the family salesman, he started his own paint and wallpaper company—"Jobbers and retailers"—across the river in St. Paul. He was replaced by yet another uncle, the "twin," who closed the store in Jacksonville to come north. In addition, her mother's youngest sister also moved to the Twin Cities, eventually marrying the owner of one of St. Paul's leading dry goods store.[24] Thirty-five years after the Civil War, the family was now mostly concentrated in the North.

The emphasis on family, on staying within family, could be stifling. As liberal as her mother was on social issues, she maintained "from civil war days, ideas and sanctions" her daughter described as "antediluvian." They lived in a house full of massive furniture protected from the light by heavy window curtains, from human touch by crocheted antimacassars. Social life amounted to the temple and visits with those who shared their beliefs and values. "The fun when we were children," the diary reports, "[was] family get-togethers!" The uncles had wives and children. A notable cousin played the piano. "She always had secrets from us youngsters—secrets connected with boys."

Few outside people pierced this secluded, interrelated world. There were the maids, mostly Scandinavians. They looked different, spoke differently, had another life beyond the confines of the house. But within it, they were kept at a distance. They ate by themselves, slept in their own off-limits quarters on the third floor. During the long slow evenings in the library—when father and mother read and the children played games or sewed or studied—the servants might be the subject of conversation, but they weren't present; they were only there if you called and, then, just till their duties were done.

The other outsiders were the tenants. The daughter remembered how the "large, comfortable room in the front of our basement" was rented to a Swede, the "all service man at father's paint store." For years, he was in charge of opening the store at 7:00 A.M. for customers "[who] came to buy their paints for the day before working hours. . . . Appreciating his loyalty, [Father] had given him the free occupancy of the basement." He stayed, like the Scandinavian help, largely unseen.

And then there were the tenants who rented the other half of the double house. They were screened to be, if not quite of her family's status, respectable. The diary notes one family in particular that had a daughter around her age. "Nosey we called her because she knew everybody's business. If anyone lost anything or wanted anything, she knew where it was. . . . I remember her well—and her smile and her red hair and her freckles and her big teeth, far apart. . . . [S]he went on errands and did favors for everyone." The diary writer's younger sister had shown an early aptitude for music, encouraged by both parents. "When she practiced organ in a church late on a winter's afternoon after school, she was afraid to sit in the big old empty church alone. [Nosey] would go along and sit there with her."

The diary describes Nosey as "unusually bright and vivid." She had a way of crossing the family's strict rules of behavior. She was instigator, organizer, comic, and a somnambulist. "Each second floor [room] had a small screened-in porch. A low railing separated them. Sometimes at night, she would walk in her sleep, climb over this railing and waltz into one of our bedrooms. Mother would hear her and wake up and lead her back to her bed in her long white night-gown; her two long red braids hanging down her back."

When Nosey reached adolescence, she had "terrible pains in her legs and arms. Then the glands in her neck hurt and swelled. She wore woolen long underwear even in summer. . . ." When it got worse, "the doctor prescribed California. So her mother took her to L.A. She grew and grew those months."

The diary writer's parents decided their eldest daughter should go west, too. She had her own health issues: some breathing trouble made worse by the long Minnesota winters. "The folks thought it was a chance for her to live in a good climate for catarrh. They thought she might have pleasure out there." That was the stated reason. But she'd also come of age—old enough, that is, to "come out," to be courted and get engaged. Attractive, mixing in the right circles, she'd even fallen for the right kind of man: a respectable German Jewish merchant. Except he was ten years her elder. When he married a Wisconsin woman closer to his age, the older sister refused to admit she'd lost him. The parents decided she needed some time away.

But the trip west didn't help. "The atmosphere wasn't cheerful," the diary notes. "[My sister] had to work in the bungalow [and wrote] such unhappy letters that Mother had to go out there." As the diary saw it, the California trip cured neither the catarrh nor the infatuation. Instead, it underlined how the family's oldest surviving child was babied. "Mother always took care of her—petted her, went to her rescue when she complained . . . Mother, to the end, gave in to her." Big sister remained "spoiled and self-centered and selfish. . . . She was always a problem. Nothing that she did ever made her satisfied and happy."

Little brother, on the other hand, was a delight, unpredictable and imaginative. In the library of an evening, while the parents and the big sisters read, he drew pictures and wrote stories in his careful cursive hand. As a fifth grader, he had one of his stories published in the local paper. It described the time he was "snug and warm under the covers . . . [only to be] awakened by the shrill cry of 'Fire!'" He called to his mother and father. "They awoke and with me at their heels ran out of the house and into the open air." The diary claimed it was actually Nosey who had wakened people during a minor kitchen fire, but little brother's version had little brother as hero.

In another story, a year later, he wrote about "a very odd pet" he owned. "It was a little cinnamon bear cub which had been caught in northern Minnesota." His father built a shed for "Bruin," who became tame enough to run around the yard unchained. "As soon as I came home from school, he stood upon his hind legs with his front paws on the fence and sniffed my pockets for bits of candy or sweetmeats. . . . The neighbors' children came from all around to play with him." Soon, Bruin "grew to be too big and rough," started throwing the ten-year-old down on the ground, "and then we had to sell him. Many is the time I have missed my pet since."[25]

The newspaper printed the story on the first page of its "Journal Junior" section and awarded it a prize. Again, it was full of excitement and adventure, with little brother in the middle of it all. Again, it isn't clear how much is factual. Imagination offered one way out of a safe, predictable homelife.

The diary keeper's response to tradition and respectability was to dive deeper; she describes her adolescence as "very religious." She studied and followed what she later called "the old ritual and conventional Judaism." It wasn't as old or as conventional as in the city's Eastern European temples, which conducted orthodox "disorganized" services in a mix of Russian, Rumanian, Lithuanian and Polish. But during these years, "she was profoundly moved and stirred by the service of the Reform-Jewish congregation. . . ." She'd go to the sixty-five-member temple Friday night with her father, who was by now vice-president of the congregation, and her mother, who'd helped organize the women's auxiliary and ran a sewing circle.[26] They'd hear "intellectual sermons" in German and English.[27]

Years later, writing in the third person, she sketched a girl who "completely absorbed the beauty of the psalms, the idealism of the prophetic passages, the adoration of God. She didn't question. As perfect love seeks no return, so she gave her heart and soul and was inspired as only the young can be. She was like a violin played upon by the bow."

But the temple didn't provide a particularly satisfying part for the violin. While the National Council of Jewish Women was calling for synagogues to allow women full membership, the best their congregation could do was allow both boys and girls to attend the female-run Sunday school and be confirmed.[28] Still, she liked the feeling of inspiration, of giving heart and soul, of being played.

She had no apparent reason to be unhappy or lonely. It was, after all, the start of the American Century, the nation was prospering, and her family was carried along on the wave. Between 1890 and 1900, Minneapolis gained forty thousand people, bringing its population to over two hundred thousand.[29] That included eight thousand Jews. A local paper picked out their family business as "an example of the way in which many prosperous business establishments have developed in Minneapolis within a score of years."[30] Yes, it was facing competition from the Department Store Octopus—a downtown store was selling everything from "Ladies' Bicycle Suits" to Masury floor paint at fifty-eight cents a gallon.[31] But there was plenty of profit to go around, and the family got the benefits: stylish clothes, fine books, a comfortable home.

It was a time of gold in more ways than one. If her older sister was buffeted by health scares and caught up in her impossible infatuation, she also got to live a life of relative leisure, her time spent in drawing rooms and at small social gatherings. Her older brother was already preparing to follow his father into the family business. The younger sister concentrated on her music, and her little brother lived in a world of pet bears and daring rescues. If she, the middle sister, had her father's practical business-like attitude, she too had the luxury of studying religion. And as she got older, literature. "Writing," she told her diary, "may relieve me and may release the pent-up feeling in me."

Given the prosperous times, what was there to be relieved from? What was pent-up? Wasn't she free to do what she wanted; wasn't she an American?

The diary offers an oblique answer. When it returns to the subject of Nosey, it includes a brief glimpse of a reality beyond the golden glow. "[I]n California, [Nosey] had spinal meningitis and was out of her head. She screamed. She died at 16. I remember her," the diary adds, ". . . more vividly than I remember any single member of my family."

The person she remembered best from her childhood, her time of gold, was the neighbor with long red braids. Family was all around, seemed to be the very air she breathed, but as she entered adolescence, they were a kind of blur, blunted by comfort, all but nameless.

. 15 .

SHE WAS A GOOD GIRL who read good books.

"A good book," she wrote in tenth grade, ". . . is one which ennobles the spirit at the same time it broadens and enlightens the mind. . . ." Literature had a purpose; books, she declared, could provide "an incentive to noble actions," could teach that "injustice and cruelty shall bring on nations the wrath of Almighty God."[1] Religion had morphed into literature, and she approached it with all the devotion and intensity of a teenager. Combining her mother's sense of purpose and her father's business-like efficiency, she'd decided good books, like the Good Book, offered a moral education.

As her parents did, she believed the life of the mind elevated. It was a kind of corollary to the American promise. If all men were created equal, education was the way to separate from that equality, to get ahead. Her prime example lived just a few blocks down the street.

The Judge's home was a brick Victorian mansion constructed the year her family arrived in Minneapolis. It had a three-story turret on one corner and a stretch of pristine white steps leading to the main entrance.[2] Though the house was new, the Judge's family was old. It traced its roots back to an English rector, then an early American settler from Mayflower days, and finally a grandfather who'd fought at Bunker Hill. Born in Maine, the Judge had come west to start over after his family suffered "financial reverses." He taught himself the law, getting his degree in Illinois. After fighting on the Union side at Vicksburg, marching through Georgia with Sherman, and rising to the rank of Captain, he settled in the frontier of Minneapolis.[3]

There, he married one of the city founder's daughters and established a law practice. First, he became head of the Hennepin bar, then was elected county District judge. He soon resigned the judgeship (but held onto the title) to get back to his "extensive and lucrative" private practice. The mansion followed. Maybe education wasn't the only cause of his success. There was his marriage into a good family, as well as his British/Mayflower lineage—a lot like Charleston's plantation-owning class. But education became one of the signs of his achievement. The

Judge "reveled in the refined luxuries of culture, music, art, poetry. He possessed a choice library, literary as well as legal. . . ."[4]

The way the girls at Miss Kelley's had mesmerized her mother, the Judge's children appealed to the serious high school girl down the street. The Judge died when she was twelve, but the wife retained a certain glamor, "wearing a black widow's hat with white around her face. She was," the diary notes, "the epitome of refined elegance." There were a son and two daughters. "The younger one fascinated me. She had very brown eyes, quite close together. She was slender and of medium height. She dressed in suits and shirtwaists and to know her personally would have been for me the greatest of good fortune."

But she never did know her personally. The distance between the Judge's youngest daughter and the storekeeper's middle daughter remained. She caught glimpses of her neighbor riding by, "driven by a coachman in a carriage," but that was it. The Judge's family visited back east, spent the summers at their house on the lake, took two months for a tour of southern Europe. "To me, she was . . . living on a different plane of existence."

When the diarist was sixteen, the Judge's daughter married. Her husband was from the city's business elite, a treasurer at one of the city's biggest grain storage companies.[5] The papers reported on her long-sleeved white-satin wedding gown trimmed with her mother's "rare old point lace."[6] She went on to attend cotillion dances, was a regular in the local papers' social columns, and helped organize a "class in literature."[7] Then, seven years after marrying, "she and her husband," the diary notes, "were killed in a smash of some type—in her carriage, coming from a dance I think. . . ."

The newspapers reported they were heading for dinner with the Pillsbury family when their carriage was hit by a streetcar. Her husband sustained a concussion and internal injuries; the Judge's daughter was thrown from the vehicle.[8] They didn't die. Instead, the victims sued the streetcar company and received "the largest verdict for personal injuries" in the history of the Minnesota Supreme Court. But according to the papers, the Judge's daughter "sued through a guardian [her brother-in-law] having lost her mind as a result of [the] accident. . . ."[9]

The diary mentions none of these details. Instead, it leaves the Judge's family in the mansion at the top of the white stairs. "They were extraordinary people." They were who she wanted to be.

Her parents had taught her that the way into this different plane of existence was through learning. "My father was interested in things of the mind—in general culture. Often he and I attended lectures together. . . ." The family's devotion to education was tested her junior year in high school. Her hard work had gotten her to the verge of being named to the honor roll, when the city of Minneapolis changed district boundaries. It meant she'd be transferred to a different school her senior year and potentially lose her academic standing. "My father, to whom education meant a very great deal, picked up his family and moved across the street." The big house they'd built was put up for rent—"10-room Modern House with chandeliers"—so the middle daughter could stay in her old district.[10] "I have always thought that was quite a heroic thing for him to do, and also for my mother to be willing to comply."

Yet in the end, for all she admired her father, she never felt close to him. "I think my temperament—nervous and inclined to be worrisome—was too much like his." It was her mother who combined intellect and action, who was outgoing and caring, who despite "antediluvian" concerns about being proper, still flashed a wild streak of unpredictability. Maybe the mother's flare came from a childhood in wartime Charleston, or maybe it had something to do with not being an immigrant, with being born in America. "Always," the daughter wrote, "I adored my mother."

The comfort and security her family enjoyed was partly thanks to a booming national economy. The US had become a "mature industrial society," its manufacturing output almost equal that of England, France and Germany combined.[11] The previous decade of "great prosperity" capped forty years—since the start of the Civil War—when manufacturing increased, prices fell, workers' wages doubled.[12] It still meant labor was getting a small percentage of the profits, and Minneapolis's painters were still trying to form a union. But general prosperity quelched the urgency. "The [painters] trade remained unorganized," and the city stayed an open shop.[13]

With the spread of national products and the expansion of retailers, her family fought to keep their share of the market. Their store was no longer the exclusive dealer for Masury paint; four other city locations sold it, as did a department store.[14] "WILL PAY YOU TO GET OUR PRICES," read an ad for the family store. "We are determined to reduce our large stock and will cut prices way down to accomplish the purpose."[15]

Just after the turn of the century, the business moved again, into an impressive three-and-a-half-story storefront. "PAINTERS SUPPLIES," the big sign out front read and beneath it, "CUT PRICES." On the ground floor was the jobbing house, providing "all kinds of mixed paints and oils, both at wholesale and retail, a large variety of oil colors, leads, putty, varnish, stains, enamel, brushes . . . and decorators' supplies and sundries." It had six employees—five men and a woman—who worked ten-hour days, fifty-two weeks of the year.[16] On the upper floor was the paint manufacturing, employing eight men and a woman, who also worked ten-hour days all year long.[17]

Comfortable establishments like this supported their temple's sedate congregation. Then, the year their business moved to its new building, Temple Israel got a new young rabbi, "small, fiery, liberal."[18] Born in Russia, raised in Palestine where his parents took part in the early Zionist movement, he'd gone to Germany for his education, then come to America in 1892. Here, he got his bachelor's and master's degrees. Like her parents, he believed in education and saw America as the place to apply it.

The rabbi took an unusual philosophical stance for the times: both a Reform Jew and a Zionist. The Reform movement had rejected as old-fashioned and un-scientific the inevitable return of Jews to Palestine.[19] But the new rabbi preached that they were a displaced people with the right to a homeland. He made it sound like life in America was a temporary step in a larger plan. When a leading rabbi in Chicago advocated intermarriage—Jews could melt and become Americans—this new rabbi argued "intermarriage of the Jews and the Gentiles will only lead to the absorption and extinction of the Jewish race."[20]

That sounded like the argument of the old-fashioned, nonassimilating Eastern European immigrants, and the new rabbi was suspected of being one of them. He had, after all, been born in Russia. To her family and the temple, the Eastern European Orthodox were an embarrassment: Old World peddlers, reminders of a less prosperous past. German Jews would sometimes define themselves as "light," where Eastern Europeans were "dark:" a throwback to the distinctions of the South.[21] "Some of these people, with their long beards and long black coats and furry black hats, looked so strange that we could not 'take' them very well" is how one German Jew put it. "I remember that other jews, the older settlers used to call them 'kikes.'"[22]

The new rabbi set out to overcome what he saw as their prejudice.[23] He argued that all Jews—and all people—were created equal. "Inclusive brotherhood" was, he felt, the one "peculiarly American" feature. He defined it as "equality of nationali-ties, as well as . . . equality of individuals. . . ."[24] So, on Rosh Hashana, he'd give his first sermon in English to his own congregation, then go north on the second day and give a sermon in Yiddish to the Orthodox.[25] He started a citywide newspaper in which he editorialized, "Be a Jew, no matter what other label you wear. Be a Jew, an Orthodox or a Conservative, or a Reform, or a Zionist, or a Socialist, or even a lodge-Jew; but be a Jew."[26]

The new rabbi's Zionism especially rankled his congregation. Its president threatened to fire him. And in the diary, she remembered how her father, an of-ficer of the temple, objected to the rabbi "bringing socialistic propaganda into his sermons."[27] One of his talks even implied that "the Old Testament endorsed social-ism."[28] Helping others—the Hebrew Benevolent Society—was one thing, but to her father, issues like Zionism and shared wealth and labor unions had no place in temple.

The religious teenage daughter sat by her father at the Friday night services. Decades later, she remembered the young rabbi "vividly . . . I can see him, little man with his moustache . . . He was so tiny—his face was so bright, so alive. He danced from one foot to the other when he talked . . . He was a scholar and a specialist. . . ." The rabbi maintained that if you thought issues through—if you examined tradition calmly and rationally—you would arrive at a fact-based faith that extended beyond the temple's walls. He sat on the board of the local Equal Suffrage Association and worked to get females a voice in the synagogue's decision-making process.[29] And he became the first president of the Minneapolis chapter of the National Association for the Advancement of Colored People [NAACP].[30] "He preached a practical religion," was how she put it in her diary, "a socialistic creed of brotherhood. . . . By favoring the workers, [he] made himself hated."

Hated among the temple's businessmen, anyway. Outside, in Minneapolis and beyond, that socialistic creed was gaining popularity. The official Socialist Party was founded in 1901, her sophomore year of high school, as the nation was witnessing over two thousand union-led strikes. The American Federation of Labor grew from 278,000 members in 1898 to over 1,600,000 by 1904. Minneapolis, the open shop, might have seemed immune: between 1880 and 1900, it saw fewer than three strikes a year. But it had eleven in 1900 and would have twenty-four in 1902. During her early high school years, union membership in the city almost doubled.[31]

The young rabbi was raising the same issue Ignatius Donnelly, the Sage of Nininger, had years earlier: the plunderers versus the people.[32] By the time Donnelly died on January 1, 1901, the economic contrast had grown more extreme. US output was ten times larger than it had been at the start of the Civil War, and the labor force was five times bigger. Meanwhile, 1 percent of US corporations controlled one-third of all manufacturing.[33] Monopolies continued to take over the economic landscape. J. P. Morgan, for example, now controlled all the Northwest railroads that fed Minneapolis, fixing freight prices and angering farmers.[34]

If the growing power of big business had a vulnerable spot, it was workers. Mill City was turning out almost 15 million barrels of flour a year by 1900.[35] But to do that, it needed workers to install, operate, maintain its huge, complex machines. These were industrial workers, not the kind of craftsmen covered by trade unions. In 1901, they formed a group called the Minnesota State Federation of Labor. Declaring that "business monopoly [was] a menace to the best interests of the people," it lobbied not only for an eight-hour day and employer-funded liability pay but, ultimately, "collective ownership by the people of all means of production and distribution. . . ."[36]

In May of 1901, the International Alliance of Machinists organized a national strike, and the Minneapolis local joined, closing every shop in the city. The fifty largest milling firms united in their opposition. Bringing in replacement workers, they successfully snuffed out the strike by mid-July.[37] But it was only one battle in the modern civil war over what "free labor" meant.

A year after the machinists' strike, the city's truck drivers walked out.[38] The brief action revealed how vulnerable big business could be. Without transportation, it didn't matter if wheat was milled; it couldn't get to market. While the newly founded truckers' union couldn't sustain the strike, business owners saw the threat and decided they needed their own, antiunion organization. They created a local branch of a recent national phenomenon, the Citizens' Alliance.

The semisecret Citizens' Alliance proclaimed its goal was "individual liberty." In this case the individual was the business owner—and the liberty was to turn a profit. "The union must not undertake to assume, or to interfere with, the management of the business of the employer."[39] To defend this "right," the Alliance sent labor spies to infiltrate workers' organizations. The information was then leaked to sympathetic newspapers, the police, and city government. From the owners of giant mills to owners of local stores, Citizens' Alliance members vowed "To uphold the principle of the Open Shop" and "To discourage strikes."[40]

If assimilation in the South had meant accepting slavery, in Minneapolis, a small business owner was expected to be antiunion. Members of the Citizens' Alliance included furniture manufacturers, managers of machinery shops, printers, distributors of fuel, owners of ice and lumber companies.[41] The leaders gathered at the newly founded Commercial Club, where speakers cheered them on. "Law and order must be enforced and . . . class domination over industry is not going to be tolerated."[42] Beginning in 1903, the Citizens' Alliance would have a major hand in defusing or defeating every major Minneapolis strike for the next three decades.[43]

No wonder the new rabbi ran into opposition preaching socialism to a synagogue supported by German Jewish merchants. That they didn't fire him was probably due to an accident: their wooden synagogue burnt down barely a year after the new rabbi arrived. The congregation switched into emergency gear. At a meeting at the Phoenix Club, her father became chairman of the building committee. Fifty-two at the time, he was a sharp-featured, unsmiling man with a small white moustache and pince-nez glasses. Dressed in a heavy, proper business suit, "he maintained," according to a sanctioned profile, "an unassailable reputation for integrity and reliability."[44] Now, as well as contributing paint and other supplies, he led the campaign to raise $18,000 (about a half a million in today's dollars) for a new brick structure. Two years later, in what the local newspaper called "an occasion of solemn splendor," he ceremoniously handed the president of the congregation a key to the new building.[45]

That the new synagogue had the look of a municipal building wasn't surprising since its architects were known for city halls and courthouses. At the first service of the Jewish New Year, 1903, it was packed, "quite a number of those present being Gentiles." The building committee auctioned off pews to raise money, and the sermon, by a visiting rabbi, "expounded the doctrines of Judaism which tho not despising the doctrines of other religions, claim for itself the first place." Proudly gathered in their new home, the congregation heard Judaism called, "the Mother of Christianity."[46]

The year after the temple opened, the family's middle daughter graduated high school. Her commemorative photo shows a slim girl in a high-necked dress, her head tilted just so, her lips in a partial smile, her hair pinned up, a few escaping curls. As the second-highest ranking in her class, she was named salutatorian and addressed the crowd that filled the city's largest assembly hall, the Swedish Tabernacle.

Compared to the other speeches—"Lessons from the Life of Abraham Lincoln," "Should the Right to Vote be Restricted"—her subject was high-minded, apolitical, literary: "The Study of Poetry."[47] By then, her passion for "old-fashioned" religion had shifted almost completely to literature. "I had been interested in writing," she'd later say, "all my life." Like her mother, she saw herself as an intellectual; like her father, she pursued learning in a methodical way. Where her older brother and sister were more social creatures—and her younger brother and sister more interested in performance (both took music lessons)—she preferred being alone. She'd be a writer.

The older sister was now twenty-six. Minneapolis wasn't Charleston where girls were presented at fifteen and married soon after, but even by modern Northern standards, she was considered old to still be single. The truth is she'd never gotten over her first love, long since married to someone else. Instead of finding an alternative—or, in the old style, having her parents find one—the child who had always gotten what she wanted stayed fixated on her first beau. Single, living in the family house, she waited.

The oldest brother had followed expectations for a male child. A young capitalist, already keen about money, he'd delivered papers as a boy. In 11th grade, he'd gotten a job as a picture salesman. With a business head and a way with words, he loved being a modern peddler and was good at it. "He traveled the countryside," his sister recalled in her diary. "He didn't want to come back to finish [high school]. Mama and Papa went down to Decatur to make him come home. . . ." The next spring, when he graduated, his parents hoped he'd go east to college, fulfilling one of their dreams. But he saw himself as a go-getter in a go-getter's age and a go-getter's city. He enrolled at the University of Minnesota, where he had friends and where he could keep making local business connections. There, he excelled at public speaking. After a summer of convincing Iowa farmers that they needed a still life over their mantelpiece, winning prizes on the university debate team was easy.

To her parent's delight, their third child, the middle daughter, was eager to go away to college. For the father who'd had to stop his education in Bohemia and the mother who still talked about Miss Kelley's, having a daughter in college would be a kind of culmination—the end of the family's immigrant past, the next stage of its American future.

College was an elite experience for women. Across the nation, only a little more than 5,000 graduated, compared to 22,000 men.[48] Most of America's 38 million women worked at home. Fewer than 15 percent were wage-earners, most of those domestics (almost 2 million). Some 700,000 women worked on farms, and nearly as many in the textile industry.[49] For the girl from Minneapolis, a college education would mean joining a rarified group. It was a way not only to broaden the mind, to pursue "good books," but to go where people like the Judge's daughter had gone—to step into that other plane of existence.

. 16 .

HER FATHER CALLED BOSTON "the Athens of American culture;" his daughter would go to a fine New England college. Never mind that Jews made up only about 5 percent of students in the elite Eastern schools. Never mind that only around a tenth of those were women.[1] And never mind the cost; the family business was one of five paint manufacturers in Minneapolis, and both the local and national economy continued to grow.[2] The immigrant's daughter was accepted at Wellesley and entered in the fall of 1904.

Wellesley's expressed goal when it opened in 1870 was to prepare young women for "great conflicts, for vast reforms in social life."[3] Its founders, Henry and Pauline Durant (married first cousins) had specific reforms in mind. When their eight-year-old son died, Henry Durant stepped away from his successful law practice and "embraced Evangelicalism."[4] The Durants then put their money toward "giving to young women opportunities for education equivalent to those usually provided in colleges for young men."[5] Not incidentally, that education would be a Christian one.

At the time, the nation only had a few female colleges and seminaries. Smith was also founded in 1870, Radcliffe four years later. More typical was the College of Charleston, which would wait another decade before it admitted women.[6] The Durants located their college near their lake house, twenty miles west of Boston. At first, the whole school was housed in a single, five-hundred-foot-long, five-story wooden building. It was set on top of a hill, like an abbey or monastery, its floorplan in the shape of a papal cross and with a cross capping each of its spires.[7] The Durants had it "humbly dedicated to our Heavenly Father . . . [that] His word may be faithfully taught here; and that He will use it as a means of leading precious souls to the Lord Jesus Christ."[8]

For its first couple of decades, Wellesley functioned as a small evangelical college for women. The administration enforced periods of silence and prayer; chapel was mandatory; the library was closed on Sunday. But in 1899, with the school in financial jeopardy, a new president took over.[9] Caroline Hazard was wealthy and connected; her ancestors had helped found Rhode Island. Privately tutored as a child, she'd gone on to tour Europe, becoming friends with the millionaires of the era including John D. Rockefeller. "[E]stablished in Boston intellectual circles," by the time she took over Wellesley, Hazard brought "the ease and breadth of the cultivated woman of the world, who is yet an idealist and a Christian. . . ."[10] She also brought fresh ideas, ambition, and money. "Liberal Boston now felt at home."[11]

President Hazard said her goal was to provide "to large numbers of women, opportunities before accessible only to the gifted few."[12] While expanding the college, she kept its commitment to a predominantly female faculty and administration. But "the pressing problem which confronted Miss Hazard was monetary."[13] She helped raise funds to improve salaries, to create four new academic departments, and to double enrollment.[14] She would put up ten buildings in ten years, including four new dorms, a music hall, and an art building.

When the seventeen-year-old arrived from Minneapolis, Wellesley was in the midst of this transformation.[15] The college had two large residential halls that each slept and fed over a hundred students and eight smaller houses that accommodated between fifty and a dozen. The fall of her freshmen year, a new recital hall opened: the forty-third building on campus.[16] Wellesley's faculty included seventeen full professors in subjects ranging from chemistry to foreign languages. Hazard had revamped the curriculum to emphasize the sciences.[17] To get in, the paint store owner's daughter had to pass exams not only in history, geometry, English literature, algebra, prosody, Greek grammar and German, but chemistry and physics.[18]

Since its beginning, Wellesley had graduated a total of some two thousand women; the year she arrived, about a thousand were enrolled. Roughly two-thirds of them were from the Northeast—mostly wealthy, Christian, and White. The majority of its trustees were from in and around Boston.[19] Within the minority of students who came from outside the region, sixty-plus were from Illinois, about as many from Ohio, and a dozen from her own Minnesota—as well as one each from Japan, Mexico, and Turkey.[20] While that amounted to a kind of diversity, in its first quarter century Wellesley had only graduated two African Americans.[21]

This world of the "cultivated woman" was a long way from Minneapolis, and she was homesick her first year. There were lots of letters back and forth with family. Even her twelve-year-old brother wrote, describing the familiar quiet of the family den: "[Younger sister] is studying, Papa is reading your letter over about the fiftieth time. Mama is reading to [the older sister]." After dutifully reporting his grade on the latest geography test, he informed her that the Swedish maid was about to be fired and that the younger sister "pretty near went crazy" when she got a letter "from him." He doodled across the bottom margin—a twenty-five-dollar bill, a card-hand with four aces, smoking pipes—and signed off "Your dear little brother / that misses you so much."

Her mother's letters were full of who'd come to dinner, what concerts they'd gone to, her charity work. "My darling girlie . . . I am just as busy as I can be . . . ;" they were signed, "Your loving Mama." Her father's, more business-like, often arrived on company letterhead: "Paints, Oils, Glass, Brushes." But he, too, insisted on how much she was missed. He described bringing "card portraits" of her to temple and showing them to the young rabbi and his wife. "They all thought them excellent."

The photos of the freshman showed a fine-featured young woman, her father's gray eyes set under thin eyebrows, a heavy crown of dark hair. Composed and confident, she seems slightly removed, as if working out some interior problem or dreaming. Years later, she'd remember how her looks used "to call forth praise." More candid snapshots from college capture her mugging with a bunch of fellow dorm mates, all in long white nightgowns. In others, they're dressed for a boating trip in high-necked, long-sleeved dresses, big-brimmed hats, boots laced tight— proper ladies protected from the world with only their hands and faces showing.

She'd dreamed of an "Athens" populated by great minds, set apart from day-to-day pettiness, with ongoing discussions of higher moral issues. She found, instead, a buzzing social whirl. Her first year, the college newspaper worried that "engrossed as we are in sports, social affairs, settlement work and numberless committee meetings, academic work must needs be somewhat crowded out." But she concentrated on her academic work. And her freshman class turned out the largest percentage of honor students in the history of the college.[22]

When she went back home for the summer, she tried to readjust to Minneapolis and her peers, most of whom hadn't gone to college. It set her apart. Like her mother, she was now the family intellectual. Her older sister was still single and living at home; her big brother was coming out of university and assuming his place in the family business; her younger sister had established a local reputation as a concert pianist; and little brother was a teenager.

Not long after returning for her sophomore year, her vision of "Athens" was punctured. In a letter to her mother marked "private," she wrote how a certain "neglect" was making her second year at Wellesley "unhappy."

Her mother wrote back that while the letter "troubled me a good deal . . . the neglect of a few thoughtless girls" had to be kept in proportion. Hadn't her daughter gotten the chance to go off to college—and a fine East Coast college at that? Wasn't she among professors and writers and scientists, mingling at a level of learning her parents had only dreamed of? What did the opinion of these few thoughtless girls matter?

"In the first place," her mother wrote, "you exaggerate them I am sure, and in the second place, 'what of it.'" She called the slights "trifling . . . when you consider the real and great things of life, the love and respect of your . . . own dear ones and the . . . staunch friends you are sure of." The advice went on from there. "You have your old friends from last year and your few Jewish friends. What do you care for the rest." That last had no question mark, maybe because it wasn't a question but a statement, a directive: don't worry about them, stick to your own.

What was bothering the eighteen-year-old revolved around Wellesley's private "societies," invitation-only clubs, each with its own residential house and dining hall. These societies were key to the college's social structure. There were societies for the arts, for the classics, for athletics, for literature. A girl who got accepted to a society lived the rest of her college years in its circle and was in many ways defined by it. That fall, the college newspaper noted new members in Zeta Alpha and Alpha Kappa Chi, among others. The listed names of inductees were New England and Christian: Rogers, Ladd, Warren.[23] Despite her academic achievement and her desire to join, the sophomore from Minneapolis hadn't been invited. And neither, apparently, had her "few Jewish friends."

It might have been expected. "In accordance with the spirit of its founder," Wellesley's catalogue still proclaimed, "the College is undenominational, but distinctly and positively Christian in its influence, discipline, and instruction."[24] If Wellesley was founded to advocate for "vast reforms in social life," those didn't include opening its elite societies to Jews, or *Aliens* in general.

She turned to her mother for help. But her mother's response was "what of it." Hadn't she, in her time at Miss Kelley's, adjusted to being part and yet not part of Charleston's elite? Nothing she or her daughter could do would change the attitude at college, or for that matter, beyond. "I am sure," Mother wrote from Minneapolis, "that things are not as bad as you believe them to be."

Instead, mother decided the problem was largely her daughter's doing. If the sophomore was lonely, if she felt excluded, she'd made "the great mistake" of rooming alone. "Can you not try to get a nice roommate yet? What has become of Bertha?" She should focus on Bertha, not lofty ideas of equality and justice. The mother insisted that what her daughter had run up against was the real world. Adjust to it because it was how things worked—in Minneapolis, in Charleston, in the "Athens of America." Her daughter was simply "over sensitive and the more you imagine that people are unfriendly to you the colder and more reserved you grow."

It was the advice of a survivor, a middle-aged woman whose life had already stretched from the bombing of Fort Sumter to that year's introduction of Ford's Model F luxury automobile. For all the nation's material progress, certain things remained the same. And the way to deal with them remained the same, too. Don't be oversensitive. Take advantage of opportunities and possibilities but stay in your circle. And within that circle, rely on the only really trustworthy connections: family.

And that was that. Her mother's letter passed on to the usual—the upcoming convention of the Council of Jewish Women, "two beautiful oriental rugs" she'd bought for the living room, the party they'd been to the night before. "Good-bye, dear heart," she closed, "Cheer up and be happy and write soon and often. Your own dear, Mama."

Her daughter tried to follow the advice. She stuck with her few friends; she studied; she concentrated on literature, not social life. But in the end, it left her feeling distant from Wellesley. And to some degree, from her own family. They didn't, couldn't understand what she went through at school. Her mother asked questions from far away. "Have you simple nourishing food at the hall and have you any congenial neighbors at the table?" Communication fell off. "I wish you could write a little oftener, darling. I think it will make you feel better to have a little chat with us occasionally, especially when you are blue. When I feel depressed," her mother continued in one letter, "I generally pull myself together . . . and say to myself, 'Nothing matters but love and truth and duty. We are not here to be happy, but to make others happy.'"

There was the moral, the lesson learned, the proposed cure for loneliness: "We are not here to be happy, but to make others happy."

On her daughter's nineteenth birthday, her mother wrote: "May you always be as good and sweet and happy as you are now and may your good Father in heaven keep you and shield you from all harm." But she wasn't shielded from all harm; she couldn't be. In the birthday letter, the mother goes on to comment on the latest photographs of her daughter. "I can easily believe now that you have gained twenty pounds, as your face shows it. It is very becoming to you to be fleshy, but how about your clothes? Can you wear them all?"

We are not here to be happy.

The mother's letters continued to be full of advice and instruction. A friend had sent canned preserves all the way from Minnesota and never received a thank you note; the daughter really should write one. "I would not go to any dances in Boston if I were you. It would keep you up too late nights and divert you from your studies." Would she be sure to visit her uncle in Chicago on her way home? "Whatever you do, dearest, don't spend your money for presents." Except she should, of course, pick up something for their Minneapolis neighbor and for her little sister.

Above all, the mother kept coming back to the question of marriage and children. Those remained a woman's primary concerns. Had she heard that the rabbi's wife had given birth to a son? Everyone was pleased. A high school classmate had gotten engaged "to a rich girl in Duluth"; another had just had a baby boy. The hints were obvious: the daughter had reached the age when she had to concern herself with such things. And make smart decisions. "Did anybody write you that M.C. is married to a chauffeur? Her marriage created quite a sensation in the neighborhood, as it was a surprise and we all think it was a runaway match. Her parents are heartbroken, but they are smiling and trying or pretending to make the best of it."

A good girl didn't break her parents' hearts. A good girl didn't stray too far from the family. And a good mother was ever vigilant to protect her family against such disasters. Someone had to keep spinning the "time of gold," extending the web even to a daughter far away in Massachusetts. It was the woman's job, constant, exhausting. To one letter, Father added a postscript in his tighter, more hurried hand: "Sure enough, Mama is sound asleep on the table, as you have seen her lots of times & everything is very quiet in the flat. It is still below Zero. . . ."

During the daughter's junior year, her mother succeeded to president of the local Council of Jewish Women. With her eldest son out of college and working in the family business, and her youngest now fifteen, she had more time for what she called "duty." The Council's first and founding president had been "essentially an intellectual," starting a weekly study group in Jewish history and literature, emphasizing the Council's goal of educating women so that the Jewish tradition would continue. Her mother, on the other hand, concentrated on "the actual practical laying down of the cornerstones of the national program," including outreach to the disadvantaged. She would remain president for eight years.

Senior year at Wellesley, the daughter succeeded in becoming one of her class's thirty-three College Scholars. She was proud of that but cared even more about being named a literary editor of the college magazine. Maybe she was, as her mother said, over sensitive and reserved, but beneath that—within that—was her writing. Poetry, fiction, essays. She'd always recall the moment during her senior year when a professor called in "several of the instructors to hear one story that I wrote, and another one of my instructors said, 'I'm sure we are going to hear from you some day, not in fiction, but in other writings.'" She held that as a kind of promise.

Her definition of good writing was still moral, still involved pointing out injustice. In her final year at college, she wrote a piece for the school newspaper that addressed the "neglect" that had made her so unhappy. "The privileges of society membership," she declared, "[aren't] fundamental to the complete, rich life of the spirit." After all, what club accepted you was—or should be—a minor part of a Wellesley education. "[B]ut," she went on, "this sense of the correct proportion of things does not make right the wrong principle of exclusion. . . ."

That's what her mother didn't understand: the larger principle of exclusion. And that hurt didn't go away just by "cheering up." Years later, she would write, "When I was in college at Wellesley, I was never conscious of any anti-Semitism whatsoever, although I was not asked to join a Greek sorority and only one Jewish girl was a member of the Shakespeare society." She'd remain a loyal alumna, keeping the college informed of her doings, making donations. As a middle-aged woman, she'd write, "I have belonged to the Wellesley Club and have gone regularly to our monthly meetings since I graduated from college." She'd even been the alumni club's "program chairman" for two terms. But she belonged to the Wellesley Club without really belonging. "I never feel at ease there. No one talks to me . . . I feel they are conscious of the religious difference. . . ."

She'd expected college to challenge her intellectually, and it had. She'd expected to meet women like the Judge's daughter, and she had. But she'd also expected Wellesley to offer an opening into that "different plane of existence," and it hadn't. It would be another half century before the college's elite societies accepted the principle of open admissions—and even then, charges of anti-Semitism continued to plague Wellesley.[25]

In fact, the most common way a woman was included in the world was still through marriage. And for many, education was still a means of making these connections. Wellesley was described as "astir with girlish life, girls a-tiptoe in the evergreen thicket . . . girls wandering hand in hand down the beloved path. . . ."[26] That girlish life drew boys from the Ivy League, potential suitors from Harvard, Dartmouth, Brown, Yale, who seemed to offer entrée to that "different plane," to becoming a real American. Sophomore year, she'd written home about a young man who'd recited Shakespeare to her. Her mother was more amused than impressed. "We had a good laugh . . . How did you manage to keep a straight face?"

In her diary, she described another suitor, telling the story of a courtship in the third person, as fiction. "He came out to her college dorm with another fellow—a friend of hers. They had a date with a girl in the next dorm to hers. . . . She liked him and his broad smile and his perfect white teeth. He said he would come to see her soon. He did.

"They walked up the road across the lovely lake. They sat on the hill over there and looked back on the towers of her college buildings. . . . Spring of her senior year approached. He took her to several baseball games. He had her to teas in his house.

"He came again to her campus on a wonderful spring night. He told her she was the most loveable girl he ever knew.

"Once he came out Easter Sunday to hear services. Then they missed the train back to town . . . They had waffles in Boston and walked all the way out to Brookline where she stayed with friends.

"He told her she was unapproachable. They sat on the steps and he asked her to give him something to remember the evening by. She was so naïve she didn't know he meant a kiss. . . ."

If this is fiction (did she go to Easter services?), it's still filled with what might have been, with possibility.

The denouement comes the night of her commencement supper, "the last assembling of the class before the Baccalaureate service." The girl's parents have traveled east for the event. "After the supper, the seniors would serenade everyone, up and down from one dorm to another. Her parents would watch the line of black-robed figures." That was the plan: the proud midwestern family witnessing their daughter's triumphant graduation. But early that evening—before the supper and serenading—she was called to the shared phone in her dorm's common room. It was him. "He wanted to come out for one last evening together."

In the story, the girl thinks of his "white dazzling teeth," how he was "so healthy and strong and virile, and the teasing smile that seemed to burst from [him] and to envelop her in a great gay happiness that embraced her like arms. . . ."

She hesitates.

If she goes with him, what will her parents do? They'll scan the rows of black-robed figures, and she won't be there. "Or they might see her with him, alone on the road to Tupelo Point, or down by the lake. She didn't want that. Somehow," she wrote in the story, "she was afraid of that." And so she answers him: "Not tonight."

"'But when can I see you again? I'm leaving the day after tomorrow.'"

He outlines his schedule. His parents are here for his graduation, too. And there's also a girl from his hometown. That's why he needs to see her now, immediately. Because a decision has to be made. They have to decide on their future. This is their only chance.

With "an empty hole where her breath should be," she asks when she'll see him if she doesn't see him now.

"'I don't know. Can't you possibly cut the supper. It'll be our last evening. . . . I have a date, but I'll break it.'

"Hundreds of times afterward," the story goes on, "she had wished she'd had the courage to say, 'Come.' Her whole life might have been different if they'd walked down to Tupelo Point and sat on the log bench overlooking the lake.

"But she was afraid not to conform, afraid her parents would see her and question. So she sat through the class supper, hearing nothing, seeing nothing, dumb misery filling every crevice and cranny of her body."

In this short story—this fiction—the incident is the culmination of the woman's college experience. With her "no," her chance to enter a different world closed.

"The next day he came to her outdoor exercises. With him his mother and E., the hometown girl. The minute she saw E. she knew. . . . She asked to go home early. She hadn't the courage to fight E. for him. . . ."

It's a story about fear, among other things: "Somehow she was afraid. . . ." A story about a good girl, a proper girl, who chooses the known over the unknown, chooses family over romance. It was written thirty years after her graduation by a middle-aged woman with a husband and three grown children. She copied it out in longhand in the old business ledger that served as her diary. The last line read: "It was like a wound that—long, long after—remains sore to the touch."

. 17 .

SHE CAME HOME WITH A COLLEGE degree. She came home a feminist with progressive ideals. She came home to a city taking part in "the most rapid advances in average wealth . . . the world has seen," advances that were the product of "a predatory social economy" driven by "self-seeking interests" and "an elaborate system of unproductive consumption."[1]

That, anyway, was what one Minnesota observer thought: Thorstein Veblen, born the year after her mother. Veblen saw the nation through the eyes of a child of Norwegian immigrants. He'd been born in a "frontier town" in Wisconsin and grown up on a Minnesota farm, some of the raw acreage that emerged when the pine forests were lumbered out. His family's community near Norstrand, Minnesota was known as Little Norway, and its immigrant farmers didn't try very hard to become Americans. Isolated and self-sufficient, rejecting English for Norwegian, resenting the "contemptuous attitude of Yankees," they went so far as to start their own schools, convinced that "the culture of the American school is mainly that of New England."[2] They refused to melt.

Veblen didn't learn English till he was seventeen. By then, he believed that the "simple scheme of self-sufficient farming was being crushed by a series of revolutionary technological processes." Specifically, the railroads and milling companies—"robber corporations"—were overcharging and destroying family farms like his family's. He saw industrialism ending "the ancient human instinct of workmanship."[3]

Veblen studied economics at nearby Carleton College but found Carleton to be part of the problem, too much in the "Dartmouth-Amherst New England tradition." Yet in 1889, he went east and got his PhD at Yale. As a first-generation "Norskie," Veblen ran up against the Ivy League gatekeepers. Unable to get a university teaching job, he wound up back on the family farm. There, according to his brother, he "read and loafed" till his midthirties. Around him, farmers organized the Northwestern Farmers Alliance, blaming falling wheat prices on Eastern conglomerates and "corporate organizations." Veblen finally found work in academia and at age forty-two published his first and most popular work, *The Theory of the Leisure Class*. It came out her junior year of high school.[4]

The book worked from the premise that America had, indeed, established distinct and permanent classes. And that the economy, rather than operating on need, or the usefulness of various goods, ran on greed and the desire for status. Sardonic, biting, observant, it paid particular attention to that "higher plane" of society occupied by people like the Judge and his daughter, the Leisure Class. To Veblen, their turreted mansions, fine carriages, suits and shirtwaists were examples of what he called "conspicuous consumption," a way for the leisure class to signal superiority. His book read as a smart midwestern farm boy's reaction to America's new elite.

"The material framework of modern civilization," Veblen wrote the year she went off to college, "is the industrial system, and the directing force which animates this framework is business enterprise."[5] Veblen described a twentieth century America where the old model of "workmanship" and "personal contact" had given way to "the machine process and investment for profit."[6] The key was efficiency. Businesses like her father's paint store were holdovers from another era. With its unadorned ads—"Manufacturers and Jobbers of Ready Mixed Paints, White Lead, Brushes, Etc."—it presented itself as honest and familiar.[7] But the personal touch, loyalty, and long-established connections had become, in Veblen's words, "sentimental considerations."[8] To greet a customer at the door, to inquire after his family and remember what kind of paint he'd last ordered was, in the end, a waste of time: less efficient, therefore less profitable.[9]

Maybe the democratic system was based on all men being equal, but the economy wasn't; the economy, according to Veblen, separated and isolated people. A modern businessman saw his customers not as associates but as "another inferior class."[10] A 1908 study of the paint industry underlined these changes. Of the five hundred or so paint factories in the US, there were still many small local manufacturers, like her family's. Such a manufacturer, the study said, "turns out an honest old-fashioned product that gives fair satisfaction." It had the advantage of "local acquaintance, low fixed charges, cheap labor and low cost of living." But it was "at a rather high price . . . [and] generally somewhat behind the times in its range of applicability as well as in variety. It is commonly a country painter's paint. . . ."[11]

Hadn't her family come north to catch up with the times, to join the modern age and ride its wave of profitability? Yet here they were running a country painter's paint store—at least in comparison to the department store that had opened on Hennepin. Its ads boasted that it carried all the "Leading Brands," including Sherwin-Williams, Masury, and American Paint.[12] And its cofounders were what Veblen called the new all-purpose businessmen—not peddlers, certainly, or even merchants in the old sense, but economic "organizers."[13] First-generation Irish immigrants, they set about creating a network of connections, not only running their store but serving on the boards of a local bank and a drug manufacturing company.[14]

This, Veblen argued, was the distinction that marked turn-of-the century society. "[N]o single factor [was more important than] the business man and his work."[15] Not religion or culture, or where you came from, but where you fell in Ignatius Donnelly's division of plunderers versus people.

Though Veblen was more academic and less populist than Donnelly, they shared a common point of view: rural outsiders who believed in "old-fashioned" egalitarian values. As Veblen saw it, the idea of honesty as the best policy had gone the way of the family farm—and the Mom-and-Pop business wasn't far behind. As the American empire expanded after the Spanish-American War, its rapidly accelerating economy shredded the old arrangements. What was left, in Veblen's view, was "competitive friction between the combined business capital and the combined workmen."[16]

That friction was more and more evident. During her college years, the Minneapolis Socialist Party had run its first candidate for mayor. He'd pulled less than 7 percent of the vote, and the Socialists wouldn't do any better in the next two mayoral elections. But immigrants were still arriving in the city and "a considerable number of them," according to one observer, "were already socialists when they arrived. . . ." Many joined Eugene Debs's Socialist Party, where instead of melting, they formed separate ethnic "language federations."[17] Minneapolis's machinists went out on strike during her junior year. Though the Citizens' Alliance snuffed the action, the strike revealed that the city's police chief had been in cahoots with antiunion interests.[18] A progressive, reform coalition began to form.

Her perspective had changed some during her four years in the East. "My imagination," she wrote, "was broadened and vitalized." She gave credit to faculty members, friends, "acquaintance with great books and the knowledge and wisdom of those who wrote them. . . ." Among other things, she'd permanently altered her connection to "the old ritual and conventional Judaism." She still went to temple, but it was more to keep up appearances, to please her parents; she no longer had their abiding faith. As she wrote about it—again turning it into fiction, again using the third person—"It was a slow, torturous transition . . . She felt lost . . . The religion of the Bible . . . became to her myth, symbols . . . fancies, superstition. . . . How absurd," she wrote, "how childish the idea of a personal God, of a supernatural being, a magnified man on whom men must lean for support."

The twenty-two-year-old college graduate came home a modern woman, liberated from the idea that she needed a "magnified man" to shield her from harm. And she wasn't alone. Between 1910 and 1930, single women aged twenty

to twenty-four were the largest group migrating into Minneapolis.[19] If the suffragist movement seemed slightly outdated—it had been almost forty years since
the founding of the first national organization—it continued to draw support.
"These courageous women," as one Minnesota woman wrote, "set a pattern not
understood yet, standing in their prim strength, in their sweetness and sobriety
against cruel ridicule, moral censure, charges of insanity; for there is no cruelty
like that of the oppressor who feels his loss of the bit on those it had been his gain
to oppress."[20] College had helped her throw that bit, and the family registered her
convictions. Beneath her photograph in one of the albums, someone scribbled
"women's rights."

Along with heightened feminism and a loss of religion, she came home a
confirmed pacifist. Industrialism was changing the face of not just America but
Europe and Russia. As the old monarchies failed, the beginnings of a new world
order prompted military buildups and a diplomatic crisis.[21] Organizations like the
National Council of Jewish Women believed the correct response was "to promote
world peace," and she counted herself among them.[22] Peace would be achieved not
through magnified men, superior force, or prayer, but negotiation. Surely modern humans could solve their problems by rational discussion, the way modern
businessmen ironed out deals? She saw herself as part of a new internationalist
movement that was proposing a world peace-keeping federation, using the term
"United Nations."[23]

Her dream was to help usher in this future as a writer. "Most of my ambition,"
she wrote, "stems back to that intense and persistent desire to become part of the
beauty and the glory of Life itself." But how? "Teachers of writing say the first requirement for creative writing is you must have something important to say. . . .
Have I anything important to communicate?" They seemed to think so at Wellesley; hadn't her English professor said she'd be heard from?

She came home to the same house, the same parlor with its same occupants.
Her parents were now in their fifties. Her older sister, twenty-seven, was still
unmarried, still living at home—an example of what might happen to her, to any
woman, who staked her future on marriage. Her older brother was immersed in
the family business, a salesman determined to get ahead. Her younger sister had
become a serious musician; she'd go off to Berlin in the summer to study with a re-
nowned pianist, taking along her younger, teenage brother. Meanwhile, the same
quiet evenings descended on the house: doing embroidery, reading "good books,"
her sister practicing piano, her father looking at the paper, mother doing Council
business before falling asleep at the table.

Minneapolis offered her few options. The number of women going to college
tripled between 1890 and 1910 but having an education didn't automatically mean
having more opportunities. Instead, it seemed to set you apart, to cut you off from

the traditional female occupation. Half of the nation's college-educated women never married.[24] In Minneapolis, the job possibilities were limited, especially if the woman wasn't Christian. It was well-known that Jews weren't allowed to teach in the city school system or work in its hospitals.[25]

All her higher education seemed to lead her toward was . . . more education. She graduated in June and enrolled that summer in the University of Minnesota. She'd grown up in a house with a German-speaking immigrant father; now, she became a "scholar in German," volunteering to tutor others. It wasn't clear where this would get her. She already had more formal education than most women of her time. But school was where she'd excelled. And in the bustling, business-oriented midwestern city, the university offered a haven of sorts.

University of Minnesota prided itself on "a lack of prejudice . . . [a] fairmindedness. . . . [and a] really democratic spirit." A faculty member declared a "striking difference between the attitude of the University of Minnesota and the city in which it was located."[26] But this "really democratic spirit" only went so far. While the U of M admitted Jews and Blacks, there seemed to have been quotas on how many. When a Jew became a celebrity halfback on the football team, a university publication described him as having "overcome his religious scruples enough to mix up with the insidious pigskin." And the same paper called an African American player "[a] lank-limbed child of sunny Ethiopia." Like Wellesley, the University of Minnesota's Greek societies were "largely segregated by race and religion."[27]

Still, her older brother had won awards at the U of M, singled out as "a gifted student of oratory."[28] And the university could work as a launching pad for an ambitious Jewish woman. Fanny Fligelman was an example. Two years younger than the diary keeper, Fligelman had come to Minneapolis from Romania. She would graduate from U of M Phi Betta Kappa and go on to become president of, first, the local Council of Jewish Women, then the national organization. A fellow pacifist, Fligelman led citywide disarmament protests and would eventually serve on the US delegation to the United Nations.[29] All this while maintaining the traditional role of wife and mother. When Fligelman was honored as one of the nation's "ten most influential clubwomen," she used her married name, Mrs. Arthur Brin. And she happily explained that despite, or along with, her club work, her husband expected her home each day for the noon meal.[30]

To Thorstein Veblen, a woman's limited options were tied into the economic system. In an essay called "The Economic Theory of Woman's Dress," Veblen set out cause and effect. The true point of the economy, he argued, wasn't to accumulate wealth but to show off the accumulation of wealth. A woman might be educated, might be a vital member of church, synagogue or club, might hold down a job, but "women must appear to be idle in order to be respectable. . . ."[31] A proper lady's dress had to show she was "not engaged in any kind of productive labor . . . ; [it] must not only be conspicuously expensive; it must also be 'inconvenient.'"[32] Hence the yards of fabric she and her classmates wore on their excursions at Wellesley.

"[U]nder the patriarchal organization of society . . ." Veblen went on, "the dress of the women was an exponent of the wealth of the man. . . ."[33] How she appeared and spoke and behaved in polite society served "as an advertisement . . . that the wearer is backed by sufficient means" not to have to work.[34] "[T]here is that about the dress of women, which suggests that the wearer is something in the nature of a chattel," Veblen concluded, adding that, "[in] the predatory social economy . . . women and other slaves are highly valued."[35]

In this way, North and South, her mother's generation and her own, were similar: women remained secondary citizens, maybe not slaves but advertisements for (male) wealth. If college had promised something different, better, she'd now left its ivory tower behind.

She came home to limited options.

She graduated in June, enrolled at the University of Minnesota that summer, and by the fall was engaged to be married.

. 18 .

"ALMOST ONE OF OUR FAMILY throughout our childhood and youth."

That's how she described her fiancée. A round-faced twenty-five-year-old, sociable, supportive, funny, he'd gone to her same temple, been in her same elementary and high schools, and was, she remarked, "a very close friend of my older brother." When she was away at college, he'd been a regular guest in her family's house, listening as her letters home were read aloud, sometimes spending the night. Their mothers had known each other for almost twenty-five years, taking part in the same charitable activities, running a booth together at the annual Hebrew Fair.[1] Their fathers had worked together at the temple.

"Almost one of our family."

The "almost" was important. They weren't cousins. And this wasn't an old-fashioned arranged marriage. It may not have had the spark of strangers meeting at an inn, but nor was it a business alliance. This was the modern age, and they were two forward-thinking, progressive adults. Even if the engagement fit the conventions for women her age, even if it pleased her parents and satisfied the community—a "good" girl making a "good" match—even if their families had a similar enough history to make the engagement seem almost inevitable, it was an American marriage: free choice between equals.

Her fiancée's family were also Jews from the South. His grandparents had emigrated from Posen around 1850, a decade after her own grandfather left Bohemia. Posen in what is now Poland was a major trade center annexed to the Kingdom of Prussia in the late eighteenth century.[2] In the period of liberalization that followed, Prussian Jews were granted full citizenship, allowed to work at any occupation, and became eligible for academic positions. Except none of those freedoms were allowed within the district of Posen, home to over 40 percent of all Prussian Jews. As late as 1846, 80 percent of Posen's Jews weren't official citizens.[3]

During the "Spring of Nations" uprising in 1848, rebels in Posen attempted to "throw off the iron leading strings of the aristocracy."[4] The insurgents demanded parliamentary elections, freedom of the press, an end to economic and political inequalities.[5] The Prussian military responded by placing the city under siege.

Across Europe, Jews joined the anti-ruling-class protests, hoping to benefit from the battle for human rights. "A consequence of our new law," wrote one leading German Jew, "will be that marriages will be mixed, and that religion will no longer be a permanent and insuperable dividing wall preventing a union of peoples."[6]

But even before the rebellion was crushed, the crowds turned on Jews. In Prague, mobs tried to loot the ghetto.[7] A Czech leader of the democratic movement called Jews "a separate-Semitic—nation. . . . Therefore, anyone who wants to be a Czech must cease to be a Jew."[8] The uprisings only seemed to accentuate old prejudices. "[I]n the very hour that brought freedom to the fatherland," wrote one Jew, "we have no other wish than to avoid <u>this</u> sort of Freedom!"[9]

Two years after the rebellions of 1848, her fiancée's grandfather left Prussia, a man of fifty, married almost twenty years, with a family of five. Men like him, "refugees from revolution," were called Forty-Eighters.[10] He eventually settled in Fredericksburg, Virginia, halfway between Washington, DC, and Richmond, Virginia. He followed his brother there. The brother had emigrated from Prussia to Mobile, Alabama, where he'd run a liquor store in the 1840s, selling "champagne Cider," "Havana honey," "Monongahela Whiskey."[11] From there, he'd moved to Fredericksburg where, by 1860, he listed himself as a merchant.[12]

Fredericksburg was a market town of about five thousand people. "Market," in this case, included not only produce from neighboring farms but slaves. In 1810, Fredericksburg was home to "several regular traders" and by 1835 had become a distribution center for slaves bred in Virginia to be shipped to the deeper South.[13] Jews had lived in Fredericksburg since the American Revolution, and the family moved right into the local business community. Both brothers became members of Fredericksburg's venerable Masonic Lodge #4, where George Washington and seven other Revolutionary War generals had been "initiated, passed, and raised."[14] Their eldest sons started a general store together in downtown Fredericksburg.

Like the diary keeper's family, her fiancé's seemed to function as a protective unit. But the son who would one day become her father-in-law was something of an outlier, a traveler. At twenty-one, he was living in a little town in southwestern Alabama called Burnt Corn. Originally a Creek Indian settlement, Burnt Corn's scattering of buildings (population 770) stood at the crossroads of the Great Pensacola Trading Path, which ran west out of Florida, and the Federal Road that ran south to Mobile.[15] The twenty-one-year-old stayed in a boarding house with a mix of workers: an Italian shoemaker, a British housepainter, a native Alabama bookkeeper. He was working as a clerk, and by late September 1860, he'd managed to save about three hundred dollars.[16]

Then war broke out. Up in Virginia, both young partners in the general store were eligible to fight. One placed a want ad promising "a liberal price" for a "substitute" to take his place in the army, the other enlisted as a private in the Army of

Northern Virginia.[17] Down in Alabama, the clerk in Burnt Corn joined the Second Alabama infantry, Company C out of Monroe County, known as the Claiborne Guards. They were assigned to man the heavy artillery at Fort Morgan, providing cover for Confederate supply ships coming in and out of Mobile Bay.[18]

The young Prussian private went from small town Alabama to the relative sophistication of Mobile, called the Paris of the Confederacy. In their single-breasted gray frock coats and gray trousers with wide blue stripes, the Guards were wined and dined. One lieutenant wrote how he'd "been out every night and sat up till past 12 o'clock. . . . I am booked for tonight again and will be probably for tomorrow night."[19]

Mobile's small Jewish community, like Charleston's, went out of its way to support the war effort. "For Southern Jews," wrote historian Howard M. Sacher, "loyalty to the Confederacy often was a matter of intense personal gratitude. Nowhere else in America had they experienced such fullness of opportunity or achieved comparable political and social acceptance."[20] All told, of the twenty-five thousand Southern Jews, twelve to fifteen hundred fought to preserve the slave system.[21] A rabbi in Richmond prayed: "Be unto the Army of the Confederacy as thou wert of old, unto us, the chosen people. . . ."[22]

Her fiancé's father—square-faced, mustachioed—stayed in Mobile for a year, defending the port and living with the Alabama regulars, till his regiment was removed to Tennessee, where it was disbanded.[23] Back in Fredericksburg, the family business had failed at the very start of the war; the day before Fort Sumter was bombed, the father had overseen selling off a store's worth of "CLOTHING, DRY GOODS, BOOTS, SHOES, FANCY ARTICLES, ETC."[24] The family left Fredericksburg for Richmond, a much larger city of 40,000.[25] A month after they moved there, it became the new Confederate capital. A couple months later, the first major land battle of the war was fought in Manassas, Virginia, about seventy-five miles from Richmond.

Like the diary keeper's grandfather in blockaded Charleston, her fiancée's grandfather tried to profit from the wartime market. That fall, he joined various business partners in a lawsuit to obtain legal possession of over six hundred thousand dollars of "enemy" property: property, that is, owned by Southerners living in the North. He had his eye specifically on the inventory of a large clothing store based in Mobile but eventually lost the case.[26]

In the meantime, he was involved in the slave trade. Richmond's Jewish population, which dated back to the late eighteenth century, included slave auctioneers and traders; its rabbis were vocal supporters of slavery.[27] After the start of the war, "[it had] become a well known fact," wrote one Virginian, "that slaves were daily making their Escape into the union lines."[28] Her fiancé's grandfather got involved in their recapture. He posted a notice in the Richmond paper under the heading, "Ranaway":

> From the undersigned, a negro girl named Elmira, belonging to the Fitzhugh's estate, in Fredericksburg. Said girl is 15 years old, very dark and likely, and clothed in a blue checked dress and is supposed to have taken the road to Fredericksburg. Any information which may lead to her recovery will meet with a liberal reward.

A month after the "Ranaway" notice was posted, President Lincoln issued the preliminary Emancipation Proclamation. It gave the Confederacy until the new year to rejoin the union, or all slaves would be declared free. To back up the threat, General Ambrose Burnside, commander of the Union Army of the Potomac, was ordered to move his army toward rebel-held territory in Fredericksburg. The plan was to go from there to take the Confederate capital in Richmond, crush the rebel army, liberate the slaves, and destroy the society that included the family of Prussian immigrants.

In October, Confederate President Jefferson Davis petitioned his Congress to draft 4500 Black men to build defenses around Richmond. Her fiancée's grandfather put out a call for "Fifty NEGRO MEN to cut wood in the neighborhood of Richmond. Also, a WHITE MAN to oversee them. Liberal Wages paid."[29] He ran his operation out of an office opposite the Richmond House, a slightly rundown hotel in the Confederate capitol.[30] He seemed to be doing anything, everything, to bring in some cash during wartime.

In late 1862, Burnside's army crossed the Rappahannock River and attacked Fredericksburg. It was the first time America had shelled one of its own cities (as compared to rebel Charleston shelling Fort Sumter.) "Here at our feet," a Union observer wrote, "lies the once beautiful city of Fredericksburg . . . [covered in a] black pall of smoke from which at time could be seen . . . tongues of fire, darting upward from the exploding shells & from burning houses. Beyond the doomed city, on the opposite hills could be seen the frowning battlements of the enemy & in rear their numerous camps."[31]

One of the largest battles of the war—some two hundred thousand soldiers were involved—it was also one of the deadliest. The rebels lost more than fifty-three hundred men, the Union almost thirteen thousand.[32] It was during this battle, at Fredricksburg's Lodge #4, that Masons from opposing armies "dropped off their weapons and equipment, hugged one another and attended Lodge together."[33]

Fredericksburg held. And when the Union tried to take the city the next spring, it was again turned back. For most of May, 1864, the new Union commander,

Ulysses S. Grant, fought the Confederate Army around Spotsylvania Court House, ten miles from Fredericksburg. Here, the Union suffered some 36,000 losses, the Confederacy about half that. Fredericksburg became "a city of hospitals," with women volunteers caring for the wounded. "Men are brought in and stowed away in filthy places," one wrote in her diary. "We go about and feed them . . . No confusion was ever greater."[34]

When the war ended, there was little left of Fredericksburg. Only, as a visitor wrote, "many chimneys, showing us the waste places and burned houses. . . ."[35] Her fiancé's family didn't have much reason to remain. Their store was gone, and reopening it would have been a struggle in a region where Jews were "increasingly targeted as profiteers, interlopers, exploiters, and outsiders."[36] They'd been loyal Confederates—two sons fighting for the rebels and the father helping in the defense of Richmond—but now they wanted to start a new life. The family decided to move north, petitioning the federal government for amnesty. They wanted their record wiped clean, wanted to start over, to forget.

They settled in Aurora, Illinois, a new industrial town forty miles outside of Chicago. Incorporated in 1857, by 1860 Aurora had six thousand residents, and that would nearly double in the next decade. The family arrived in 1865, the year of Lee's surrender. Unlike the Southern towns they'd been in, Aurora didn't have an established Jewish community. In 1868, her fiancée's grandfather helped host the town's first service, and the fifty-eight-year-old went on to organize local believers to close their businesses on the Jewish New Year and the Day of Atonement.[37] One of the sons started a real estate operation, then partnered with a brother in a "mercantile undertaking." But that only lasted a few years. And the father had to file for bankruptcy.[38] By 1870, the family had relocated to the larger, more prosperous Chicago.

Here was an America, a huge northern city, that they ought to be able to blend into, to lose at least their southerness. They moved onto a street in the 10th Ward near an Irish tailor, a German fisherman, a doctor from Kentucky, a Prussian cigar maker.[39] Compared to the cities of the South, Chicago had come out of the war strengthened, a manufacturing and railroad hub. In 1860, it was already home to a hundred thousand people, and its diverse population tripled over the next decade.[40]

In his sixties, the family patriarch found work as a "commission merchant," living off a percentage of whatever he sold for others. His net worth of $300 (roughly $5000 in today's money) was no more than his son had as a clerk in Burnt Cotton. While his eldest lived next door with a wife and three small children, his twenty-six-year-old daughter remained with him, as did the youngest son, employed as a traveling salesman. Meanwhile, her fiancé's father, the ex-soldier, had gone back to clerking but this time in a northern store that operated on a whole other scale from Burnt Corn, Alabama.[41]

M. Gimbel's hat and glove business had been founded by Moses Gimbel, a Bavarian Jew. He'd arrived in America in the 1840s, part of the same wave of German Jewish immigrants as her grandfather, and he, too, began as a peddler—in Philadelphia. But Moses went west rather than south. He ran general stores in Indiana and Illinois and then, toward the end of the Civil War, the thirty-five-year-old relocated to Chicago where his sister lived. Here, he started a wholesale hat, cap, and glove business.[42] By 1870, Gimbel and his two partners were operating on Wabash Avenue, and he was worth some $35,000, about two-thirds of a million in today's dollars.[43]

Soon after hiring her fiancé's father, Gimbel offered him a promotion to salesman. A generation earlier, the job description might have been peddler. It meant going from town to town, store to store, soliciting orders, making connections, then moving on: establishing a circuit. He'd still be a foreigner, still be viewed with a certain amount of suspicion, his accent a mix of German and the deep South, But instead of a pack bulging with goods, he'd carry samples of M. Gimbel's high-quality hats and gloves. And instead of talking to farm wives, he'd be speaking with store owners as a salaried "sales representative" for a modern manufacturer. He was twenty-seven, single, a "typical young bachelor." He was already a traveler, a lot of his American life spent with other rootless, hustling men in the Alabama boarding house, then in the army. This was more of the same but with a chance to get ahead. He took the job.

Open-faced, with short-cut dark hair, the new salesman sported a carefully trimmed black moustache and dressed in a proper, middle-class manner. "He had," his son would recall, "a military bearing and was, in his way, a very personable individual." As a salesman, he needed to be able to meet and win over a broad spectrum of Americans. As the child of another salesman from the same period wrote, "Dad's horizon broadened. . . . He was traveling a good deal. He met some of the big businessmen in the country. He visited many new and interesting communities and he liked that kind of life."[44]

The salesman's chances of advancing were slowed by the Chicago fire of October, 1871. Whether started by Mrs. O'Leary's cow or not, the flames engulfed the city's south side and then spread north, becoming nine separate fires. By 11:30 at night, it had reached the 10th ward where their family lived. A half hour later, a gas works exploded, and the city courthouse was in flames.

The blaze killed between a 120 and 300 people, destroyed more than seventeen thousand buildings, left ninety thousand homeless. Gimbel's inventory was wiped out. But unlike when Charleston burned, it was peacetime, and Chicago had the resources to start over.[45] Soon, downtown had doubled its previous size, adding taller, modern buildings. Newcomers flocked in to fill job openings. The 5000 Jews still residing in the city after the fire were joined by 10,000 more in the next decade.[46]

In the midst of the rebuilding, the panic of 1873 hit. The economic collapse left a third of Chicago's workers unemployed. Demonstrations sprung up in the streets, newly arrived German craftsmen organized a Socialist Labor Party, and a broad base of immigrants helped elect a People's Party candidate as mayor.[47] Another fire struck the city in July, 1874. According to the Fire Marshal, this one started on Wabash Avenue, not far from Gimbels' store. Rumor had it the tinder point was a small barn owned by a Jew; he was charged with arson but never convicted.[48]

Despite the setbacks, Moses Gimbel continued to grow his business. After being burnt out, he moved the company to four floors on another part of Wabash Avenue. "Their trade," a newspaper noted, "extends all through the West and Northwest."[49] In 1875, Gimbel offered his thirty-six-year-old salesman a promotion: company representative in charge of the Dakotas, Iowa, Wisconsin, and Minnesota. To better cover his new territory, he left his father and siblings and moved to Minneapolis.

The two family stories, hers and her fiancé's, were variations on a theme. Both had come out of the defeated South; both had started over again in the North. Looking at the bigger picture, maybe the similarities shouldn't be surprising. It's the American story, after all: immigrants arrive in a strange land, try to make it, move to where the odds seem better. Where her family in Minnesota had achieved the peddler's dream, her fiancée's family hadn't: had never amassed much capital, had never succeeded in that sense. The bachelor salesman continued to crisscross the prairie from one town to the next, living in hotels and boarding houses. If that created a certain loneliness—the loneliness of not just an immigrant but an itinerant—wasn't the constant moving, the road life, part of what it meant to be an American?

. 19 .

AT FIRST, THE TRAVELING SALESMAN was based in the Nicollet House, an impressive yellow brick hotel that dated back to the founding of Minneapolis. Later, he set up a more permanent (and cheaper) arrangement, taking a room with a German-born Union Army veteran who'd been in the Minneapolis clothing trade.

The salesman spent enough time in town to become an active member of the Jewish community. A year after arriving, he was one of a handful who organized the Montefiore Burial Association, and a couple of years later, he helped found Shaarai Tov temple. But his family and the company he represented were back in Chicago.

Gimbel's was thriving. "There is no city in the United States where the hat and cap trade is on a better or firmer basis than in Chicago." In 1876, estimated overall sales for the trade were at $3.5 million. Immigrant labor made for a cheap workforce, and the region west of the Mississippi was seen as "an unlimited market."[1] While his company was a leading player in that market, the salesman's future in the company must have seemed unclear. As he continued to work the far outposts of the trade, Moses Gimbel was gradually bringing his sons in as partners.

There was an alternative: the peddler's dream. The sales rep could break from the parent company and start his own. It's what his two brothers had done. They'd also ended up working for Gimbel, but in 1876, amidst the depression, they'd started a competing hat business—on the same street as Gimbel's. Also occupying four floors, the brothers' business not only sold men's hats and caps but buckskin gloves, linen towels, and ladies' hats in "the Latest Leading shapes."[2] The Minneapolis salesman could have joined the startup but declined. Instead, his brothers took an outside partner. A year later, they bought the partner out, giving their brother a second chance to buy in, but again he played it safe. He kept his job with Gimbel and continued traveling, selling.

By the time her family opened the city's first paint store (not far from his rented room), the salesman had turned forty and was still spending most nights in hotels. In the Spring of 1880, his immigrant parents celebrated their golden wedding anniversary with 150 friends, four of the couple's children, and ten grandchildren.[3]

His younger brother, who had been married a few years, kept telling the salesman he had to settle down and start his own family.

This same little brother even recommended a particular girl, the eldest daughter of a Jewish family that had come from Dusseldorf to Pekin, Illinois, in the 1840s. The father was a successful, forward-looking clothing merchant. In 1876, he'd taken his oldest daughter, fifteen, to Philadelphia to see the United States' Centennial exhibition. Father and daughter got a glimpse of the future: an Agricultural Hall, a Machinery Hall, a Woman's Pavilion, and prototypes of new inventions like typewriters, steam engines, electric lights. The gleaming, industrial promise of a new age. Not long after, the father decided to send his daughter to a finishing school in New York City. And soon after that, the rest of the family followed. They packed up their comfortable small-town life in Pekin, had their friends sign ornate "Farewell" albums, and moved to New York's Upper East Side.

That's where the Minneapolis hat salesman went to meet the eldest daughter, now a serious-looking twenty-two-year-old. He was almost twice her age, a respectable man with a carefully kept beard and mustache and an established if not dazzling career. From her point of view, he must have seemed a sensible, slightly retrograde match, offering her a familiar, smaller midwestern life. For him, it meant a connection with a stable, prosperous family (the father had become a manufacturer of industrial shelving) and a hedge against loneliness.

Maybe it was their engagement that gave him confidence to finally invest in his brothers' hat business. If it worked, he'd have some capital to start his married life with, an ownership share in a family business, a chance to cash in on the Gilded Age.

The marriage took place in 1883 with a ceremony at the Wisconsin Dells, after which the middle-aged groom took his young bride to Minneapolis. At first, they stayed with the same childless couple he'd been renting from for years. Or, more accurately, she stayed with them. He went back to his long sales trips out of town. The young wife set up house in a rented room in a city she barely knew. Eleven months later, they had their first and only child.

By the time the boy was born, the salesman had not only invested his own money in his brothers' hat business but had convinced his New York in-laws and his seventy-four-year-old, recently widowed mother to do the same. It seemed like a sure thing. According to the *Chicago Tribune*, "the house was generally considered in excellent financial condition."[4] The brothers' business was purportedly worth around $50,000, with his brothers' stock totaling another $75,000. Thanks, perhaps, to the sales rep in Minneapolis, their trade was reportedly improving, "for they were shipping large quantities of goods to customers at Western points," including three truckloads to Davenport, Iowa. To meet this demand, the firm had ordered "an unusually large stock from Eastern manufacturers, a purchase done on credit.[5] That was accepted business practice; wasn't easy credit part of what was propelling the Gilded Age?

Then, in what one article called "a surprise to the firm's business neighbors," its "paper" turned out to be no good. The brothers found themselves with outstanding debt of some $145,000. In early November 1894, creditors started weighing in. The business owed sums from $2500 to $5000 to some fifteen manufacturers and distributors. One accused the brothers not only of being insolvent but of knowing that they were "long prior to the time of incurring the . . . indebtedness. . . ."[6] If that was true, they'd taken their relatives' money in a vain attempt to bail out a foundering business. The assets were nearly wiped out by nine confessions of judgement in the Superior Court, mostly to members of the family of the firm.[7] Those included over $4000 to their mother, nearly $5000 to the salesman's in-laws, and almost $9000 to the salesman himself. One article about the collapse was headlined, A BAD LOOKING FAILURE.[8]

In a desperate last move, the brothers shifted the firm into the hands of a solvent businessman, the shelf manufacturer on New York's Upper East Side. If they hoped his solid credit rating would prop them up, it didn't work. The Chicago sheriff's office came in and auctioned off the brothers' remaining inventory—the same way, years before, their father's inventory had been auctioned off in Fredericksburg. Up for sale went the four floors of "Men's, Youth's, Boy's, Children's Hats and Caps," as well as "100 dozen linen towels . . . 100 dozen ladies' bonnets . . . 200 CASES Ladies' Fine Fur Felt, Velvet and Satin"—all sold at "A Fearful Slaughter."[9]

Debts and litigation would haunt the investors into the next decade. His brothers eventually recovered, the older going into real estate, the younger becoming a dry goods representative. The salesman in Minneapolis had lost more than $220,000 in today's dollars. To provide for his young wife and five-month-old son, he went back to his route in the northwest territories, selling another man's hats.

For the baby's first year-and-a-half, they stayed in their rented rooms at his friend's house. Then they took a place in a residential neighborhood southwest of the city center. The salesman remained a member of the temple, its burial association, the B'nai B'rith, and an immigrant-aid group, the Free Sons of Israel. Like the Charleston paint store owner, he had his portrait done, though in a nod to new technology, it wasn't an oil painting but a large black-and-white photolithograph. It showed a substantial citizen in a dark suit with just a glimmer of adventure in his eyes. The local paper described him as "widely known"; his son would later comment that he was "away from Minneapolis most of the time on business."[10] The couple never had another child, never had enough capital to own a house.

Childcare was left to the mother from Pekin. The diary describes her as "suspicious, inquisitive, . . . positiveness combined with . . . fear . . . diligent, systematic, punctual to a fault; sentimental, easily moved to tears." And judgmental. She would declare she "didn't want to have anything to do with so & so because she lived with a man she wasn't married to or because he didn't pay his bills promptly." She pronounced these judgements in a voice, the diary says, "with no rounded corners—each sound is sharp like a German word, harsh. [She once entered] a strange room & she said, first thing, looking around . . . 'This one is after my own heart. She is a wonderful housekeeper.' That is what counts."

The mother from Pekin shared the childcare with the salesman's aged mother, a thin wraith of a Polish immigrant who would spend her last sixteen years with them, dying at age 92. The two women doted on the only son. A photo portrait, taken when he was around four, has him posed with a big toy hoop in one hand; behind him is a painted set of an ivy-draped fence. The precious, nineteenth century rustic look is reinforced by dressing the toddler in a plaid jacket with brass buttons, a matching plaid skirt that comes to his knees, and midcalf leather boots. Years later, his wife would write in her diary that he was brought up "with kid gloves, within narrow limits, [taking] no chances." In her phrase, "he didn't know the red light district."

He grew up in the same small circle as his future wife. When he was nine, his mother was secretary to the local Council of Jewish Women that her mother cofounded. The future husband and wife went to the same neighborhood school, where he became close friends with her big brother. The two boys were confirmed at the same ceremony in 1899. Her fiancée-to-be delivered the opening address, "Israel and His Revelation;" her brother spoke on "Judaism in the Present and Future."[11] Both received certificates urging them to "Hear, my son, the instructions of the father, and forsake not the teachings of the mother." After the confirmation, the salesman's wife threw a 50-person party for her only child. It had a green and gold theme highlighted by a centerpiece of yellow jonquils in a cut-glass vase. The woman from Pekin made sure the local paper printed all the details.[12]

As she was raised to be a good girl, he was raised to be a good boy. But where she was often solitary and worried, he was easygoing, eager to please, sure that things would work out for the better. They both liked words. Quick-witted and verbal, he coauthored what the local paper called a "clever little skit" for his high school graduation.[13] But he didn't go on to college or, for that matter, leave Minneapolis. Maybe it was because his father, the travelling salesman, was sixty by then and in declining health. Maybe it was because his mother wanted her only child to stay near. Or maybe the family couldn't afford it.

Five days after high school graduation, the seventeen-year-old started work for the Palace Clothing Company.

The success story of his boss, Maurice Rothschild, was like Moses Gimbel's, like the immigrant founders of the Octopus stores: one story, really, with variations. Rothschild arrived in Chicago in 1878, worked at one of the city's wholesale clothing outlets as a teenager, then filled "a covered wagon with goods" and headed out to Seneca, Kansas, where he started his own store. According to one chronicler, "When customers initially failed to materialize, he brought an armful of overcoats to the roof of his store and threw them to the people below as a publicity stunt."[14]

From then on, Rothschild believed in advertising. Three years later, in 1887, he sold his thriving concern to move to Minneapolis, where the twenty-three-year-old founded Palace Clothing, "the first retail store in Minneapolis' downtown to feature electric lights."[15] Thanks to a new technology called chromolithography, he could afford to print and give away thousands of sixteen-by-eleven-inch-colored engravings known as trade cards. One featured a pretty girl in a Santa's elf cap and a fur-trimmed gown, white feather fan in her hand. Another had a more complicated appeal: a Black boy in frock coat and top hat played violin on the sidewalk, while a White family watched him through a window. That there were few Blacks in the Twin Cities, that the scene was nostalgically outdated, that it appeared to transpose the old South to the North, only made it more eye-catching. On the back it read, "Palace Clothing Co. High Art Clothiers."[16]

At the time, Thorstein Veblen characterized advertising as "parasitic."[17] According to Veblen's Minnesota farm boy values, promotion was "unproductive work. . . . Each concern must advertise chiefly because the others do."[18] Maurice Rothschild, on the other hand, saw it as essential. He took out three-quarter page spreads in the newspapers touting "Top Coats! Rain Coats! . . . 1,300 Pairs of Trousers . . . Lowest prices on record. . . ."[19] With manufacturers constantly turning out new product, advertising was a way to expand the consumer base and separate the High Art Clothier from its competitors. As early as 1897, Rothschild was thanking the Minneapolis evening paper for how it had "helped us to build up the largest exclusive men's and boy's clothing business in the entire Western country."[20]

Her fiancé-to-be joined Palace Clothing as "an advertising man." The job, as he described it, "was in and out of newspapers, up and down their stairs, for several years, and wrote some things in an amateur way for the papers." The writing was ad copy, not the kind of literary work she'd done at Wellesley. "Writing," he declared, "was a calling, a business, because I was engaged in advertising." A Palace Clothing ad for men's suits began: "Did you hear something drop just now? We just cut off another price chunk. . . ."[21]

Like other businesses, Palace Clothing had to deal with the ongoing Labor Wars. Two years after he joined the firm, union workers started a boycott of hats made by nonunion workers. The Citizens' Alliance called it "coercion of reputable merchants of Minneapolis." It only got in the way, the Alliance insisted, of "the success and advancement to which we are all mutually interested. . . ."[22]

But what if all weren't "mutually interested" in the same goals? What if definitions of success and advancement differed depending on where you stood in the line of profit? Palace Clothing held an "open meeting" at the Phoenix Club in the spring of 1904. It included "officers, buyers, department managers, salespeople, factory superintendents and office help," 240 people in all. "The prime object," the *Minneapolis Journal* reported, "was to promote a feeling of fellowship and a better understanding between the various persons that go to make up a great mercantile organization." The subheadline read, "Employer and Employee Talk It Over for Mutual Benefit."[23]

At the meeting, management proposed an employee insurance program, paid for by employees but with the company's "moral and financial support." If that was a "mutually agreed" objective, the bulk of the meeting was taken up by inspirational speeches on "Congeniality," "Salesmanship," "Push," "Advertising." Then came refreshments and music. "The first meeting was voted such an unqualified success," the *Journal* reported, "that the company has decided to hold others at intervals of about four weeks. . . . [It marked] an epoch in Minneapolis business advancement."[24]

The story reads like a puff piece, the kind a young advertising man might be commissioned to write. Those gathered to define Palace Clothing's "Mutual Benefit" didn't include factory workers, or delivery men, seamstresses, cashiers. The "feeling of fellowship" sounds top-down, a kind of patriarchy, with upper management rallying middle and lower management to increase profits.

Palace Clothing continued to expand, buying a prime Minneapolis location where it built an eight-story skyscraper. "Our business," Maurice Rothschild said, "is developing into larger spheres . . . constantly pushing us higher. . . . [d]emanding a class of merchandise which makes increased foreign facilities necessary. . . ."[25] That translated into establishing a foreign office, moving manufacturing jobs overseas, plus setting up a new flagship outlet in Chicago.

When the advertising man was twenty-one, his father died. The salesman, sixty-six, had come a long way from Burnt Corn, Alabama, but he ended up with no property or business to leave to his widow, still only in her midforties. She would eventually leave Minneapolis to return to New York City's Upper East Side. But the salesman did pass on a legacy; the year he died, his son joined the Ancient and Accepted Order of Freemasons.

For the young advertising man, Freemasonry was a reassuring family tradition. When he wrote that Masons "recognize that events repeat themselves and that man's nature does not change greatly from generation to generation; grandfather to son to grandson," he was speaking personally. The same way Masonry had offered his grandfather a way into Fredericksburg's Southern society, it offered him entrance into Minneapolis's business world.

The handbook the young advertising man received when he joined Minneapolis Lodge #19 proclaimed, "Masonry is a beautiful system of morality, veiled in allegory and illustrated by symbols. . . . It is but another name for that pure spirit of Brotherly Love, which should unite all men. . . ."[26] That not only left women out, but in practice, Masonry only united some men. The cost of initiation and annual fees ruled out most of the working class. And while it claimed to be religiously neutral, membership was predominantly Protestant.[27] Prayers were often delivered "in the name of Jesus."[28]

By the end of the nineteenth century, Masonry was a huge, fundamentally conservative organization with over a million members, about 7 percent of the nation's male, adult, White, "native-born" population.[29] According to his lodge's constitution, " . . . obedience to law and civil government, is the rule and guide to every Mason. . . ."[30] That meant the milling magnates, small businessmen, white-collar workers who joined mostly opposed strikes and demonstrations. Lodge #19 had a history of only including the "best" people. When it received its charter in 1858, one of its early Imperial Potentates was treasurer and general manager of the Minneapolis Knitting Works.

At his initiation, a member-to-be was supposed to identify himself as "a lover of wisdom, and an apostle of liberty, equality and fraternity."[31] But it was a particular kind of equality. Most fraternal orders (and by this time the US had 460, claiming five million members) were middle class: carefully selected societies that valued sobriety, thrift, industry, self-improvement.[32] That way, if you were a travelling salesman or a young, up-and-coming advertising man, once you'd exchanged the secret handshakes and signs, you'd identified yourself as someone with the right values.

Her fiancé-to-be threw himself into Masonry. He enjoyed the camaraderie, the feeling of belonging, of being in a club. At the age when Maurice Rothschild had founded his Minneapolis store, the genial and curious only son of the hat salesman showed few signs of ambition. He lived with his mother, stayed mostly within the Jewish community, participated in temple and Masonic rituals. Bound to the known and the comfortable, he was delighted to marry the daughter of family friends, a girl he'd grown up with and admired.

Both young people had been born in America; it was the first marriage in their family trees where that was true. If she worried about her place in society, if she wished she'd known the Judge's daughter, he'd inherited his father's gift of gab and the belief that everyone could be talked to and was, at some level, equal. Where she railed at slights and prejudice, he was more in the "what of it" school of thought. As she would write, decades later, "You believed in Happiness. Many times I heard you say: 'Our business is to be happy.'"

. 20 .

THE DAUGHTER RAISED UNDER the credo "We are not here to be happy" married the son who believed "Our business is to be happy."

The wedding took place at her parents' house. The young rabbi presided before eighty guests, including relatives from both sides: the groom's uncle who'd been partners in the ill-fated Chicago hat business, the bride's uncle who'd been partners in the successful Florida paint store, aunts, cousins. She wore a white satin gown, carried a bouquet of lily of the valley. Her father presented her; her older brother served as best man; her older sister maid of honor; her younger sister played the wedding march. It was a family affair.

They honeymooned out West, seeing America as Americans. They'd both been born and raised in the New World, after all; if they weren't Americans, who was?

When they returned to Minneapolis, the twenty-three-year-old bride left her family home to move in with him. That is, she left her family home for his family home, moving in with his mother, a forty-five-year-old widow, in her meticulously kept house out near Lake Calhoun and Lyndale Park.

The same way she moved but stayed within the confines of family, the old neighborhood near Shaarai Tov had dissolved only to reassemble elsewhere. Even as membership in the synagogue rose from 125 families to 275, the area's "once-haughty houses . . . became rooming houses, funeral homes, and private academies"[1] Middle-class families moved out of the inner-city business area for more suburban settings, but instead of melting into the general population, they tended to travel as a community. Many German Jews, for example, relocated to the lake district, maintaining old ties in a new neighborhood with access to open space and recreation.[2]

In the decade ending in 1910, the number of Jews in the state more than doubled, from 6,000 to 13,000, even as the population of Minneapolis increased by almost half.[3] Like the nation, the region was being changed by industrialization. Where 50 percent of all American workers had been farmers or farm laborers in 1870, by 1910 two-thirds worked in industry.[4] From Maurice Rothschild making overseas business connections for Palace Clothing to the family paint store leasing new and larger space downtown, the local economy - like the national - was predicated on expansion. No wonder many businessmen supported open immigration; they needed workers. Almost 10 million entered the country between 1905 and 1914 as immigration peaked.[5] The "huddled masses" helped propel a nation destined, many said, to be great, to rule the world.

At the same time, the question many asked was where the expansion would leave them: with a house in the lake district or a shrinking percentage of the profits?

In the election of 1910, a socialist again ran for mayor of Minneapolis. Thomas Van Lear, once a member of the Knights of Labor, had risen up through the city's machinists' union. His campaign denounced both major parties as representing the plunderers. "[W]hen fat, slick, well-fed, well-dressed men, who never missed a meal in their lives, come down here," Van Lear called out to a cheering crowd, "and tell you workingmen that you should be patient and satisfied with things as they are, I think you ought to tell them to go to hell."[6]

Van Lear came within a thousand votes of winning, and socialists followed up with more organizing, sponsoring dances, picnics, rallies. Seeing the emerging threat, the city's Democrats and Republicans collaborated on a bill designed to rule out third party candidates. "It was a time of conflict," wrote an historian of the era, "and polarization."[7]

In her diary, she called it a second "time of gold." A year after the marriage, their first child was born, a boy they named after his deceased salesman grandfather. As young bride and mother, the Wellesley graduate postponed her literary ambitions. She did join the Liberal Union of Minnesota Women, giving a talk the year her son was born on "The Growth of Human Ideals." But motherhood was consuming—and satisfying. "For several years," she'd write, "I wasn't too active. . . ."

Her husband spent much of his spare time with his fraternal order. He'd proceeded through the rituals and tests to become a Master Mason and, in 1907, entered the Order of the Mystic Shrine.[8] Shriners were their own subgroup of Masons. They dressed in oriental robes, a signature red fez (like the kind they made in Strakonice, Bohemia), long-sleeved satin shirts, wide trousers bloused below the knee, white spats.[9] While the Shrine had once had a reputation as the "playground of Masonry," by the early twentieth century, it was changing into a charitable organization, known for its ability to raise funds for "Crippled Children."[10] The advertising man became the local Shrine's first chairman of publicity. He spent evenings in its red brick, neo-Gothic lodge with vaulted ceilings, ornate meeting rooms, banquet hall, billiards room.[11] A cartoon showed him wearing his fez and beating a drum for Shriner causes.

At Palace Clothing, he was busy producing what he called "effective ads . . . individually prepared, on a clear conception of your needs, expressed in personal style." In one, an elegant line drawing showcased a man in a bowler hat and three-piece suit, one foot on the running board of a roadster. Another featured a gentleman with walking cane wearing a knee-length raincoat dubbed "The English." The ads were designed to appeal to a nation entering the modern age. Mass production, increased trade, emerging technologies seemed to guarantee the high fashion of Veblen's leisure class—the indicators of wealth—would be available to all. Advertising's job was to increase demand by promising consumers they could live like the Judge's family down the block.

Advertising men (and they were mostly men) proclaimed it "an age of faith," of alchemy.[12] "*Advertising,*" advertisers told each other in italics, "*turns human faith into an asset. . . .* It is a form of progress, and it *interests only progressive people.* That's why [it] thrives in America as in no land under the sun."[13] By this definition, the shift from the Gilded Age to the Progressive era was a function of the economy. Advertising men were "part of the emergent managerial-professional class," their jingles and ad copy "the folklore of industrial society."[14]

The department store on Hennepin took out ads boasting how its paint inventory was "the most complete of its kind in the country."[15] When John W. Masury's Brooklyn Paint Company began scouting for a Minneapolis location, ambitions merged; the department store became Masury's exclusive city distributor. To celebrate, a thousand painters and decorators were invited to a party at the Orpheum Theater. There, they were wooed with free gifts, entertained by a stand-up comic, listened to a specially commissioned song, "The Painter's Parade."[16] There was no way her family's store could compete; it was a whole new scale of merged corporate operations.

Instead, her father, who turned fifty-nine in 1910, continued to run things much as always, the firm predicting hopefully that "this year's business has exceeded last year's."[17] The eldest brother, twenty-eight, was now store manager, positioned to take over. He'd fall sick in early 1911 and have to have a kidney removed. The go-getter would remain in compromised health the rest of his life. Single, he lived with his parents, as did the rest of her siblings: her thirty-one and twenty-one-year-old sisters and the baby brother, now eighteen.

Three years after their first son, she was pregnant again. With the family growing and her husband holding down a steady job, they developed a plan to move out of his mother's and into their own place. The twenty-nine and twenty-seven-year-old decided to celebrate their American independence by building a dream house. They made the bold move bolder by choosing the modernist architect, William Purcell. Purcell's Minneapolis firm was part of the Prairie School, following the master, Frank Lloyd Wright.[18]

Purcell later described his young clients as examples of "that fine type of Jewish idealists with progressive and liberal minds."[19] They wanted a house that would reflect those values, and that was Purcell's specialty. He was in the middle of constructing his own home, which featured a radically open floor plan, a spare Japanese-looking exterior, and minimalist furniture designed specifically for the space. Now he drew up something similar for the young Jewish couple: an austere, box-like exterior with a flat, hipped roof and minimal detailing. Plain concrete steps would lead to the entrance, with an open, glassy sunroom out back. Her husband called it "functional, plain, cubiform and squared." A break from their families' ornate nineteenth century values, it had some of the straightforwardness, the expansiveness that they associated with the coming American Century: a declaration.

And then they realized they couldn't afford it. So, they compromised. After their second son was born (named to honor her piano-playing sister), they rented a place, filing the blueprints away. If prosperity continued, they could return to the design. And prosperity seemed built into this century.

The "rapidly rising tide" of Progressivism marked the presidential race of 1912. The Socialist Party's Eugene Debs pulled over 900,000 votes, and the winner, Thomas Woodrow Wilson, vowed to curb trusts and fight "special privileges."[20] Campaigning in Minneapolis, he declared "that property . . . compared with humanity, as compared with the vital red blood of the American people, must take second place. . . ."[21]

An intellectual, a professor at elite Eastern colleges, Woodrow Wilson seemed to embody the young couple's "progressive and liberal" values. And Wilson, too, was a Southerner come North, the first Southerner to become President since the Civil War. As a proponent of "reasonableness [and] virtue," he seemed to offer a way to reconcile the nation's divisions—racial, economic, social—and the loneliness that came with.[22] The day before his inauguration, eight thousand suffragists marched down Washington's Pennsylvania Avenue, demanding the vote.[23] Mobs pushed and blocked the marchers; cavalry troops had to be called out to maintain order; hundreds were injured.[24] "A government which denies expression to one-half of the people," as the Mayor of Chicago put it, "cannot be termed a democracy."[25] The next day, Wilson declared: "We have been proud of our industrial achievements, but we have not hitherto stopped thoughtfully enough to count the human cost. . . . There has been something crude and heartless and unfeeling in our haste to succeed and be great."[26]

He assumed the presidency of a nation that was now producing almost a third of the world's manufactured items.[27] Growing demand from overseas markets was creating the first inklings of a modern global economy, and its effects rippled to the local level. In the Twin Cities, the business manager of the city's Brotherhood of Painters, Decorators, and Paperhangers reported that "Minneapolis and St. Paul and the rest of the middle north-west, for the past year, have been the most prosperous part of our country. . . ."[28]

Her family used the good times as an opportunity to enjoy life; they bought a summer cottage out west on the lakes near Crystal Bay.[29] Her mother had shifted the focus of the local Council of Jewish Women from study groups to charitable action. She helped start a fresh air camp at Lake Minnetonka that would serve some six hundred low-income mothers and children, mostly Eastern European Jews. The goal was to "Americanize the newcomers so that foreign ways . . . would not jeopardize" Jewish gains and acceptance.[30] But it was also to change the system, opposing poverty through "scientific philanthropy" in the hope that immigrants would be treated as "fellow citizens," as equals.[31]

In the midst of this push for assimilation, word came that one of their own—a "thoroughly assimilated" Jew from the South—had been indicted for murder.

Leo Frank was born the same year as her husband, the Minneapolis advertising man. Raised in New York, educated at Cornell University, Frank, too, benefitted from America's prosperity. His father was a textile manufacturer in Atlanta, Georgia, a member of that city's Reform Temple, and president of its Chamber of Commerce. Leo Frank, in his turn, got a white-collar job as supervisor of an Atlanta pencil factory. Then on April 26, 1913, the body of a thirteen-year-old girl was found in the basement of the factory; she'd been sexually molested and killed.

Though there was little evidence against him, Frank was indicted. "Even before Frank went on trial," writes historian Sarah Imhoff, "the media began to emphasize how he was different from normative Southern men. . . ."[32] A Georgia paper declared, that he was a "lascivious pervert;" anyone could tell by "those bulging satyr eyes . . . the protruding fearfully sexual lips; and also the animal jaw."[33] One Southern commentator found Frank to be an example of immigrant minorities that refused to "amalgamate and be assimilated. . . ." In such a case, "the melting pot becomes a huge bomb, loaded with deadly explosives."[34]

Jews were no longer considered honorary Southern Whites. In the 1890s, night-riders in Mississippi had burned Jewish-owned properties, and threats had driven Jewish businessmen out of Louisiana.[35] William Faulkner captured the mood in *The Sound and the Fury*, when one of the characters meets a traveling salesman with a big nose. "I've known some jews who were fine citizens. You might be one yourself." The salesman answers, "No, I'm an American. . . . My folks have some French blood, why I have a nose like this. I'm an American."[36]

Leo Frank maintained that he, too, was an American, innocent until proven guilty. But in August, the day before the young Minneapolis couple's second son was born, the jury ruled against him. The case became national news. A coalition of Reform Jews and other progressives claimed the Southern prosecutors had "terrorized the public officials" and "made democracy hideous."[37] A call for a retrial was met with accusations that "the rich Jews" were trying to save one of their own.[38] When *The New York Times* supported Frank's innocence, Georgians accused it of being "Jew-*owned* . . . [and] Jew-*hired*. . . ."[39]

In response to thousands of requests for clemency, the Governor issued a last-minute commutation of Frank's death sentence. A cry went up for "another Ku Klux Klan." On the night of August 16, 1915, a mob grabbed Frank from his prison cell, drove him across state, and lynched him, leaving his body on public display.[40] Lynching was as old as the slave economy, except this time it was a Jew who had supposedly befouled Southern womanhood. As the "fiery" rabbi at her Minnesota temple editorialized: "Yesterday a human being was lynched, and we were told it was only a negro [*sic*]; today it is a Jew; tomorrow it will be an Italian, or a German. . . ."[41]

The leaders of the lynch mob went on to rebuild the Ku Klux Klan. And the new Klan targeted not just Blacks and Jews but Catholics. If second generation Italians, Irish, Poles thought being born in America made them Americans—if they thought prosperity led to equality—the KKK aimed to prove them wrong.

Far from healing these divides, President Wilson had already signaled which side he was on. Not long after entering office, he'd segregated the federal civil service. Six months before Frank's lynching, he'd given a special White House screening of the controversial pro-Klan film, "Birth of A Nation."

America's ethnic clashes and Labor Wars were mirrored by the war in Europe. Sparked by the assassination of an Austrian archduke, it played out old nationalistic rivalries. To the young mother in Minneapolis, it seemed a distant throwback to the unenlightened, tribal thinking of their grandparents' day.[42] She signed up for the female-driven Peace Party, started by Jane Addams, founder of Hull House, who believed women were "committed to both nonviolence and social and economic justice."[43] The party's slogan was "Listen to the Women for a Change." It sent a delegate to an international congress with the goal, endorsed by the National Council of Jewish Women, to create a new world order through mediation, not war.[44] And President Wilson seemed to agree. Wilson kept the nation out of the conflict, speaking of mankind's "common origins" and "universal sympathies." His stated goal was "peace without victory."[45]

In Minnesota, farmers organized the pacifist Non-Partisan League. Loosely aligned with the Socialist Party, the League's main goals were domestic: public ownership of grain elevators and mills, of packing and storage plants.[46] The Citizens' Alliance reacted by declaring, "A Non-Partisan League lecturer is a traitor every time."[47] But in the elections of 1916, the League's candidates swept into office and ended up controlling much of state government.[48]

With almost half Minnesota's population now urban, industrial workers demanded their share as well. In Minneapolis, the city's teamsters called a general strike.[49] Begun in June, it was crushed by July as some 2500 of the city's businesses set up "councils of defense," patriotic paramilitary groups armed with clubs and guns and protected by the city police.[50] In the aftermath, the Socialist Party again nominated Thomas Van Lear for mayor.

Van Lear presented himself as an antidote to the Citizens' Alliance and an alternative to continued corruption. He proposed replacing the present system with a "cooperative commonwealth." He emphasized that "the final disappearance of the evils of *capitalism* will be hastened by . . . bettering the lives of the workers, and strengthening their position in society."[51] The Citizens' Alliance countered by declaring Van Lear meant to "overthrow the present organization of society, to destroy individualism, to abolish wages and the private employer, and to substitute the state as the sole employer."[52] But Van Lear was mainstream enough to form an unofficial coalition with President Wilson, and the socialist became mayor of Minneapolis by a margin of almost two thousand votes.[53]

In his campaign for reelection, Wilson had appealed to voters like the young Progressive couple in Minneapolis. Their rabbi called Wilson "the most enlightened statesman of the present age."[54] Meanwhile, suffragists continued to hold marches and rallies, hoping to convince the President to endorse the federal amendment guaranteeing women the vote.[55] In early 1916, Wilson nominated Louis Brandeis for a seat on the Supreme Court. Brandeis, a Jew from the South, was the child of Bohemian Jews who'd emigrated to Louisville, Kentucky.[56] Born the same year as the diarist's mother, Brandeis went on to Harvard Law School and established a law practice in Boston. Though "conservative" on civil rights and with a history of helping to suppress strikes, Brandeis represented what Wilson called "a new freedom."[57] Just before his nomination, Brandeis came out in favor of women's equality.[58]

The nomination helped balance the horror of Leo Frank's lynching. Her rabbi called it "a great surprise" and concluded "[t]he really worthy Jew can always get his deserts in this country. . . ."[59] Maybe ethnic and racial problems, here and abroad, could still be solved by rational, peaceful means?

Then on April 2, 1917, arguing the world must be "made safe for democracy" and positioning America as the worldwide "arbiter of human freedom," Wilson reversed his position and led the country into war.[60]

. 21 .

THE GAUGE OF A "TRUE" AMERICAN quickly became support of the nation's war effort. Minnesota sent over 123,000 men into the military.[1] Her husband, thirty-four, got a deferment as the family's sole provider. Her older brother's health was too compromised for him to serve, but her baby brother, twenty-five, ended up a sergeant in the aviation corps. Across America, women stepped up, too. Volunteers rolled bandages; others moved into the factory jobs that opened when men departed for the front. The "Army of American Housewives" pledged to conserve food and wear plain clothing.[2]

The day after the United States entered the war, Minnesota established a Commission of Public Safety that set out to suppress labor agitation. Under the Espionage Act, passed in June of 1917, leaders of the Industrial Workers of the World out on Minnesota's Mesabi iron range were jailed and socialists arrested. The postmaster of New York City declared the latest book by Thorstein Veblen "unmailable."[3] A socialist group was banned from holding their national conference in St. Paul, while a "rally in defense [of the war]" was permitted in Minneapolis.[4] Across the nation, immigrants faced accusations not only of being un-American but of taking jobs from "true Americans." This despite the fact that almost a quarter of the draftees in 1918 were so-called "foreigners."[5]

In November, ten thousand people gathered in St. Paul to found the America First Association. It went on to hold loyalty meetings and denounce socialists as ruling "by virtue of force and terror."[6] So-called scientific racism trumpeted the superiority of Nordic people. A popular wartime author proclaimed that "[t]he crossing between any of the three European races and a Jew is a Jew."[7] In 1918, this patriotic revival helped defeat Socialist Mayor Van Lear; the insurance salesman who succeeded him ran on the Republican platform of "Americanism, undiluted and unhyphenated."[8]

Minneapolis had grown to almost 380,000 people.[9] In the accelerating war time economy, her family paint store bought the space it had been leasing on Marquette Avenue and gave itself a more contemporary name. But it couldn't afford the sort of large-scale ads that Octopus stores used, and modern wisdom insisted that mass advertising was key. "It Pays To Advertise!" is how a prominent Minneapolis salesman put it. "Some are born advertising. Some attain advertising. Some have advertising thrust upon them. . . . The only person who does not advertise is dead." Her husband, the ad man, agreed. "Got to hand it to you," he wrote the speaker, "you're certainly there with the stuff, all right. . . ."[10]

In late 1918, the diary keeper was asked to take on the Presidency of the Minneapolis branch of the National Council of Jewish Women. The founding generation, including her mother and mother-in-law, had aged out of official positions, and the organization needed temporary wartime leadership. "It was a very difficult time," she'd recall. Thousands of Jews were caught between the Russian and German fronts.[11] She and her husband both sat on the board of the Minneapolis Committee for the Relief of Jewish Sufferers from the War. "Many immigrants," she wrote, "were coming here, and from Ellis Island, some of them were sent here to Minneapolis, and the Council was trying to take care of them as best we could." Her real interests were still writing and family—her boys were eight and five—but she felt obligated to accept the position.

The Council tried to maintain its programs. It continued to steer immigrant Jewish women to safe harbor and find jobs for them when possible. It ran Sabbath Schools and "a very successful" child psychology class. It worked with the juvenile court system, distributed health pamphlets, and hosted light entertainments, including members posing as "living pictures" in a program called "Women of the Bible."[12] "It was her aim and purpose during her year of stewardship," the Council noted later, "to keep constructive education and social progress out of the maelstrom of the war."[13]

That proved next to impossible. "[P]ractically everybody," she noted, "thought only of doing war-work. . . . We were affiliated with Civil Defense and Red Cross Home Service. One of the most successful contributions in the war-effort and the most popular . . . was the class in surgical dressing." She was a failure at it, her bandages as unconvincing as her support of the war. "I, at that time, was a very ardent pacifist, so much so that it was very difficult for me to adjust to the things that we were called upon as a member of the community to do."

As historian Melissa R. Klapper has written, there was "significant Jewish membership" in national peace organizations, but those who didn't actively support the war were "excoriated by some elements of an American Jewish community still unsure of its welcome and security. . . ."[14]

For many, to be prowar was to be anti-German.[15] Before the US entered, many of the nine million German Americans and four-and-a-half million Irish Americans were against going into the war.[16] Afterward, "Huns" had to prove their loyalty, no matter how long their families had been in America. According to

Thorstein Veblen, "a German miner today may feel that he is an alien in another culture. He may know a great deal about American institutions but yet feel he is not of them."[17]

In August of 1918, in a small Minnesota town, abductors in masks kidnapped a German farmer who'd come under suspicion as a member of the Non-Partisan League.[18] They drove him to the South Dakota border, where they "assaulted him, whipped him, threatened to shoot him, besmeared his body with tar and feathers, and told him to cross the line into South Dakota, and that if he ever returned to Minnesota he would be hanged."[19]

In this storm of wartime patriotism, the National Council for Jewish Women had come out against the war. They were promptly accused of being communists.[20] To counter that, to prove it was as patriotic as the next organization, the Council composed an editorial. "We Jews," it read, "are working with all the rest these days to spread, to deepen, and to insure the best Americanism. If our people are to be truly part of America, all Jews must become familiar with the language, the laws, and the ideals of the United States. Ours of the second and third generations is the duty of assimilating our newcomers into the great melting pot."[21]

As the temporary president of the Minneapolis Council, she felt more strongly about pacifism than Americanism. She didn't want her little brother injured fighting a senseless war, or her sons to grow up in a militaristic nation. There had to be a way to settle differences without killing, to place shared values over regionalism. The hope was that President Wilson's "war to end all wars" would establish what he called a new "community of power . . . an organized common peace."[22]

In Wilson's words, the goal of the First World War was to take international conflicts and "lift them out of the haze and distraction of passion, of hostility, out into the calm spaces. . . ." There would be no more territorial invasions; disputes would be settled through compulsory arbitration. "The more men you get into a great discussion," the President declared, "is the more you exclude passion."[23] In many ways, it was a religious vision. Wilson described it as an international covenant where people would awaken from "national sovereignty" to realize "the sovereignty of mankind."[24]

The other way to think of it was as the ultimate assimilation. The Great War was being fought to erase national and ethnic differences, to unite as one people. "Only a peace between equals can last," Wilson declared and then proposed a League of Nations: a kind of fraternal organization to which all the world would belong. The very concept of a nation-state would melt away.

The more radical wing of the suffragist movement was insisting their cause be part of this progressive agenda. As the diarist assumed the presidency of the Council, she declared, "All over the world women are taking their place side by side with men. Like all other women, today, the Council asks the power to meet its opportunity."[25] In 1916, the National Women's Party began picketing Congress, the Supreme Court, and the White House. "MR. PRESIDENT," their banners read, "HOW LONG MUST WOMEN WAIT FOR LIBERTY."[26] In the fall of 1918, President Wilson appeared before the Senate. "We have made partners of women in this war," he declared, "shall we admit them to a partnership of sacrifice and suffering and not to a partnership of privilege and right?"[27] Almost eighty years after the suffragists' meeting in Seneca Falls, women would finally get the vote. Except for Native American women. And African American women in the South.

Armistice was declared in November 1918. The war had left some eight-and-a-half-million dead, around 100,000 from the United States.[28] Veterans returned to work; women were expected to go back to their domestic duties; things were supposed to return to normal. That included urging Blacks who had migrated north to come home. "We people of the South," wrote the head of the Chamber of Commerce in Jacksonville, Florida "understand the Negro laborer and . . . prefer [them] to the white man, especially in the turpentine camps, saw mills, and upon the plantations. . . ."[29] But Black veterans didn't want to return to normal. They were, as writer Jean Toomer put it, "openly resolved and prepared to resist attacks."[30] Violence surged. Near Jacksonville, in the late winter of 1919, a returning Black veteran was falsely accused of assaulting a White woman, hauled out of a police car by a mob of angry Whites, chained to a stake, and burnt alive.[31]

A few months later, Charleston exploded. The city had stayed sleepy since Reconstruction, its population only increasing by 20 percent in four decades. It jumped almost that much during the war years after the addition of a Navy Yard. In the process, parts of Black Charleston had become party centers for the sailors on leave. One night off King Street, in the neighborhood of the old paint store, when some enlisted men claimed they'd been shortchanged over a bottle of whiskey, fighting broke out. A thousand sailors showed up, and by the next morning, five Blacks had been killed.[32]

It was only the beginning of what would be called Red Summer. That July, Chicago erupted over Blacks "trespassing" on an all-White beach. Like Minneapolis and New York, like many American cities, Chicago had divided up into immigrant enclaves. "Go that way, past the viaduct, and the wops will jump you, or chase you into Jew town. Go the other way, beyond the park, and the Pollacks will stomp you. Cross those streetcar tracks, and the Micks will shower you with Irish confetti from the brickyards. And who can tell what the niggers might do?"[33] By the time the militia stifled the Chicago uprising, twenty-three Blacks and fifteen Whites had been killed and over five hundred people seriously wounded.[34]

"Brother," W. E. B. Du Bois wrote that fall, "we are on the Great Deep. We have cast off on the vast voyage which will lead to Freedom or Death."[35] Freedom was linked to equality, which was linked to peace. But even as President Wilson toured the country trying to garner support for the League of Nations, he was okaying the Palmer Raids, led by Attorney General A. Mitchell Palmer. This national purge of American citizens deemed un-American led to the arrest of some ten thousand and the deportation of five hundred "foreign citizens" as threats to national security.

Thorstein Veblen called it "official hysteria," a "Red Terror . . . running wild among the guardians of Business as usual. . . ."[36] At the same time, anti-Japanese sentiment rose in California.[37] And the terror wasn't just aimed at the foreign-born. President Wilson predicted that "the American negro from abroad would be our greatest medium in conveying Bolshevism to America."[38] A political cartoon of the time showed a Black mother asking a stone-faced Wilson, "Mr. President, why not make <u>America</u> safe for democracy?"[39]

In reaction, there was a surge in labor actions. 1919 saw the biggest increase in strikes in American history.[40] The government deployed army tanks to stop workers' protests in Cleveland, and Gary, Indiana ended up under martial law.[41] Between 1916 and 1919, about half Minnesota's industrial workers signed up to join unions—though some were "company unions," set up by the big mills like Pillsbury under the credo "Labor and Capital are partners, not enemies."[42]

The middle-class, properly dressed mother of two in Minneapolis was among those who didn't want to return to normal. She stood with her fellow Council member, Fanny Fligelman Brin: "We must not seek to modify war, but to outlaw it; to make it an international crime."[43] After stepping down as president, the diary keeper volunteered as the Council's local representative to the newly formed League to Enforce Peace. She would participate in the Council's "No More War Day." And when the Council passed a resolution in favor of world disarmament, a Minneapolis paper featured her as a spokesperson for the cause. "All nations have testified they cannot afford to go on arming themselves in preparation for war. The United States alone has taken actions increasing war appropriations." She declared wars were "not only military and naval but industrial" and identified the "biggest argument" against war as "the economic waste." The next conflict, she predicted, "will be fought with chemicals and gases . . . All the black and brown races will be involved."[44]

Despite—or within—the social upheaval, the couple's private life seems to have been calm enough. She was thirty-two, her husband thirty-four, their school-age children prospering. He'd been at the same Palace Clothing job since he was a teenager. It didn't promise enormous advancement, but the pay was fine, his position secure. As an advertising man, he was busy invoking larger-than-life ambitions—1919's "New idea in men's suits" was "Fiber silk shirts with the Easter 'gleam'"—but he was a modest man.[45] What he really enjoyed was the social side of business, "making folks understand," as he put it, "who you are." He liked chatting up clients and colleagues, hanging around a newspaper office, giving courses in beginning advertising at the University of Minnesota, being a Shriner. He'd contributed his skills to the War Savings Stamps campaign, Liberty Loans, Red Cross drives, as well as serving on the mayor's playground commission: all noncontroversial, "apolitical" community causes.[46]

A portrait of father and sons, taken around this time, shows him in *pince nez* glasses with a clipped moustache and sporty bowtie: the muted flair of an advertising man. His two sons—nine and six—are in old-fashioned pinafores and bowl haircuts; they could have stepped out of his childhood. The round, open-faced father is the center of the picture, and the boys cling to him as if to a boulder in a strong current.

Then the boulder moved.

There was a generational shift going on at the family paint store. His father-in-law was now approaching seventy. A portrait of him shows a self-contained, apparently content man with a slight smile. (The companion portrait of his bride, her mother, is full-length in a Victorian gown and with an expression of resolution mixed with sadness.) The uncle who'd come north nearly forty years earlier to partner in the Minneapolis store was near retirement. The younger uncle had long since split off to run his own paint and wallpaper enterprise in St. Paul. Leadership had shifted to her big brother, thirty-five, who despite his kidney illness, had assumed much of the day-to-day responsibilities. Her younger brother, twenty-seven, had returned from the war and promptly become the company's head salesman. It was the born-in-America generation leading the family business into the modern era. They offered her husband a newly created position, Head of Advertising and Sales.

Was the offer made in recognition of the advertising man's skills and the business's need to incorporate modern sales techniques? Or was it, more simply, the older brother wanting his sister's husband by his side? The engine of the firm's success, after all, had always been family—from South Carolina through Florida to Minnesota.

The advertising man's present employer, Palace Clothing, had shifted its focus to Chicago. Still, it was an expanding, dynamic business; in some ways leaving Palace Clothing for the paint store would be going backward to the smaller, the more old-fashioned, the more personal. And then there was the cautionary example of his own father investing in the brothers' hat company and losing everything.

On the other hand, while the paint firm may no longer have been "one of the important manufacturing industries of Minneapolis," it offered him the chance to be a company officer, to own a piece of the business: the peddler's dream.[47]

And with the majority of stock in the hands of his wife's parents, it promised even stronger job security. In a nation sorting itself out after a world war, in a city facing continuing labor troubles, with the definition of who was and wasn't an American being challenged, family seemed to offer a safe haven.

The man who believed "Our business is to be happy" accepted.

. 22 .

WITH HIS NEW JOB, WITH THE WAR over, the couple could make their move. They went back to the blueprints and started construction on their Prairie School house, symbol of both their progressive views and their move up in the world.

After armistice, the fierce patriotism of the war years only grew fiercer. Congress had threatened since 1897 to pass limits on immigration but had met with repeated presidential vetoes. In 1917, at the height of the war, it overrode President Wilson, banning Southeast Asians, tightening the net that kept out "radicals," and instituting a literacy test to determine which huddled masses America would consider letting in.[1] One commentator called it "deportation delirium."[2] With unemployment at 12 percent, new immigrants were seen as taking jobs from true Americans—the descendants, that is, of earlier immigrants.

Jews were, according to some, part of the problem. A Congressman from the state of Washington called them "abnormally twisted . . . unassimilable . . . filthy un-American[s]."[3] Henry Ford began associating Jews with an international economic plot.[4] Postwar anti-Semitism was seen as "much more widespread and tenacious."[5] In 1919, a Minneapolis Journal editorial questioned whether "German Jews and others besides [were] psychologically unfit to be citizens of an Anglo-Saxon state or country?"[6] In that climate, building their modernist house was making a statement. Spare, functional, free of tired conventions and Old-World values, it wouldn't just represent new ideas; it would be one.

Though they worked from the plans, they proceeded without the architect, William Purcell. The result, in Purcell's view, was that the young "Jewish idealists" cut corners, spending about half what they should have. "Not only were the details cheaply and incidentally carried out," he wrote, "but we had no control over the construction. . . . The result is a pretty disappointing building, within and without."[7]

They didn't think so. Rather than furnish it in the modernist style the architect wanted, she brought in the kind of heavy nineteenth century furniture she'd grown up with—the kind, for that matter, her mother had grown up with in Charleston.

The clean, light, glassy interior was filled with high-backed chairs and horsehair sofas, ottomans and thick carpets. Part of that was practical: they couldn't afford the furnishings and the detail he'd designed. To the architect, the result was "awkward and unpleasant."[8] But the young couple liked it. To them, the place ended up both daring and familiar, a progressive exterior with a conservative inside.

She prided herself on keeping a proper middle-class house. "Before people come into my home to enjoy themselves I want the setting perfect." His salary and her dividends from the paint business were enough to provide not only for the new house but for a Swedish girl to help with chores. And the wife could afford carefully chosen, fashionable clothes—not furs or expensive jewelry, not yet anyway—but nice things, proper things. "I expect to be dressed," she wrote, "so as to be one harmonious, suitable, pleasing whole before I do anything or contact people."

Years later, after this second time of gold had ended, she wondered about those values. She asked in her diary if she wasn't "starting at the wrong end . . . sacrificing the spiritual to the material. Always I have gotten clothes first." She'd eventually come to think that the code she'd been raised with—to keep up appearances, to care about what others thought, to be "proper"—was almost murderously self-involved. "Had I had money in reserve I could have had it on hand for doctors for mother." But in the rising postwar economy, people bought houses and cars; it was almost a patriotic duty. America ran on consumption, on credit.

Wasn't that, after all, the basis of her husband's work—to expand people's desire for things? "Advertising and selling methods and propaganda have created demand," she'd write, sounding like Thorstein Veblen, "have spurred the people on. . . ." It wasn't that she and her family were greedy; no greedier, anyway, than the next. In an equation almost too fundamental to explore, buying things seemed to be a way of putting the past behind, of forgetting, of blending in. "All the world," she wrote, "America first and, following us, all the world, even the Far East, places Money first. I DO TOO." She called it, with emphasis, "THE Great Problem."

It nagged at her. It was as if the war effort—the bandage-folding, victory-gardening, Army of American Housewives—had shifted seamlessly into a nationwide purchasing effort. As if the point of the bloodshed had been to smooth the way for this new booming market. In Veblen's view, Wilson's postwar "pacific league" of nations could only work if it included the "revision, reconstruction, realignment" of the economy. "[T]he meaning of 'reconstruction,'" he added, "is that America is to be made safer for the common man. . . ."[9] A new Reconstruction, then.

She was more personal about it. "Had I saved money and not kept my mind disturbed by the question of how to pay for clothes," she wrote, "I would have lived in greater inner harmony." But what she'd called an "industrial war" seemed to have led to an industrial peace. For all her later regrets, she would remember the era for "the warmth and fluidity" of her love. It was the start of the Roaring Twenties; they were young; they had their health; they had a good income. And they had their family.

Her older brother now described himself as a Manufacturer of Paints. In 1919, he got engaged to a twenty-eight-year-old Jewish woman formerly from the Twin Cities. They were married the next year, and at thirty-seven, he moved out of the family home for the first time, renting a nearby apartment.

Her younger sister had turned her piano skills into a career. In her midtwenties, she'd spent a year studying in New York, given well-received recitals there, and performed with the Minneapolis Symphony Orchestra. She'd been recognized as "a bright particular star," and one magazine insisted "the name will no doubt be classed among those of the great pianists."[10] But instead, she'd followed the traditional route. She'd put her career to the side and married a nice Jewish man in the business of "smelting and refining" for dental inlays. Their reception at the Radisson had 200 guests.[11] She, too, moved out of the family house.

The baby brother was twenty-seven now. His fantasies about an adventurous life—raising a pet bear, rescuing his family from raging fires—were things of the past. A small man, 5' 3", with brown hair and the family's gray eyes, he described himself as "Salesman, Paint & Oil." He was still living at home.

So was the oldest sister, thirty-nine and single. The ugly, whispered words were "spinster" and "old maid." Her family and friends knew she continued to carry a torch for the man she'd met as a teenager, the one she'd gone to California to forget. And he—attractive, boyish in middle-age, long-since married—still flirted with her. "He sent her a card about sex appeal," her sister noted in the diary. "He asked her to go driving with him. He took her in his arms once. . . ." It was an awkward if not quite scandalous situation. The older sister would go out with the married couple, claiming her relationship to the man's wife was based on "loyalty and friendship." Nothing overt happened, but the single woman couldn't leave it, couldn't leave him alone. "She went on playing," the diary notes, "flattered by his interest, straddling the situation, patting herself on the back but all the time proud of her conquest. . . ."

Her father was still the ostensible head of the company and maintained his position in local society. In the midst of anti-German, anti-Jewish sentiments, he posted the biographical entry where he described himself as "thoroughly American in spirit and interests. . . ." And confirmed his belief that "America has been to him the land of opportunity." He was no longer immigrant or peddler or even store owner; business had made him American. "[H]e exemplifies the spirit of progress and enterprise which has been the chief factor in the upbuilding of the Northwest." In return, "through his membership with the Civic & Commerce Association, he does all in his power to promote the welfare and prosperity of his adopted city."[12]

Of all the associations he could have joined, this was a telling one. Founded back in 1892, the Civic & Commerce Association began like a kind of rotary club: promoting the city, encouraging new businesses, supporting "commercial supremacy." The advertising man had been involved even before her father; it was the kind of popular boosterism they both believed in. During the war—with socialism spreading both among farmers and city residents—the Association shifted from pro-business to anti–organized-labor. Its "Patriotic, Preparedness and Prosperity" tour covered fifty-nine Minnesota cities, emphasizing the connections between love of country, support for the war, and getting ahead.[13] To belong to the Association was to oppose the Socialist mayor, to rally against the Farmer-Labor Party, to help quell the city's streetcar strike in 1917. Soon, the anti-labor Citizens' Alliance was made up "almost exclusively" of members of the Civic & Commerce Association.[14]

Her mother, meanwhile, had gone from being president of the Council of Jewish Women to president of the Hebrew Ladies Benevolent Society. She remained an active member of her temple's Bible Study group, where the family "intellectual" stood out for her close analysis and her ability to memorize psalms. Then on Yom Kippur, 1921, as the congregation gathered for the day of atonement, their "socialistic" rabbi died suddenly of a heart attack, age forty-eight. He was eulogized as "that valiant spirit, that indefatigable worker, that wise leader and affectionate friend. . . ."[15] Soon, Temple Israel shifted from his left-leaning, inclusive ways back to a more moderate, isolated position. Her mother was among those in the community who helped the replacement rabbi find his way. Years later, he would remember her as "a very remarkable woman."[16]

After the war (and a worldwide flu pandemic), the US saw a surge in population.[17] Both her elder brother and younger sister had daughters in 1921. The next year, she had their third child. She was thirty-six, her husband thirty-eight, their youngest son nine. A new child meant taking time from her writing, again, and pulling back from the social engagement she'd just begun to revive. But the baby came and was a girl. Now she could be a mother as her mother had been to her, extending the female line, but in a new era with new values.

The daughter would grow up able to vote and with a broader range of opportunity—if not equality. In 1923, suffragist/feminist Alice Paul returned to Seneca Falls for the 75th anniversary of the women's convention there. She introduced a resolution that went beyond just voting; it became known as the Equal Rights

Amendment. "Men and women shall have equal rights throughout the United States and every place subject to its jurisdiction." Until such a law passed, Paul declared, "We shall not be safe. . . ."[18]

Opposition remained strong. In the South, women's rights were feared as a step toward racial equality. And Northeastern industrialists tended to see the issue as a wedge toward unionism, opening the question of working hours, wages, and job conditions for all.[19] Already, women's votes were affecting child labor laws, among other issues. But the worry that women's enfranchisement would open the door to revolution proved baseless. The new Reconstruction didn't happen; many women put their efforts, instead, into "clubs" like the League of Women Voters and the Parents Teachers Association.[20]

There's a photograph of the extended family taken in the early '20s, a professional portrait made on the occasion of her parents' fiftieth wedding anniversary. Three generations are posed at the parents' home. In the long dark living room, trimmed with oak molding, a mirror glints in the background over a central fireplace. Sofas and high-backed chairs are grouped in a semicircle; on a deeply varnished side-table, a potted fern. It has the feel if not of the tomb then of fixed formality.

The white-haired matriarch from Charleston sits on one side, smiling and looking across the room at her white-haired husband, her cousin. Her broad hands are poised on the chair's armrests as if she's ready to rise and assist if anyone needs anything. The middle daughter, the diarist, sits nearby, her posture a little stiff, her hair already showing gray. Her husband, the advertising man, stands behind her. In bowtie and glasses, he holds their dark-haired infant daughter on one arm. Her second son is nearby; the oldest son faces them from another stiff sofa across the room.

Around them are the rest of the relatives. Her younger brother is a short, intense man in glasses, with a small black moustache, his shoulders slightly stooped. Her younger sister, the former pianist, holds a small child. The eldest sister sits in unadorned dark clothing next to the older brother's wife and infant daughter. The older brother stands behind them, slouched slightly, more informal than the rest, or more sickly.

At the end of the semicircle, in a high-backed chair, sits her father, the patriarch, a grandchild on each knee. The toddlers look at the camera, full of life; he looks away, fragile.

The photograph memorializes the family as it was and never would be again. The "thoroughly American" patriarch would die a year later, age seventy-three, and be buried in the temple graveyard. A week of sitting *shiva* followed, bringing the family back to the large formal room, this time with friends and relatives in mourning clothes, sweet lily-scented air, silence.

Life and the family business went on. Her widowed mother was now the majority stockholder, the oldest son finally and officially in charge. Though small local paint manufacturers like theirs were "being gradually superseded by the larger, better equipped factory," he actively pushed their line, touring the state, placing it with other jobbers in other towns.[21] He became treasurer, then president, of the Minneapolis–St. Paul Paint, Oil and Varnish Club. Her husband, meantime, ran for office at the Minnesota Advertising Club.[22] Both men were positioning their company and themselves to get ahead, though her husband, as always, was more sociable than ambitious. His transition from selling clothes to selling paint had gone smoothly. It was still a question of attracting consumers, and peace time prosperity helped.

In the Twenties, there was a "conviction," according to economist John Kenneth Galbraith, "that God intended the American middle class to be rich." It was inevitable and would be all but "effortless."[23] Wages kept rising, prices on mass-produced items fell, and spending on advertising reached an all-time high.[24] Real estate was booming. In their old hometown of Jacksonville, for example, out-of-staters were snapping up thousands of acres of building lots, often sight-unseen. Two-thirds were bought by mail through flyers and newspaper ads.[25] The 1925 *Miami Herald* claimed it was packed with more advertising than any paper "in the history of the world."[26]

And there were examples closer to home. On South Marquette Avenue in Minneapolis, passersby could stop and gawk at the construction of a thirty-two story Art Deco building designed as a symbol of success and ambition. Foshay Tower was to be the tallest skyscraper not only in the city but between Chicago and the west coast. Its owner, Wilbur Foshay, was one of the era's self-made men. Born back east in 1882, he'd started out as an electrician, worked his way up to managing a power-and-light company in Kansas, then married the owner's daughter and moved to Minneapolis. Borrowing $6000, he then bought an electric supplier in Nebraska and parlayed it into the hot investment scheme of the day, a holding company.

Holding companies didn't manufacture anything or even provide services; they held shares in other companies that did.[27] In flush times, as stocks rose, finance itself became a way to get rich. In Thorstein Veblen's definition, a holding company amounted to "sufficiently few men to control a section of the community sufficiently long to make an effective monopoly."[28] By the end of the Twenties, the W.B. Foshay holding company, focused on utilities, would be worth $20 million and hold interest in operations in thirty states, Alaska, Canada, and Central America.[29]

Again, the key was mass communication. Foshay "promoted the sale of [its] various securities to all classes of people by a constant campaign of advertising, personal solicitation of salesmen, circular letters, pamphlets, newspaper and magazine advertisements. . . ."[30] Wealth rose to the top, pyramiding like the skyscraper on South Marquette. The groundbreaking for the tower was an extravaganza with half-nude dancers and a special musical composition written and played by the great band leader, John Phillip Sousa. It was the modern version of throwing overcoats out your store window.

The turn of the century had seen a "tidal wave" of corporate consolidation involving a quarter to a third of the nation's manufacturers. The country had matured into "a fully capitalist economy," where many saw the market and society as one and the same.[31] Sociologists and economists had come to accept consumerism as a large part of what united the United States. "As consumers of wealth, we exhibit an amazing mental and moral solidarity. We want the same things."[32]

In this booming atmosphere, the business of providing paint and brushes to local contractors felt old-fashioned and limited. With his father gone, her big brother began to pull money out of the business for other, more exciting investments. The largest was a partnership in a hotel on the border of North Dakota and Montana. It was the sort of investment a travelling salesman saw as a sure thing. The elegant three-story establishment had sixty-two bedrooms, an interior finished in fumed oak, and a dining room that seated over eighty guests.[33] Located in a town of five hundred people, it may not have been the Foshay Tower, but it must have seemed to him to have more growth potential, more excitement than the family business.

The Twenties roared, and anything was possible. Never mind loneliness; never mind inequality. To be American was to be on the verge of unending prosperity. It was a great financial blaze, and they were all melting.

. 23 .

SHE WROTE SHORT STORIES and poetry. She wrote essays and delivered the occasional lecture/book review at the Woman's Club, the Wellesley Club, or for a study group at the Council. All this got done in her spare time—when she wasn't raising children or keeping house--and in the hope of "being heard" in the literary world. She submitted to magazines. "[I]t is my chief satisfaction, in spite of my high pile of rejection slips."

She dreamed her writing would have the impact of someone like Sinclair Lewis. His novels of the early 1920s—*Main Street (1920), Babbitt (1922)*—were set in her part of the country, which he referred to as "that bewildered empire called the American Midwest."[1] Born and raised a hundred miles west of Minneapolis, Lewis took apart the "unsparing unapologetic ugliness" of small town Minnesota and, by extension, America.[2] "Main Street," he wrote, with some of Veblen's ironic bite, "is the climax of civilization. . . . Such is our comfortable tradition and sure faith." He went on to skewer the new American empire, declaring that only "an alien cynic . . . [would] distress the Citizens' by speculating whether there may not be other faiths."[3]

The heroine of *Main Street* is a college-educated woman trying to instill progressive ideas into midwestern society. *Babbitt* takes on a city a lot like Minneapolis, "a new type of civilization" built on "extraordinary, growing, and sane standardization of stores, offices, streets, hotels, clothes, and newspapers. . . ."[4] Lewis wrote about modern women's "discontent"—they're being "ironed into glossy mediocrity," settling for "making a comfy home and bringing up some cute kids and knowing nice homey people"—and connected it to the "ancient, stale inequalities."[5] His work challenged the American values behind the family paint store, behind the family, and she took it to heart, delivering a talk to the Council: "Mob Psychology as Exemplified in the Novels of Sinclair Lewis."[6]

Even as the economy boomed in the mid-1920s and Minneapolis expanded its population by over 20 percent, there was what was called an "agricultural depression."[7] The earlier, wartime market had exhibited an apparently bottomless appetite, with the nation planting an additional thirty million acres. The government promoted slogans like "Food Will Win the War" and "Plow to the Fence for Defense." The year peace came, Minnesota's wheat crop was up 70 percent, hog production had risen by 15 percent, and the corn crop was the largest ever.[8] But the boom depended on overseas demand. As that slowed, there started to be a surplus of wheat. Prices dropped rapidly.[9] A bushel that brought $2.58 in July 1920 was down to $1.43 by the beginning of December and a dollar by the next year.[10]

Out of necessity, Minnesota's farmers began diversifying. By 1930, the once-dominant grain crop would account for only 10 percent of Minnesota's farm output. But diversification could only help so much. As Europe rebounded and began to produce its own food, prices fell further.[11] Between 1920 and 1925, the average value of a Minnesota farm dropped more than 30 percent.[12] Residents of the Midwest's rural towns started selling farms and moving into the big cities, chasing work. For the first time in American history, the number of farms fell, even as total acreage increased; it was the beginning of more corporate agrobusiness.[13]

Minnesota's remaining family farmers realized that in order to survive, they'd need to organize and take political action. In *Main Street,* Sinclair Lewis has a character talk about "Swedes [who] . . . turn socialist or populist or some fool thing."[14] During World War I, the rural Non-Partisan League had formed a loose coalition with the state Federation of Labor to create a third party, an alternative to both Democrat and Republican called the Farmer-Labor Party. It now began drawing from a wide range of voters: progressive Republicans, socialists, and others who believed the mainstream parties couldn't deliver the change they needed. Farmer-Labor's stated goal was to have "the basic and monopolist industries owned and operated by the government: steel, oil, textiles, grain elevators, mills, railroads, etc.—the big banks also."[15] By 1922, Farmer-Labor was strong enough to win both of Minnesota's Senate seats as well as a Congressional race, and it only lost the governorship by 2 percent of the vote.[16]

In town, Minneapolis business was doing fine—Pillsbury and General Mills were expanding into giant corporations—but a lot of freight was now being diverted to the Panama Canal, which had opened in 1914. And some milling began to shift to Buffalo, New York and down into the South.[17] The Citizens' Alliance attributed Minneapolis's continuing prosperity to its ability to keep out unions. "[T]he open shop is more firmly established in private industry than at any time in the history of the city."[18] Across the nation, the total of unionized workers dropped from five million in 1920 to 3.5 million by mid-decade.[19] A union organizer called it "a sad commentary on civilization." Among industrial workers, men in the flour mills were putting in twelve-hour days and qualified as "the most underpaid next to the steel industry."[20]

By 1920, a quarter of the residents of Minneapolis were immigrants; if you added the children of immigrants, it was two-thirds.[21] In reaction, there was a wave of what people had begun calling "Americanism." *Aliens* were blamed for flooding the job market and lowering wages. The Immigration Act of 1924 contained a number of firsts, including absolute quotas on newcomers and required visas and photo id's for those entering the country. As the chief author of the act put it, "the myth of the melting pot has been discredited . . . [T]he day of indiscriminate acceptance of all races has definitely ended."[22] Even those who thought they were already assimilated had to reconsider.

The number of Italian and Polish immigrants was falling, even as the popularity of the post–Leo-Frank Ku Klux Klan surged.[23] Reorganized by a Mason and recruiting heavily in Masonic lodges, by 1921 the KKK claimed to have a presence in forty-five states; its Minnesota membership would soon pass 10,000.[24] "[O]ld stock Americans are coming to believe," according to the Klan's paper, *The Fiery Cross,* "that the Jews dominate the economic life of the nation, while the Catholics are determined to dominate the political and religious life."[25] Foremost on the list of unAmericans were the Reds. Not only corporations but major unions like the American Federation of Labor began to purge their rolls of suspected socialists and communists.[26] Sinclair Lewis mimicked the man-on-the-street's reaction: "What they ought to do is simply hang every one of these agitators. . . ."[27]

1920s Americanism included anti-Semitism. The way one historian put it, "the Jews faced a sustained agitation . . . an agitation that reckoned them the most dangerous force undermining the nation."[28] Quoting a fabricated text, *The Protocols of the Elders of Zion,* conspiracy theorists began blaming a Jewish-Masonic plot for World War I.[29] The situation had become so acute that a hundred prominent Citizens'—including Woodrow Wilson and William Howard Taft—signed a petition defending the patriotism of Jews.[30] One local rabbi noted that in 1922 "Minneapolis Jewry enjoys the painful distinction of being the lowest esteemed community in the land so far as the non-Jewish population of the city is concerned."[31]

The corporate ladder was still mostly closed to them. Downtown buildings in Minneapolis had their own quota system, making it difficult for Jewish physicians and lawyers to rent space. The city's public schools hired few Jewish teachers. Entire Minneapolis neighborhoods were redlined, making it impossible for Jews to live there. And key social clubs like the Rotary, Kiwanis, Lions stayed exclusively Christian.[32] Nationally, the Masons' "sacred asylum" began advocating for a White Protestant United States.[33]

The prevailing response among the local Jewish community was the traditional one. Like the long ago Jews in Bohemia, like Jews in the South, they kept a low profile, looked the other way, stuck to their own. It was her mother's nonquestion writ large: "What do you care for the rest." But there was a built-in contradiction. In the increasingly corporate and global economy, the idea was to network, expand, become less local. And wasn't that also the basis of Wilson's New Freedom and her pacifism: that people could no longer afford to be tribal, to be confined to their own? For peace to work, you had to "care for the rest."

The advertising man and his wife tried to walk a line between modernism and tradition. They had both boys bar mitzvahed. And though they now lived across town in their modernist home, they maintained their ties to the old family temple. By now, its congregation had outgrown the brick building her father had helped build. With the center of German Jewish culture shifted to the more fashionable southside, the congregation began raising funds for a new structure.[34] It would be less Moorish-looking, less foreign. While its twelve columns would symbolize the twelve tribes of Israel and its five doors the five books of the Torah, its overall appearance was white marble neoclassical American. At the dedication ceremony in July of 1927, her mother's "History of the Congregation" was read aloud.[35]

But for both the diarist and her husband, visits to the temple had become infrequent and largely ceremonial. They still observed the high holy days, held the Passover banquet, fasted on the Day of Atonement. They would go on the *yahrzeit* occasions, the memorial days of their parents' deaths. But when it came to religion, she "had resolved," she wrote in a thinly disguised self-portrait, "that her children should be spared the battle she had fought. As soon as they were old enough to think, she would see that no false ideas were to find a place in their minds. There would be no wasted years, no confused doubts. . . ."

If she had her way, her children would be free of the small town, small-minded parochialism that haunted Sinclair Lewis's characters—free of both the "sure faith" in America's singularity and the traditional faith in an all-knowing "magnificent man." If that left them facing the modern world without belief in higher good? "She would sense their misgivings, having experienced them herself, and would be there as a loving guide."

Education, literature, rationalism: those were her alternatives to religion; that's what she would use to guide her children. She became chairman [*sic*] of the Council's committee on education. Through their teens, the boys went to public school and, in their free time, the public park across the street. They played baseball in the summer, football in the fall, hockey through the long winter. Coordinated, outgoing, intelligent, they were judged by who they were and what they did, not where their ancestors had emigrated from, not their religion. That, anyway, was her hope and still one of the country's fundamental promises.

The eldest son joined his own national fraternal organization, the Boy Scouts. Founded the year he was born, the Boy Scouts dressed in military-like uniforms and offered their prescription for becoming an American: stay "physically strong, mentally awake and morally straight." By seventeen, he'd risen to Eagle Scout. The next year, he was accepted at an East Coast Ivy League college. It was her parents' dream, her dream, reenacted. Maybe it would be different for him, a generation later and a man. Maybe it would open doors that had stayed closed to her.

But Dartmouth, where he went, was if anything more restrictive than Wellesley. All male, the New Hampshire college admitted mostly students from the "elite Anglo-Saxon culture," the future leaders of business and government.[36] The problem was that as more *Aliens* got access to better education, more and more sons of immigrants tested well enough to qualify for admission. Dartmouth's response was to have a quota: no more than 6 percent of the incoming class could be Jewish.[37] And the office of admissions tried to make sure those were "the better types of Jews and not the Brooklyn and Flatbush crowd." To that end, it instituted a policy of a photograph with each application to screen out "Jewish students of a physical type unattractive to the average Dartmouth student."[38]

The college president, Ernest M. Hopkins, had made his position clear in the early Twenties. President Hopkins considered a "characteristic of the Jewish race at all times and under all conditions [to be] . . . unhappiness of the soul and the destructive spirit of revolt." They were, by nature, radicals. And their "jaundiced mullings" undermined both the Dartmouth tradition and "the spirit which education is supposed to produce. . . ."[39] Challenged on the admissions quota, President Hopkins told *The New York Times,* "Dartmouth College is a Christian College funded for the Christianization of its students."[40]

To be Christianized was to become American. To become American—at Dartmouth and elsewhere—was to prepare students to enter a triumphant economic system. Big business in America," the argument went, "is providing what the Socialists held up as their goal: food, shelter, and clothing for all."[41] In the summer of 1928, Herbert Hoover, the Republican nominee for president, declared: "[W]e shall soon, with the help of God, be within sight of the day when poverty will be banished from the nation."[42] Half the nation's families owned cars; the other half couldn't be far behind.

What drew less attention was that three-quarters of those cars had been bought on credit.[43] As the decade progressed, it became clear that the Roaring Twenties roared only for a small percentage of Americans. The long trend of inequality continued, with some 75 percent of families earning under $3000 a year and without savings.[44] Company profits were up, but wages had plateaued. Corporate interests were monopolizing the market, threatening both the family farm and the family business. In the Twenties, America's two hundred biggest companies grew at almost double the rate of smaller ones.[45] Big business was helped by a sharp reduction in taxes, increased tariff protection, less federal regulation.[46] The nation as a whole saw a 9 percent gain in income in the Twenties, but the top 1 percent gained 75 percent. And the top 0.1 percent of the rich held about a third of all savings.[47] In *Main Street,* Lewis suggested the United States had ended up with a permanent economic hierarchy, including a leisure class and an "American peasantry . . . settled into submission to poverty."[48]

Banks kept providing easy credit, and advertising kept urging consumers to consume. Improved technology helped turn out more wheat, more steel, more paint. During the decade, the value of the Dow Jones had increased tenfold, and it went up 20 percent just in the summer of 1929. Then in September, the British market took a fall. And on Wednesday, October 23rd, 1929, so did American stock.

The next day, Black Thursday, at the opening bell, the US market lost over 10 percent of its value. Thirteen million shares of stock proceeded to change hands. As *The New York Times* reported, "Fear struck the big speculators and little ones, big investors and little ones. Thousands of them threw their holdings into the whirling Stock Exchange pit for what they would bring."[49]

Friday, President Hoover reassured the nation, "The traditional business of the country . . . is on a sound and prosperous basis."[50] The big banks pooled their resources to halt the fall. But the next Monday became "the most devastating day in the history of the markets." The stock exchange lost another 13 percent of its value.[51] The day after saw an enormous amount of trading—and another loss of 12 percent.

In St. Paul, a Black bellboy at the "wealthy, prestigious, white Minnesota Club" noticed the newspaper headline: MARKET CRASHES—PANIC HITS NATION. "I couldn't imagine," he wrote, "such financial disaster touching my small world; it surely concerned only the rich. But by the first week of November I too knew differently; along with millions of others across the nations, I was without a job."[52]

Two months after the completion of his tower, Wilbur Foshay saw his multimillion dollar holding company collapse. He'd defied the Citizens' Alliance by building his symbol of the new economy with union labor. As punishment, the Alliance had gotten a local bank to buy up his loans and demand repayment.[53] Then came the crash. Within weeks, Foshay's loans were worthless; he was so bankrupt, the check he'd written John Phillips Sousa bounced. A few years later, he'd be convicted of running a pyramid scheme and go to federal prison.[54]

By mid-November, the Dow had lost almost half its value.[55] At the synagogue, some members cancelled their pledges to pay for the new building; others resigned, unable to come up with annual dues.[56] It was the equivalent of Charleston after the Civil War.

Her family rested in the "comfortable tradition and sure faith" that they'd be sheltered from the fall. They had the paint business, after all. She and her husband felt sure they'd be able to continue to pay the eldest son's college tuition and provide for both their sixteen-year-old, captain of the high school hockey team, and their nine-year-old daughter. They were as safe as you could be from the collapsing system.

Then on a November evening stroll, her husband broke the news.

. 24 .

"WHILE WE WERE WALKING UP the Avenue, without introduction, [my husband] told me [my brother] had buttonholed him one morning at the store and told him one or the other of them must get out of the business. The business couldn't afford to support them both. . . ."

The immediate shock hit on a number of levels. That her brother would fire her husband. That her family would turn on her. That the paint business was in such desperate straits.

If the business really couldn't support both salaries, it—and the family—were in far more trouble than anyone had admitted. Its income supported her mother and eldest sister. Both her older and younger brother worked there. She depended on it, not only for her husband's pay but through her shares of stock. If the business was truly one salary away from collapse, then nothing and none of them were secure.

Across the country, the mask of prosperity had fallen. In a matter of weeks, the economy had gone from optimism to despair. Her family had watched from a certain distance, insulated (as always?) by their business. Now, the crash had come home.

Her husband took it personally. It was a betrayal of friendship and of trust, and his first reaction was simply to walk away. "Well, of course, I'll get out."

She understood. He'd given up his position at Palace Clothing, one he'd held for almost two decades, because her big brother "had asked him in, urged and persuaded him to leave." Husband and wife had talked it over at the time, and while the move to the paint business made sense in a number of ways, it was based above all on the two men's lifelong friendship.

A decade had passed. Her husband had "worked for the firm," she wrote in her diary, "and gave what he had to give of enthusiasm and energy and ideas. . . ."

It was a measured phrase: "what he had to give." Her husband wasn't a go-getter, didn't want to be. Maybe a go-getter could have resurrected the business over the first five years when her father was still alive and the five years since when her brother was managing things. Or maybe nobody could have. The economy of size, the power of corporations, was replacing small family concerns. What had brought them this far no longer made sense.

She didn't blame her husband for quitting. She saw him as "supersensitive . . . if [my brother] wanted him out, he would go." But you didn't have to be supersensitive to understand the implications. "For ten years, working side by side, [my brother] felt [my husband] was a drain on the rest of them. . . ." A drain. As if her husband had never really been qualified for the job, had gotten it through marriage not merit.

And there was more. The way her brother broke the news—"casually"—it was as if he assumed her husband knew—knew the business had been carrying him all those years, knew his salary amounted to a kindness, knew she and the children had been living on unspoken charity. And implied, beyond that, that the family had known it, too.

Her husband's first reaction was to resign; his second was to go quiet. "[He] was hurt. So hurt he waited several days to tell me." In the interim, her brother told their mother "[who] owned the largest share of the business—controlled the major stock and the deciding vote."

The child of Charleston, now seventy-three-years-old, had "sympathy for each—too much," her middle daughter wrote, "No one ever lived who forgave so easily, so generously. . . ." The mother scolded her eldest son. "She told him it was a terrible thing to have done." Then she tried to patch things up. "She called [my husband] to her house and begged him to come back. . . ."

The round, easygoing, bow-tied forty-five-year-old met with his mother-in-law, a kindly looking woman with warm eyes and an open face, her gray hair brushed straight back, her clothes dark and simple. She asked him to return to work, and he listened to her politely, respectfully. But as the diary noted, "his pride wouldn't let him."

He'd been accused of spending a decade living off the family business, of taking a free ride. Now his mother-in-law was offering him his job back as another act of charity. No, he couldn't accept.

It was after he'd resigned and then refused to come back that he went on the evening stroll and finally told his wife. After the shock had worn off a little, she had another reaction. "I was angry," she wrote, "angrier than I'd ever been."

The rational business side of her spoke up. "I was a director and stockholder. I should have been told in advance. The other stockholders should have been advised and have considered the matter." The other stockholders were, of course, her relatives. If one of the officers of the company was an ongoing "drain," that should have been brought up at the annual meeting. What's more, if the business had gotten to the point where it had to cut management positions, they should have had some warning of that, too.

But the only people who'd known it was coming were her older brother, his wife (who "had been heckling him to get [my husband] out for years"), and her younger brother, the company's chief salesman.

That hurt. Her little brother—who had adored her, who had written her in his childish handwriting when she was away at Wellesley—had known and said nothing. "If you can't get along," he'd told her husband, "why, one of you better leave. [He] is the son of father, who built the business. He knows more about it. Nothing remains but for [you] to get out."

Little brother had sided with big brother, with continuity, with tradition. He had, she knew, his reasons. Now in his late thirties, he'd been living at home, in his parents' house, since coming back from the war. Then a few months ago, he'd gotten married. And his marriage had challenged tradition, continuity, the family itself.

Her siblings might pride themselves on being various degrees of modern and openminded, but none had married a non-Jew. It was, of course, prohibited. "Neither shalt thou make marriages with them," Deuteronomy said, "thy daughter thou shalt not give unto his son, nor his daughter shalt thou take unto thy son. . . ."[1]

That admonition held less power for their modern generation, but their family had always stuck to their own. People talked about it like it was a Jewish trait, but wasn't it how most immigrants (which is to say, most Americans) lived? An Irishman married an Irish woman and stayed in an Irish neighborhood. Germans, Poles, Blacks did the equivalent, by choice or by necessity.

Her family's definition of assimilation—from Bohemia to New York to the South to Minneapolis—was to try and fit in wherever they found themselves, but always to maintain the difference: the us and them. If you looked at her parents' case, you could argue that the taboo against marrying out was even stronger than the taboo against marrying in: better a first cousin than a non-Jew.

In the old days, a Jew who wed a Gentile received a rabbinical funeral service; such a person was dead to Judaism.[2] Her little brother had crossed that line. He'd married a Danish farm girl from North Dakota. She was part of the 20 percent of Minneapolis that was Scandinavian, more than half its foreign-born population. Described in a nineteenth century history as "a sturdy, hard working, earnest, pious class of people," they formed their own Lutheran society.[3] Thousands of these immigrant daughters had left the wheat and dairy farms to work as domestics, while the men loaded lumber and grain on the docks, did the heavy work on the railroads. They occupied the low rung of the economy, almost as out-of-bounds for a middle-class Jew as slaves had been in the South.

Her short, dark-complexioned little brother saw the fair-skinned Scandinavians in the store as customers, or in the news as socialists agitating for change, or at home as maids. Now, he'd married one: the sort of girl hired to keep house and make meals, who had to be taught how to serve and to call family members "sir" and "madam."

His wife, ten years younger, soon gave birth to a baby boy. They named the child after his deceased father, but the family split couldn't be healed that easily. Husband, young wife, their baby, and the wife's younger sister had gone to live in a rented apartment in St. Paul. He wasn't banished exactly—he still worked at the firm—but he'd become something else. Was this what it meant to be American, to break from Old-World traditions, to cross boundaries, to marry democratically? If so, it had brought another kind of loneliness.

This latest crisis—the firing of the advertising man—offered her little brother a chance to prove family loyalty, a way back in. He sided with his big brother: "the son of father who built the business."

Again, her rational side argued that anyone who looked at the situation unemotionally could see past her big brother's façade. "I knew," she wrote in her diary, "his procrastinating methods. I knew his terrific egotism, his pride that would lead him to blame others, never to admit or acknowledge his own indecency. I knew how many ventures he had wasted time and money on, stubbornly continuing at a loss despite the bank's insistence that he stop financing his private ventures at the expense of the family business."

If she knew, the others knew. The bank had sent up warning flares that the core business, the paint store, was in jeopardy. As she wrote in her diary, the oldest brother had "plugged along—physically far below par, low in energy—living with one kidney, neglecting his health, trying to keep up the family business and his own [the hotel] in another city, besides smaller investments." Ambitious, he'd wanted to make his own mark. Hadn't his father said that the Midwest was built on the "spirit of progress and enterprise?" Didn't a savvy businessman jump on opportunities and ride them? In the updraft of the Twenties, only a fool stayed grounded.

The family had pretended not to see, had chosen fiction over reality. "I knew— we all knew—credit (so firm and secure while father lived) was going. Each year," she wrote, "showed the business losing, losing." And losing even as the Twenties' economy roared. That was the real unspoken secret—not her husband's business failures but her big brother's.

The family had glossed that over, had assumed success, but the truth was the paint business had been in the red for a while. "We had appealed for a thorough professional investigation. [My older brother] put it off. He knew where the trouble lay, he said. Next year 'we will correct it.'" Next year had turned into next, and now the stock market crash had laid the whole situation bare. The economy that had run on credit, on optimism, had stopped running, and her brother's losses had become real. In desperation, he'd reached for an explanation, an excuse. "All the blame he thrust on [my husband]."

While she understood her husband's response—to resign and refuse to come back—pride didn't pay the bills. Never mind the finer things, the quality items she liked to have around; there were the basic necessities—groceries, the mortgage, college tuition for the eldest son. And in less than two years, their second son would be ready to go to college, as well.

With the economy plummeting, with her husband out of work, something had to be done. Not long after the evening stroll, she found her chance. "I went to mother's one morning when I heard [my older brother] was there talking to her." She picked a dress from her respectable wardrobe and, looking "harmonious, suitable," rang the bell to the family house.

Morning light fought its way into the dark, luxurious living room, streaked the thick rugs that seemed to muffle everything, glinted off the large family portraits. All of this—all they had—came from the paint business, which had now existed in its various forms for more than eighty-five years. From peddling on the streets of New York through the ruins of the Civil War and the extravagance of the Gilded Age, what had emerged to carry them, to allow them to survive as Americans, was the "firm."

Her mother, a child of that business, sat in one of the plush, high-backed chairs. Near her was her eldest surviving son, sick from kidney disease, no longer the young go-getter, now fighting to keep control of the business and of the family. Enter the properly dressed, gray-eyed middle daughter, here to stand up for her husband and herself.

She asked her brother to explain what had happened. "He told me [my husband] had been a drain on the business: he was inefficient; he handled customers poorly. He threw all the blame . . . on [him]. And here I knew . . . [that if my husband], coming from seventeen years under one of the great merchants of the country, offered a suggestion, urged up-to-date methods, he was dictatorially squelched. . . ."

Her brother ran the business the way their father and grandfather had: from the top down. It was her belief that "my father, physically old and sick, had wished to change. . . ." But for her brother, the firm was the firm. "He didn't investigate modern methods. He stayed in the small orbit in which our business moved 20 or 30 years earlier. He went on being led, not leading, by primitive methods. . . ." As corporations had taken hold, fed by mass production and national advertising campaigns—as socialists and others had marched in the streets to protest inequalities—her brother had kept the business as is. Within the "small orbit" that included New York, Charleston, Jacksonville, Minneapolis, connections had been established and passed down through the children and grandchildren of the founders. These "primitive methods" might no longer be functional, but her brother had been too content, or too shortsighted, or too busy with his hotel, to change them.

She sat in the darkened room, listening to her brother explain how the business was sure to rebound, how none of the failure was his doing, how her husband had never really fit in or contributed. She was well aware how a "good girl" was supposed to react: the same way her mother had. The decision belonged to the eldest male. Never mind that her mother was now majority stockholder. Business was men's domain, the son's domain. His word was final.

Back when the daughter had been at Wellesley, her mother's advice was clear: "the real and great things of life [are] the love and respect of your . . . own dear ones." Back then, her daughter had followed it, "afraid not to conform, afraid her parents would see her and question." She'd reacted as a dutiful, respectful daughter, and much had followed from it: her return to Minneapolis, her marriage to her childhood friend, her children. Now, she was expected to do that again, to stay quiet and let the incident settle into history, slip into the dark of the family, undisturbed.

But she couldn't. Her husband had been betrayed; she felt betrayed.

When her brother finished his version of events, she jumped right in. "How I went for him! . . . I told [him] what I thought. I let go. I used no restraint. I hurled unleashed anger at him, anger that had accumulated for several years of insult to which he had subjected [my husband]. . . . I let it all out."

In this civilized, educated, Old World home, voices weren't raised. Except hers was now. "That morning stands out in my memory—harsh, unrestrained, a sharp burst of long suppressed resentment." Suppressed how long? Back to her big brother being treated as if he would inevitably, eventually, run things? Back to her adolescence and the assumption that her life—that all her sisters' lives—would center around finding an acceptable Jewish man and settling down to their real occupation: raising a family? Never mind her younger sister's brief career in music. Or, for that matter, her own Eastern education. Maybe that had been a kind of charity, too—her parents sending her to college, letting her pursue her dream of an intellectual life, knowing all along that, as surely as the brothers would take over the family business, she'd eventually come back to their home, their circle, their values.

"Mother tried to placate me. What I remember most of that day was her effort to have me lower my voice." The daughter shouting in the quiet living room, the brother maintaining a studied calm, the mother insisting that propriety must be kept: a certain Southern—or was it Jewish? or simply old fashioned?—propriety. Family didn't raise its voice. Family kept up appearances. Family overlooked slights, failures, differences of opinion. Family stuck together. "And it angered me the more that her chief consideration was then—and always—what will people think?"

There was worse. "I know she was sorry for me. . . ." That stung: the realization that she was being treated the way her husband had been, as a charity case. The daughter spoke up, tried to tell the truth, and the mother's reaction was to feel sorry for her. "I was stubborn, too," she wrote later, "stubborn in that I kept on expecting them to see and to admit and to ask to be forgiven. . . ." It was like the League of Nations. They were warring countries, stuck with their own prejudices and perspectives—and the parlor should have been one of the "calm spaces" President Wilson had proposed, "where men look at things without passion." Except they couldn't find a calm middle ground. And Wilson had died unable to get Congress to endorse his dream.

Her brother remained unemotional. "He never gets angry," was her analysis; "He's too sure of his own superiority. There are people whose egotism has gradually taken the place of conscience. They can't be wrong. They won't be wrong. Their pride and blind arrogance won't let them." Winner of a college oratory prize, schooled in being the even-tempered businessman, his silence made her look irrational. Like a hysterical woman. Like a radical.

Her mother kept asking her to lower her voice, but instead she went back over it, again and again. She kept repeating her side of the argument, sure that her mother would eventually get it. The business was failing. It was because of her brother, the manager, not her husband. They couldn't keep deceiving themselves. Forget politeness; forget family loyalty. They had to step forward and do something. "I took a stand. That much I did."

Her mother wanted her to accept her husband's firing. To restore peace the way it had always been restored, by going along with the men's decision.

Not this time.

"I asserted myself. Anger blotted out love."

Her big brother maintained his reasonable tone, as if the facts were on his side, as if he somehow owned the facts. From her side, she appealed to her mother's sense of justice. She did it emotionally; she blazed in the dark, curtained room. "Therein," she continues, "was my blame in the whole matter. It's possible if I had remained calm and reasoning. . . ."

Later, her husband assured her that it wouldn't have made a difference: what she said or how she said it. Their minds were made up. "And it is true they wouldn't see. . . ." Or couldn't. The same way her husband's pride wouldn't let him go back to work for the best friend who'd betrayed him. In this, what amounted to a family war, all their roles seemed fixed, preordained, nonnegotiable. Is this what nations felt like: tied into their positions, unable to see common ground? Was this what happened between bosses and workers; what led to strikes?

Years later, in her diary, she concluded that her mother—as controlling stockholder, as surviving head of the family, as their mother—could have made a kind of peace just by acknowledging that the advertising man wasn't to blame, that the business was failing for other reasons. Her husband still would have been out a job, but they might have gone on from there. Except that would have been admitting her son's failure. Instead, she sided with the eldest male. And then tried to smooth it over with money. "The next day she sent me a check of $200, thinking of the financial end, knowing I was distressed at the thought of [my husband] being without a salary and, God, to placate me. . . ."

As if she hadn't been placated enough.

Nearly a decade after the check arrived—and with her mother buried in the temple's cemetery—the daughter wrote, "Poor soul! She knew of no other way to help me. . . . Once after, she told me she didn't want me to think [my big brother] was right; but she was so sorry for him. He had nothing: owed much more than he could ever redress to creditors of his own business. He was ill and she was his mother."

. 25 .

The diary keeps coming back to the incident, analyzing it, looking at what led to it and its aftermath. "I resented [older brother's] arrogance and conceit, his dodging the issue of his own responsibility, his pride of egotism serving for a sense of duty and trust." Calmly, effectively, he'd dismiss her complaints, and their mother went along with him. "Then he said if I thought that—if he was accused of being to blame for that state of the business—he would hire a man to investigate the business. So sure was he of his infallibility."

The family took him up on it. They hired an examiner, but he couldn't come for a couple of months. That prolonged her husband's stay on the job: "[He] wouldn't leave until the man came and he was exonerated. . . . I remember little but crackling anger and disappointment and shock those first weeks. . . ."

Finally, the examiner arrived: a Mr. Blankly, respectable, conservative. "On the first or second day," she reports, "he told [my brother] he was running the business on old-fashioned methods. He advised him to install a cost [analysis] system and so reduce the expenses of his country salesmen. [My brother] resented this and dismissed him from further service."

Word of the dismissal got back to her husband. "[He] telephoned the news to me. I to mother." This time, the mother overrode her son's order. "The family decided that since the man was here, he should finish his job."

When the report was done, the board of directors assembled at the family house. The relatives gathered in the same big formal room where they'd posed for their family portrait, back when her father was still alive. Now the house was occupied by the eldest surviving male and chief officer of the company. He, his wife and two young daughters, were renting for a nominal fee from the widowed mother, who still owned the house. She'd moved ten blocks east, where she leased a place for herself and her eldest daughter, now fifty.

The board of directors was all family: the mother, the eldest son, and the other siblings. Before getting to business, Mother insisted they have dinner. They sat at the table, observing the proprieties, waited on by the help, using the family silver brought up from the South, trying to be civil.

After dinner, Mr. Blankly handed the report to the company secretary—the eldest sister—to read aloud.

"In the report," the diary writes, "he said the manager ran a one-man business. . . . [and] ran it on old-fashioned business methods. . . ." The methods dated back to her grandfather in Charleston and his immigrant mentors in New York's Lower East Side. Decisions were made unilaterally, a one-man hands-on approach with the company manager as patriarch, the suppliers as friends, the workers as loyal and obedient children under a "magnified man."

It was an approach that had carried them through the South and then north to Minneapolis, but modern business valued efficiency above all. It examined procedures in a so-called objective, scientific manner, measuring workers' productivity, manufacturing techniques, distribution, sales strategies, the effectiveness of advertising. It operated in a constant state of streamlining: identifying and cutting excess. Her big brother inherited old methods and old employees, and he couldn't or wouldn't modernize.

"[Mr. Blankly] advised getting [my brother] out as manager . . . He advised getting [him] out as manager [and getting] a new manager before all was lost. To me privately he advised, 'Take your mother's money out or she will have nothing.' . . . [He] took a personal approach, said he wanted to give us—[my brother] rather—a bit of personal advice. He could see [my brother] was sick, that accounted for the things he did, such as . . . the hotel business and . . . [claiming] the failure of [the] business was [my husband's] fault. . . . [He] suggested [my brother] take a rest. [His wife should] take him away for a vacation."

According to the diary, the examiner was confident the board "now would see the light and . . . would put a stop to [my brother's] selfish doings for the sake of all concerned. . . ." The family thanked Mr. Blankly politely and wished him good night. When he left, her brother began his rebuttal.

There was no doubt the business was in trouble. The books made that clear. But he could explain that. "[He] gave a long talk about [my husband's] mistakes and inefficiency. He made him the goat. . . ." Her husband tried to respond. "[He] talked about [my brother]—but [my husband] isn't good at fighting. . . . I wanted to urge him on to more telling, incisive accusations. . . ." But she didn't. She remained in the background, silent. Having exploded the one time, weeks ago— "hurling" her anger at mother and brother—this time, she controlled herself.

"All agreed the report was fair." Of course, it was the Depression, but Mr. Blankly hadn't blamed the economic times; he'd blamed management. In the end, the board (which was the family) "resolved to sell out the business."

The advertising man hadn't exactly been exonerated. "From that day to this," she wrote in her diary, fifteen years later, "no word of defense or support was uttered in [his] behalf. They saw [my older brother's] business going. They knew his record in several attempts . . . Yet they supported him—they protected him. . . ."

Still, the implication was clear. The operation that her big brother had been in charge of was no longer viable. The paint business—the peddler's dream—would be sold off. The stockholders would get paid what their shares were worth (at Depression prices), and the workers, including her husband, would have to look for other jobs.

When the meeting finally drew to a close, the family got their coats and went out into the Minnesota night: she and her husband to their modernist home, her younger sister to her place, her younger brother to his in St. Paul, mother and the eldest sister to their rental. Her big brother remained in the family home. "That very night, [my brother] . . . moved to liquidate . . . moved to form a committee to price the goods. Another to hire a lawyer. Another to arrange for sales, etc."

Then the next day, "[he] changed his mind. . . ."

If the paint business were sold, people would know its true worth—or lack of worth. In the close-knit financial world of the city, that would reflect on its managing officer. The former president of the Paint, Oil and Varnish Club would look incompetent. Even in the Depression, when scores of businesses were closing, her brother's reputation might never recover. And his standing in the even smaller Jewish community would be ruined. What, as his mother might say, would people think? How would his wife and daughters go out in society? How, for that matter, would he find another job?

So he decided, instead, to wage a countercampaign against the board's decision. "He went around in the store and the factory appealing to all the employees on the basis of holding their jobs, to come up to mother's house; attest to his popularity and efficacy and to [my husband's] incompetence and unpopularity." The key to canceling the sale of the business lay in the hands of the majority stockholder. Her big brother organized the employees to appeal to his mother directly.

"The meeting was held at 8 A.M." The board was to assemble at the family house to hear the workers' plea. The diary keeper writes: "We were told by Mother it was to be at 8 o'clock. Of course we assumed it was 8 P.M." Was it a sign of how communication had broken down that no one corrected them? She and her husband missed the morning meeting.

"All but 2 of the office-force went to mother's—2 workers refused to go." When the meeting began, the employees rose one by one and asked that the business not be sold. They were familiar faces. Now they stood in the family home and, hats in hands, asked the widow to spare their jobs.

It was the opposite of a strike—not workers demanding their rights or trying to change the system but humbly requesting that the business stay as is. Hadn't the family always taken care of them, and hadn't they been loyal in return? The patriarch was gone a decade now, but they were asking for the patriarchy to go on.

It worked. Faced with turning familiar faces out on the street (including her sons), the mother changed her mind. And the majority of the stockholders, her children, went along. The business would continue. Her eldest would continue to run it. Only the son-in-law would be out.

"I wish," the diary says, "I could write naturally and unrestrainedly, without ill-will or intolerance or blame or self-excuse or self-glorification or throwing a stone. I wish I might write about it as simply as a mirror: clearly, truthfully." But she couldn't. She wasn't a mirror; if anything, she was a window into her family.

In the diary, she called the event—the failure of the business, her husband's resignation, the family disagreements that followed—a "bare tragedy."

She'd studied tragedy at Wellesley. She knew Aristotle defined it as "an action which has serious implications, is complete, and possesses magnitude."[1] To be a tragedy, one action must be "a consequence of the other . . . [making] the result inevitable."[2] Maybe a man getting fired from a midwestern paint company didn't possess magnitude. It was common, almost anonymous. But looking back, it did seem inevitable. Not because the gods willed it—the Greek or Judeo/Christian gods—but because of the people involved. Her family was made up of "human beings," as the diary put it, " . . . crushed by their own weaknesses—good people, sweet kind people—kind but not just or fair." They were motivated, she concluded, by "drives in themselves that they either do not see or will not recognize." Thus the inevitable result, the bare tragedy without ornament or nobility.

Was this what Tolstoy called the tragedy of the bedroom: small, domestic, unavoidable? Did people everywhere act this way, operating within a small circle of family and friends? Or was a man getting fired from a midwestern paint company part of a larger drama, particularly American, a product of the free-market system that had populated and propelled the continent?

By the start of 1930, several million people across the country were out of work. Henry Ford, who had proclaimed in November, "Things are better today than they were yesterday,"began the new year by laying off about a third of his workforce.[3] Not only were jobs disappearing and wages dropping, but those who'd managed to stay employed were working fewer hours. The economic failure affected everything, including education. Funds for public schools were cut so that fewer teachers taught larger classes. Some three million kids simply stopped attending.[4]

The Depression struck Minneapolis's 22,000 Jews hard.[5] "[S]ince so much of Jewish energy and man-power is devoted to trade and business," a local rabbi observed, "the strain of economic reverses is felt more heavily by the children of Israel."[6] Not only did trade dry up, but the Depression saw a "disturbing rise" in anti-Semitism.[7] Minneapolis residents, desperate for something or someone to blame, settled on the familiar: outsiders, *Aliens,* unAmericans. According to a local observer, "This was one of the worst Jew-hating communities in the world through the Thirties and into the Forties. . . ."[8]

It wasn't—didn't need to be—disguised. In the papers each day, the help-wanted ads read: "Gentile" or "Gentile preferred."[9] Jews were "the last to get the jobs," observed a Minneapolis Jew." Young men never had an opportunity to work in a bank or with the major railroads, and a young woman had no chance at all. . . . The few people that were accepted in the post office and the state were so infini-tesimal against the population that it isn't even worth accounting. . . . We saw the pattern, it was very clear. . . ."[10]

Her husband hovered at the edge of this abyss. In the Thirties, for the first time, the nation had more native-born Jews than immigrants.[11] But two genera-tions of striving—of selling door-to-door, of opening stores, of buying wholesale and selling retail, of becoming American—seemed about to disappear. For mil-lions, the Depression was erasing the idea of "individual achievement," of making your own way. It threw people back to a time when there was no protection, no escape, almost as if they'd never reached the New World. Almost as if the status of full-fledged American citizen could be taken away. Or had never really existed.

Her husband was lucky. By the spring of 1930, just six months after resigning, he'd found work as a secretary at a printing company.[12] Was it through friends, Masonic brothers, connections in the business world? He wasn't an advertising man anymore or even management. But it was a job at a time when some thirty-five thousand Minneapolis residents were out of work. As unemployment soared above 20 percent, the city's historic Gateway Park at Nicollet and Hennepin be-came a new kind of skid row.[13] Compared to that, compared to those shuffling through Gateway Park - or even the whispered hardships among other members of his temple - he was lucky.

The other factor that kept him from becoming one of "the masses" went be-yond luck: the family business continued to throw off some dollars. Right after the advertising man was let go, he wrote the board of directors asking, "if I am not yet employed" in three months, to allow his wife to draw $440 a month against her stock holdings. That stock had been made over to a new corporation. It was a way to shake old debts and make a fresh start, but the basic operation stayed the same. So did the problem of competing with larger national companies. The firm's value kept falling.

The diarist wanted out. She told her mother "she would never be satisfied with the situation where [my eldest brother] was managing a business in which [my] money was invested." She demanded a buyout. Her brother, she wrote, "derided it, said it was an absurdity, [the business had] no money to pay out to minority stockholders." Instead, he authorized "remittances" on her shares: $100 a month, less than a quarter what they'd asked for. It wasn't clear what these payments were—the company buying back stock, or money owed them as stockholders, or simply another form of charity. Within a year, the payments had dropped to $75 a month (about $1200 a month in today's money). Every little bit helped.

The Crash of 1929 didn't apply to Minneapolis in quite the same way it did much of the rest of the country. The city's agricultural-based economy had entered hard times through a gradual, decades-long slide. Earlier in the Twenties, when national wages were going up 11 percent, Minneapolis only rose 2 percent.[14] The extended stagnation convinced many that the system needed radical change.

In 1930, the Farmer-Labor party ran Floyd B. Olson for governor, and Minnesota elected him by a landslide. Olson, child of a Norwegian father and Swedish mother, had grown up on Minneapolis' north side in its "heavily Jewish" community.[15] He learned Yiddish from his Eastern European neighbors and served as a *Shabbos goy*, performing tasks Jews were forbidden to do during Sabbath. After dropping out of the University of Minnesota, he became a lawyer and, eventually, county attorney, obtaining indictments against local KKK leaders and prosecuting corrupt Minneapolis politicians.[16] His statewide reputation came from going up against the Citizens' Alliance. "If private organizations which undertake to enforce the law without cooperating with the duly constituted authorities, and in disregard of the police, are not wiped out," he declared, "this country will soon reach a condition where factions and class violence will be the rule. . . ."[17]

To some, the country was already there. Not long after Olson became Governor, several hundred hungry citizens broke the windows of a Minneapolis grocery store and made off with whatever they could carry. It took a hundred policemen to restore order.[18] That March, a Communist rally turned into a riot when the police tried to disperse the crowd.[19]

Her husband's firing, the bare tragedy, overlapped and intermingled with the Great Depression. Not just business, but government institutions were failing. When the basis of the economic system drops away—when the family fails to support —what's left to melt into? Where and to what did they belong?

. 26 .

PEOPLE NEEDED HELP.

Up until now, American charity had been the responsibility of private agencies, like the Hebrew Benevolent Association and the Ladies Benevolent Society of Charleston. But the scope of the Depression overwhelmed. In New York, Governor Franklin Delano Roosevelt argued that some sort of unemployment relief "must be extended by Government, not as a matter of charity, but as a matter of social duty."[1] Minnesota Governor Olson agreed.

The number of relief cases in Minneapolis in 1932 was six times what it had been just four years earlier.[2] The out-of-work who were camped in Gateway Park began showing up at city council meetings, confronting aldermen, demanding help.[3] They were, they declared, American Citizens'. Among the leisure class, some fretted that "relief" was the first step toward socialism. As Veblen put it, the "predatory social economy" was about individual achievement—each man for himself—and helping the down-and-out was seen as "unnatural."[4] Rural residents also tended to be leery, equating larger government with higher taxes and more regulation.[5] But the situation continued to deteriorate. As food prices dropped, banks and insurance companies cut credit.[6] One observer testified to "a great exodus of girls from the farms into the city now. Thousands of farms have been vacated completely. . . ."[7]

In the fall of 1932, farmers responded by organizing a "holiday." They stopped the harvest, set up pickets outside Minneapolis, and successfully prevented produce from reaching the city. The strategy was to starve the market, forcing prices up. 1932 was an election year. Olson, the Farmer-Labor governor, tried to take a middle ground that wouldn't alienate liberals, including Democratic Presidential nominee Roosevelt. Olson endorsed the goals of the farmers' holiday, but called out the State Highway Patrol to break up protests.[8]

By the winter of 1932–33, when Roosevelt was elected, national unemployment had climbed to 25 percent: twelve million people out of work. The country's gross production had dropped by a third since 1929. There were more strikes in the spring of '33 than in the entire previous decade. The number of workers involved in labor disputes would triple in a year.[9]

In Minneapolis's Hennepin County, a quarter of the factories closed, and some seventy thousand people were jobless. Almost 90 percent of Minnesota's businesses were reporting losses.[10] Those, like her husband, who managed to find work continued to see drops in wages and hours. Over 60 percent of the employed were trying to survive on $20 a week or less.[11] Convinced "the present economic system has shown its inability to provide," Governor Olson declared, "The old pioneer idea of government as confined to police power has passed off the stage. We have now reached the socialized state."[12] Even moderates were calling for some form of government relief. What one historian called the "sophisticated network" of Jewish charity was overwhelmed, and the shift from taking private aid to accepting governmental help began to be seen as a good thing, a democratic thing, "an opportunity for Jews to become fully American."[13]

The Depression stretched worldwide, and the reaction overseas was, if anything, even more intense. In the homeland of German Jews—Germany, Poland, Austria—one in five was unemployed. Industrial output was down 40 percent. Banks and other financial institutions were on the verge of collapse.[14] Adolf Hitler's rise to power followed. In January 1933, he was appointed chancellor; by March, he was given unilateral power to deal with labor unrest and protest in general. That led to the purging of political opponents. By July, all opposing parties had been abolished. Anti-Jewish rhetoric—older than her family's roots in Bohemia—turned into official decrees. Jewish shops were boycotted; Jewish books were burned; the government established a Department of Racial Hygiene.[15]

In Minneapolis, her husband added to his secretary's salary with pieced together work as a freelance advertising man. She was the bill-payer in the family. Her younger son remembered her sitting at her desk in the sunroom, trying to decide if she could put off the butcher another week because they hadn't paid the grocer in a month. He was about to add to family expenses; before his brother graduated from Dartmouth, he would follow him there.

The Ivy League colleges, desperate for paying students, had lowered their admission requirements and seemed to be overlooking their ethnic quotas. But when it seemed the incoming class at Dartmouth might be as much as 15 percent Jewish—almost triple the usual quota—President Hopkins wrote his director of admissions. "I think I would rather take the hazards of what appears to be a group of less scholastic promise, distributed among Anglo-Saxons, Hibernians, Scandinavians and those from other outlying districts, than to let the Jewish population again rise."[16] Still, the second son was accepted. They ended up borrowing money from a family friend for tuition.

Over the next couple years, the payments from her stock in the paint business went down to $35 a month. Her husband's dismissal, their money squeeze, the systemic failure of the economy colored everything. Her sons couldn't afford to make the long trip home very often, but she managed to get east at least once. There, she compared her sons to the other Ivy Leaguers. "When the boys were young," she wrote, "I admired them, was proud of them. I didn't see deficiencies. They made me very happy. And they grew in the light of my praise." But now she found some of their classmates "handsomer . . . more perfect in frame and physique. More poised. They fell in my estimation. Never since have I seen them as wonderful. My eyes were opened to their imperfections. I have never since been as contented about them or as satisfied or as happy. And I think unconsciously sensing criticism, they have been less at ease with me."

Her time of gold had ended.

It was more than a mother reacting to her empty nest. There was also a kind of distance from her family that was hard to explain, a loneliness.

The nest wasn't actually empty—she still had a young daughter at home—but "[i]t was different with her," she wrote, different because "I always saw flaws." The daughter was supposed to have been the culmination of the female line that ran from the immigrant grandmother who'd braved a new country alone—through the Charleston intellectual—to the Minneapolis housewife yearning to be a writer. But the child had never lived up to those expectations, and in some way, she knew it. "You love me but you don't like me," she told her mother. And the mother had to agree. "I never glowed with pride about her."

It had started in infancy. "How you clung to me," the mother wrote. "I felt it was wrong; there should be children your own age to occupy you and satisfy your need for companionship; but except to send you to nursery school, I didn't know of any way to pursue. And I wasn't comfortable either." Instead of the mother/daughter bond she'd imagined, "I felt bound. I couldn't do the things outside the home, in the community, I wanted to. There were many proofs of [the daughter's] energy and initiatives," but somehow she needed more care than the others.

It got worse after her husband's firing. After he was let go, she'd gone to St. Paul with her daughter to talk over the situation with her favorite uncle, the former salesman who'd lived on the third floor all those years. They'd been close when she was a girl, and he knew the family and the business. She hoped to outline the whole break in a rational, dispassionate way; then he'd see her side, and she'd finally have an ally within the family.

But as she told the story, it turned into an emotional outpouring. And then a harangue. "In a little room in [my uncle's] apartment I talked with hatred about Mother—about them all. I heaved and spat figuratively. I can feel myself letting out venom." She went through the family members one by one, "analyzing their acts; telling spectators (for they were that compared to my mother) what wrongs they had done."

She all but forgot her ten-year-old daughter was in the room. "She sat there, looking at me, glowering, her sensitive little soul confused, upset. She sat hearing her mother speak, breathe hatred. She felt, I know it, some of the blame must be mine.

"When a child hears, sees, her mother whom she loves show antagonism to <u>her</u> mother, what can she feel? The fundamentals of life shake." Instead of a proud female lineage, the daughter heard this story of resentment and betrayal. "She sat there—dark. Like a storm cloud. She wasn't old enough to reason one way or the other. She was confused. She, she above all children, should have been bathed in love. Instead, she sat speechless, and heard me almost hiss hate."

The daughter tried to follow in her mother's and grandmother's footsteps. She was the youngest speaker at one of the temple's Mothers and Daughters Luncheons. At a fundraiser for the Federation of Jewish Services, the eleven-year-old appeared in an historical sketch. That same year, 1932, the city paper ran a letter over her name that echoed her mother's pacifism. "[T]he majority of boys . . . consider war an adventure, a chance to show their bravery . . . Suppose two thousand of these men said, 'No, I shall not go . . . I won't go to war to be killed or kill someone else . . . I would rather go to prison . . . [T]here could be no more war. . . . And so, we the women and children of America," the eleven-year-old concluded, "plead with the men for peace."[17]

If her mother didn't actually dictate this—if this was the daughter's voice—it was the voice of a child trying to please her parent. But they all now operated within a family whose wounds wouldn't heal.

The struggling paint business was still managed by the oldest brother, sickly, aging, renting the family house with his wife and two daughters, trying to fill the role of family patriarch.

Mother, in her late seventies, still lived with the eldest daughter, now in her fifties. This middle-aged daughter continued to see her former beau and his wife, still—as the diary put it—"straddling" her desire for the married man. The man's wife had got a skin disease. She went to a string of experts from local doctors to the Mayo Clinic, but "treatments failed; her skin peeled off. She looked," the diary noted, "like a death's head or like nothing describable . . . like a leper." The oldest sister was with her every day, comforting her, "part of the family."

The youngest daughter—the former pianist—had given up her career to raise three daughters, the oldest now a teenager, the youngest seven. With her husband's income from dentistry work, they were weathering the Depression.

The baby brother continued to live in St. Paul with his Danish wife. They had a son in 1931 and a daughter two years later. He tried to support his family as a salesman for the all but defunct paint business.

By the spring of 1934, almost a third of workers in the greater Minneapolis area were without a job.[18] The five years of Depression had worn away at them. "When you look at the unemployed women and girls," one Minneapolis resident wrote, "you think that there must be some kind of war."[19] The president of the national League of Women Voters maintained that women weren't any more hard hit than the men, that "nearly all discriminations [against women] had been removed." But the Women's Party listed some one thousand discriminatory state laws. And the Equal Rights Amendment was still stuck in House and Senate committees. Its opponents were convinced that equal rights for women would open the way to broader rights for workers in general, dropping "the governmental shield [against] labor evils." Many argued that in a time of overwhelming unemployment, women should stay home. The number of working married women increased by 50 percent in the 1930s, but over a third of those took low-paying domestic jobs.[20]

In Minneapolis, the Citizens' Alliance maintained the answer to a healthy economy was the same now as in the past: open shops. "With a permanent and well-paid staff," one observer wrote, "a corps of undercover informers, and a membership of eight hundred businessmen, [the Alliance] had for nearly a generation successfully fought and broken every major strike in Minneapolis."[21] It had been formed in response to a teamsters' strike thirty years earlier. Now, in the depths of the Depression, the city's teamsters, specifically its coal yard truckers, were reorganizing.

Driving a truck was one of the few jobs the out-of-work could hope for. Granted, it was part-time, seasonal. The coal yards needed drivers during Minnesota's long winter, then would lay them off in spring and summer. And it was badly paid. "I would get fifty cents a ton," one driver reminisced. "If I was lucky . . . I'd make a dollar [a day]."[22] Coal drivers had no contracts and no union. The International Brotherhood of Teamsters, established back when drivers were handling teams of horses, operated as a craft union, organizing the elite drivers who had steady work, making no attempt to include the part-time men or the other workers on the loading docks. Strongly anticommunist, the Teamsters held to a strategy of negotiating wage increases rather than resorting to strikes. A strategy, that is, of working within the system.

But a handful of Minneapolis coal truck drivers disagreed. They thought the way out of Depression lay in direct action and worldwide "permanent revolution." Carl Skoglund had been a political activist in Sweden (where he was born), a founder of the American Communist Party, and a railroad worker blacklisted for helping to organize a major strike.[23] Vincent Ray Dunne, son of an Irish immigrant, was raised on a Minnesota farm and worked in the lumber camps before he and his brothers, Grant and Miles, found jobs in the Minneapolis coal yards.[24] These leaders had been thrown out of the AF of L as "reds," banned from the Farmer-Labor Party for the same reason, purged from the Communist Party as anti-Stalinist Trotskyites. They'd helped found their own Communist League of America.[25]

Following Trotsky's principals, they believed the only way to beat the Alliance was to take to the streets. They set out to form an industrial union that included not just the coal drivers but the men who loaded and unloaded, the guys who cleaned up, any worker connected to the industry. That strategy fit their larger goal: to change not just the Minneapolis coal business but business in general. "It is the natural right of all labor," read the preamble to their union by-laws, "to own and enjoy the wealth created by it." Seeing the Depression as "a moment of capitalist crisis," they believed the time had come to realize the dream that went back to Ignatius Donnelly and beyond.[26] The bottom had fallen out of the economy; family and friends couldn't sustain. The solution was union, a way of organizing, something to belong to in both a local and a larger sense. And the organizer's best tool was the strike.

Thanks to 1933's National Recovery Act, the fledgling truck drivers' Local 574 had the right to "organize and bargain collectively." But early in 1934, the head of the national Teamsters cautioned 574 that it would lose support funds—and risk losing their charter—if it struck.[27] The coal yard owners jumped on this statement, maintaining the Trotskyites weren't duly recognized. A local coal executive declared the union meant "just exactly nothing to me."[28]

In the dead of winter, with temperatures below zero, the demand for heat—which meant coal—which meant coal trucks—which meant drivers—was high.[29] That's when a strike would be most effective. But it was unusually warm in January, 1934 with an average temperature of 40 degrees. Finally, in February, the cold rolled in. The strike began on the 7th, in 12-degree weather. Within a few hours, seven hundred truckers walked out, shutting sixty-five of the city's sixty-seven coal yards.[30] "My God," one worker recalled, "they were practically starving to death anyway. What did they have to lose . . . ?"[31]

Local 574's strategy was direct and physical. They put two-men teams on the street. When they got wind of a driver trying to break the strike, one man would jump on the running board, reach through the window, and pull the emergency brake; the other would then run up and pull the release that dumped the load of coal—often in the middle of the street.

It only took three days for coal companies to give in. A number of them agreed to have a union-elected representative negotiate the issues. In addition, they promised better wages and, ultimately, union recognition.[32] "[W]orkers have demonstrated their power," Vince Dunn announced, calling the strike "a victory of no mean proportions."[33] But the Citizens' Alliance continued to warn of "Communists capturing our streets."[34] And by April, the coal companies had gone back on their promises.

Local 574 now represented some two thousand workers. The drivers believed they had a sympathetic ear in Governor Olson. And the Farmer-Labor Party offered them the possibility of statewide support.[35] "Only by all the sections of the trucking industry acting together," one union leader emphasized, "did we have a chance to win anything for any one of them. We knew very well that would tie up the city."[36] What united the protestors was simple enough: the need to make a decent living. Even a cop declared, "I didn't blame those men for striking. For many years a common laborer in this city was nothing better than a serf."[37]

Serfs: did that describe the workers in her father's paint business? The immigrant owner would have vehemently denied it. But if he didn't treat them as Old-World serfs, they certainly weren't considered New World equals. Like the Scandinavian girls who kept house for them, the firm's drivers, factory workers, custodians had worked and lived alongside the family but were always kept at a certain distance. Her older brother maintained that distance. The diarist, on the other hand—with her admiration for the young "socialistic" rabbi and her Eastern education—took a more progressive view. "Colored races held down," she shorthanded in her diary. "Groups of working men and women, people held in ignorance by those governing until they can't stand it any longer." The result? As she saw it, "When human beings are denied equality, they protest silently for a while—suffer—complain—chafe—murmur—grow rabid and blind to the other side and finally driven mad, strike to save themselves. . . ."

If that was more progressive than her family's values, she still saw a strike as a kind of madness. A madness she didn't—couldn't—belong to. She, too, kept her distance from the strikes. It was a distance as old as Charleston: watching the colored union troops from behind drawn blinds.

In April 1934, some of the Minneapolis's 30,000 homeless held their own protest. They marched to the courthouse where they were teargassed by the police.[38] Later that month, Local 574 held a mass meeting at the downtown Schubert Theater. There, Governor Olson himself endorsed the "union idea" as "fundamentally sound:" a key tool, he said, in the fight against "vested interests."[39] The truckers' union issued a new set of demands—or, rather, repeated the demands that had never been addressed: shorter hours, higher wages, extra pay for overtime, and recognition of the union. The Citizens' Alliance responded by calling it a "Closed Shop and Communist revolution."[40] When the city's official employers committee (largely made up of Alliance members) again refused to meet with Local 574, the truckers held a mass meeting and decided to reestablish the strike.

This time, five thousand walked out.[41] The city stopped working. It was the local climax to the decades-long Labor Wars, a never-say-die moment which would attempt to define (again? once and for all?) what it meant to be an American.

. 27 .

ONE OBSERVER CALLED IT "virtually civil war."[1]

The truckers shut down city businesses from grocery stores to factories to manufacturers of "all building materials," anyone who depended on drivers to get their products in or out.[2] If bombing Fort Sumter had signaled the start of the war over slave versus free labor, this action—seventy years later—challenged what free meant. Free to make a decent wage? Free to share in profits, to have a say in decision making? Free to organize?

The strike started with three days of peaceful picketing. The truckers' strategy was to blockade Minneapolis: three thousand protestors closed all city entrances.[3] Like the recent farmers' holiday, like the siege of Charleston, the idea was to create shortages. By the fourth day, the newspapers worried that 750,000 people were "threatened . . . with complete shut off of their perishable food supply, gasoline for their automobiles and all transportation other than street cars."[4]

To implement the blockade, organizers deployed so-called flying squadrons of picketers who could appear when needed, blocking scabs from filling jobs. "They had the town tied up tight," is how the sheriff put it. "Not a truck could run in Minneapolis."[5] Workers around the city rallied to the cause. Taxi drivers refused to carry fares; construction workers left their job sites; farmers provided free food to strikers. The hope of uniting people, of reaching beyond truck drivers, seemed to be coming true. "It is not a strike of men alone but of women, also. [W]omen hold up half the sky," is how Carl Skoglund put it, "they're entitled to half the jobs."[6]

Headquarters for the strike was a garage at 1900 Chicago Avenue, four blocks south of the house her parents had built, that she'd grown up in. Across the building a banner had been strung up proclaiming "STRIKE HEADQUARTERS FOR GENERAL DRIVERS' UNION LOCAL 574." Compared to her family's careful privacy, strike headquarters had a constant stream of workers coming and going. Pickets were dispatched, thousands of meals served, preparations made to treat the injured.[7] The volunteers of the Women's auxiliary kept headquarters running but were also ready to march on the frontlines; one commentator called them "the secret of Local 574."[8]

As preparations were being made, a committee addressed "the whole question of publicity statements for the press, full-page advertisements to be written telling the truth about the strike."[9] It was a little like selling hats, or paint, except the final objective was not to spur on consumers but change their view of the marketplace. Expenses were covered through contributions from various city unions and citizens. Governor Olson sent in $500.[10]

The immediate response of the Citizens' Alliance was to label the strikers communists. But instead of putting workers off, the accusation attracted some. One recalled coming up to a strike leader in a bar and asking, "Are you a communist?"

"What the hell's it to you?"

". . . If it's so, I guess that's what I want to be."[11]

Business leaders called for "law and order" and demanded that their elected officials quash the action immediately. Minneapolis police were put on twelve-hour shifts to "protect" grocery and meat dealers. Following the strategy that had kept Minneapolis an open shop for decades, the Alliance deputized five hundred citizens as "special officers." In the first few days, a hundred strikers were arrested.[12]

This wasn't a winter strike, designed for quick settlement. Called in the spring, this was to be a prolonged campaign, aimed at winning over the general population and enacting broad-scale, permanent change. Local 574 had reason to expect some sympathy from the government. Governor Olson was up for reelection in November. And the mayor, a Republican, was the son of a housepainter who had been a member of the Knights of Labor and an active officer in the Brotherhood of Painters and Decorators.[13]

The first confrontation came on Saturday, May 19, 1934. Rumors began that a truck was going to try to break the embargo by making a delivery from "Tribune alley" in the newspaper district (where the paint store had once been). Union leaders suspected a trap. But three trucks of strikers, male and female, were dispatched to the scene. There they found cops waiting with billy clubs.

The violence that followed changed the city. Thorstein Veblen had long ago suggested that "law and order" used the police as "weapons of industrial warfare."[14] But in the America many Americans imagined—a country that promised all were equal—police were peace officers, on the people's side. The beatings in Tribune alley rewrote that definition. A half dozen of the strikers had to be hospitalized. Of those who were carried back to headquarters, "All the women" Carl Skoglund reported, "were mutilated and covered with blood. . . ."[15] What had started as a matter of wages and hours had quickly escalated." [To] me at least," one striker recalled, "(and I was very young, twenty-two), the employers were ready and determined to kill if needed to maintain their control."[16]

The action that had begun nonviolently—a protest of the system but within the rules of the system—shifted gears. One union member recalled how, originally,

"We went unarmed, but we'd learned our lesson. All over headquarters you'd see guys making saps or sawing off lead pipe. . . ."[17] Sections of garden hose were cut, weighted with washers, and taped shut. Strikers wanted immediate and violent revenge. Leadership told them, "We'll prepare for a real battle, and we'll pick our own battleground next time."[18] Sunday was occupied with rallies and strategy meetings.

Before dawn the next Monday, strikers arrived at one of the city's main markets. Police and deputized Citizens' formed a defensive circle. At 9 A.M., the first set of delivery trucks tried to pull out of the docks. A union leader recounted the strategy they'd devised: "The special deputies [deputized Citizens'] were gradually pushed by our pickets to one side and isolated from the cops."[19] That left about three hundred police circled by some six hundred protestors.

A stand-off followed. Neither side was willing to back down or make the first move. Most of Minneapolis kept its distance, steering clear—like her family—of the "madness." They didn't want or need change badly enough to be standing out in the May sun with weighted slugs of garden hose. Those who had gone that far now hesitated to take the next step. For three hours, they jeered at the police, milling about but not willing to cross that line where the peace officers—and the government they represented—became the enemy.

Finally, the shouting from the protestors reached such a din that the police drew their guns. That, strike leaders had agreed, was their cue for action. A truck loaded with protestors drove toward the thin blue line.[20] "We figured by intermixing with the cops in hand-to-hand fighting, they would not use their guns because they would have to shoot cops as well as strikers."[21] The fight that followed was "a free-for-all," according to one policeman. "I mean with everything from brick bats to iron pipes. . . ."[22] Three protestors were injured, compared to thirty-seven police. By that count, in this modern civil war, it was considered an initial union victory.

The next day, Tuesday, May 22, both sides knew better what was coming. Twenty to thirty thousand workers from all over the city showed up at the market. Before them stood three-quarters of the city's uniformed police and a thousand deputized citizens.[23] A radio station set up a live broadcast from the scene. This wouldn't be a protest, a demonstration, a "holiday"; this would be a battle. Again, there was the tense, silent stand-off, the moment of wondering if citizens were really going to battle authority. Then someone threw a crate of tomatoes through a storefront window, and it began.[24]

There's a news photo of a worker, in cap and heavy pants, swinging a baseball bat. It could be from the sports page except what he's hit—what his follow-through carries him away from—is a special deputy, head down, dropped to his knees on the cobblestone street, his hand still on his billy club. Other protestors close in, carrying sticks and iron rods.

Another photo shows two women, both in hats and overcoats as if headed out on an errand, except one with a club in her hand is gouging at the eyes of the other. They stand in a cleared space, surrounded by men, their shadows dark against the street.

Workers fought police for an hour in what one commentator called "a demonstration that the American workers are willing and able to fight in their own interests."[25] They drove the armed cops out of the market and then continued the running battle through the streets of Minneapolis. As one policeman put it, "They just took over the town that day."[26] Later dubbed "The Battle of Deputies Run," it was one of the most violent confrontations of the Depression. Two deputized Citizens' were killed. One of them, Ceylon Arthur Lyman, the son of a wealthy lumberman, was an attorney who'd served on the board of the Citizens' Alliance. He reportedly showed up for the confrontation in jodhpurs and a polo helmet.[27] He left behind three children under twelve.

The strike's slogan, "Make Minneapolis a Union Town," seemed innocuous enough. But it was calling for major changes in how the city worked, how it saw itself. To become a Union Town was to acknowledge that Minneapolis was made up of different classes: separate, semipermanent, antagonistic. When the national press carried pictures of local workers toe-to-toe with cops, it underscored fundamental questions—and they were being asked in more than one city. Dock workers' strikes in Portland and San Francisco threatened violence; two were killed in a strike in Toledo, Ohio; workers in packing plants in Oklahoma and St. Louis as well as steel workers nationwide were on the verge of walking out.[28]

To make sure Mill City didn't become a Union Town, authorities asked Governor Olson to call up the National Guard. He did but, trying to hold a political middle ground, refused to deploy them. Instead, he declared a twenty-four-hour truce.[29] During that time, an agreement was negotiated at the Nicollet Hotel. In it, the union was promised recognition, including representation for "inside workers" (who didn't drive trucks) and guarantees that strikers could get their jobs back. It appeared to be a rational, nonviolent solution.

The Farmer-Labor Party hailed it as a victory for the workingman, giving credit to their own Governor Olson for brokering it. The national Teamsters union celebrated the "peaceful resolution" of a violent strike it had never authorized.[30] The Communist Party, meanwhile, denounced it as a sellout, a chance for revolution negotiated away. Local 574 saw it as a "limited victory," a step along the way in a larger war.

The first phase of the strike ended May 25th, after eleven days. Three weeks later, the Citizens' Alliance was urging employers to defy the agreement. Companies refused to recognize inside workers and began bringing in outside truckers. The Employers Committee, formed to negotiate disputes like this, wouldn't.

According to one of its members, the Committee consisted of men who had "helped to make Minneapolis"—the business leaders that defined it as a modified New England town—"and they felt that this strike was a terrible thing for their city. . . . [The] great rallying cry for employers [was:] This is a fight against Communism. . . ."[31]

Wasn't that, after all, what union leadership kept saying? That the strike was about more than jobs and wages? "We see the issue between capital and labor," Local 574 wrote in a strike bulletin, "as an unceasing struggle between the class of exploited workers and the class of exploiting parasites. It is a war."[32] What the city's businessmen heard was that those who owned a business wouldn't have the right to manage it the way they wanted. As one member of the Employer's Committee put it, "It was, when you boiled it down, a question of property rights."[33] Like Charleston's plantation owners in their civil war, the business owners in Minneapolis saw the fight as a threat to a whole way of life, from well-furnished homes to social clubs to quiet residential blocks. All of that was being attacked. Media sympathetic to big business proclaimed that the unions' real goal was to set up a soviet right there in Mill City.[34]

As spring ended and summer began, the issues simmered. The Citizens' Alliance made sure that the press contained "hundreds of full-page advertisements and columns . . . attacking the union."[35] The Employers' Advisory Committee drew lines between "legitimate" unions and the "Communist" ones that had led the strike.[36] "It is still a marvel to me," remarked one member of the committee, "that people couldn't sit down and talk their problems out and eliminate this ill-will." But they couldn't. It wasn't just ill-will; it was a different way of looking at the country, a fundamental split. Ninety-five percent of workers in the city supported the strike. On the other side, two-thirds of the employers backed the Citizens' Alliance.[37]

Through May and June, there were worker rallies out at the parade grounds west of Hennepin. By early summer, truckers' wages had fallen back from the $17 agreed to for a thirty-four-hour week to $12.40 for forty-one hours.[38] Local 574 opened its membership to the unemployed, and five thousand new members rushed to join. In July, Minneapolis witnessed the largest mass meeting in its history. Union supporters, including farmers' groups, garment workers, machinists, marched through the streets, ending with a rally at Municipal Auditorium. "I contend this:" the president of 574 told the crowd, "that the working class, they are the taxpayers. We don't want to have our agency, the Police Department, used against us. If they do, if they do, God darn it, we have enough people to remove the Police Department."[39]

The AF of L heard that as an invitation to anarchy. "If you love the union," it cautioned, ". . . get busy and stifle such radicals."[40] The national union demanded

Local 574 come up with past dues or face bankruptcy.[41] But on July 16th, in defiance of the city fathers, the Citizens' Alliance, and the AF of L, 574 called for another strike—the third phase of the extended battle.

This time, headquarters was on South 8th Street, opposite the swanky Minneapolis Club, one class facing another.[42] "It sure is good," a woman at strike headquarters announced, "to see the enemy plain like that."[43] Another vowed to "fight side by side with the men to the finish."[44]

If you were a certain sort of progressive woman—an educated woman, a woman who believed a better world was possible—it was time to take sides. The sons and daughters of the middle class, of shop owners, made their position clear by staying away. Minnesota writer Meridel Le Sueur thought she understood why. Women like the paint store owner's daughter were raised believing in an "individualistic . . . merchant society [built on] a cut-throat competition which sets one man against the other. . . ."[45]

Le Sueur, a decade and a half younger than the diary writer, had grown up in a more radical environment. With a stepfather from Nininger, her family believed in Ignatius Donnelly's rallying cry: "Return the land to the American people, rescue the rich earth from predatory plutocrats. . . ."[46] Still, as she stood across the street from Local 574's strike headquarters—that "dark old building " with its "lean, dark young faces leaning from the upstairs windows"—it scared her. "I was afraid," she wrote. "Not of the physical danger . . . but an awful fright of mixing, of losing myself. . . ."[47]

To protest, to join the strikers, might be a way to fight loneliness. But for an educated, middle-class, middle-aged, White woman to cross the street and enter headquarters was to abandon what she'd gained. It was to give up comforts and acknowledge what Le Sueur called America's "curious and muffled violence."[48]

In the end, Le Sueur decided, "No one can be neutral. . . ."[49] She made the move, crossed the street, joined the strikers. "I am one of them," she wrote, "yet I don't feel myself at all. . . . It is curious. I feel most alive and yet for the first time in my life I do not feel myself as separate. . . ." Instead, she experienced "a close and growing cohesion . . . [a] mass feeling."[50]

The paint store owner's daughter never crossed that line. Was it fear? "Somehow," as she'd written about defying convention back at Wellesley, "she was afraid of that." She remained in her modern home across town. She remained in her family.

The July strike began as the first phase had: peacefully. Again, Governor Olson called up the National Guard; again, he didn't deploy them. It was a murky, ninety-degree afternoon when the employers sent out a single truck to break the embargo. It carried a few sacks of oatmeal and corn flakes, but fifty armed policemen accompanied it.[51] When a strikers' truck with ten unarmed men turned to follow, the police didn't hesitate. "[They] direct aim at the pickets and fired to kill." So, anyway, a Governor's commission would conclude.

The storm of gunfire injured sixty-seven protestors, many shot in the back trying to escape.[52] For ten minutes, the police "just went wild," one striker reported. "Actually they shot at anybody that moved. . . ."[53] Le Sueur witnessed the scene. "Lines of living, solid men fell, broke, wavering, flinging up, breaking over with the curious and awful abandon of despairing gestures. . . ."[54] Two were killed, including Henry Ness, a WWI veteran and father of four.[55]

The guns were meant to stop the protest before it started. "There are very few men," the secretary of the Citizens' Alliance declared, later, "who will stand up in a strike when there is a question of they themselves getting killed."[56] The Governor's commission concluded that "[t]he police department did not act as an impartial police force to enforce law and order, but rather became an agency to break the strike."[57] The union newspaper called it a "war of poverty against wealth," Donnelly's plunderers versus the people.[58] It wasn't just the negotiated strike settlement but the larger social agreement—the rules of behavior, the proprieties—that had been tossed aside.

Social clubs—the Rotary, Kiwanis, Lions—issued statements supporting the police. They urged employers not to "compromise with Communist propogandists or agitators."[59] The night after the shooting, the strikers staged a mass meeting in a parking lot two blocks from their headquarters. "The smell of blood," in Le Sueur's words, "hangs in the hot, still air." They gathered round the "bullet-ridden truck of the afternoon fray . . . the center of a wide massed circle that stretched as far as we could see. . . . My heart hammers terrifically. My hands are swollen and hot."[60] The meeting climaxed in a march on City Hall, with workers shouting they were out to lynch the mayor and the police chief, calling them "would-be Hitlers."[61]

The next Tuesday, July 24th, the funeral procession for Henry Ness headed down 8th Street. Some thirty thousand strong, "[t]he great mass uncurled like a serpent" from downtown several miles through residential Minneapolis to the cemetery.[62] It felt larger than the people involved, larger than the city. All traffic and business stopped. People watched from behind pulled blinds.[63]

The next day, the union signed an agreement, again brokered by the Governor, recognizing its right to bargain for both drivers and inside workers. But employers, again, refused to endorse it. Where the strikers were determined to change the city or else, Governor Olson had the upcoming election to worry about. Trying to balance sympathy for workers with the need to appear tough on law and order, he declared martial law, deployed the National Guard, and instituted a curfew. Minneapolis, he vowed, would be "quiet as a Sunday school picnic."[64]

Some strikers believed the Governor had brought out the National Guard to support them. After all, he'd warned the Citizens' Alliance that "responsibility for what occurs in the City of Minneapolis if the strike continues is entirely upon your shoulders."[65] And he'd added that it was absurd and inhumane "that the plea for a living wage by a family man receiving $12.00 a week is answered by calling him a communist."[66]

The Alliance, on the other hand, assumed the National Guard was there, as usual, to be strike-breakers. In every past action, government had supported big business. "We'll run . . . bayonets up the rumps of those red agitators," declared the police chief, "and then pull the triggers."[67] After twenty-four hours of martial law, the strike was essentially government-controlled; it was up to the National Guard if deliveries were still blocked. The Guard—quietly, without fanfare—began allowing trucks to pass, breaking the embargo.[68] "Scab drivers are operating," union leadership declared, "with Military Permits in ever increasing numbers."[69] The Governor appeared to have sided with the open shop. Soon, nine thousand of a total of thirteen thousand trucks were moving under military protection.[70]

On July 31st, twenty-five thousand workers rallied at the Parade Grounds, determined to battle the National Guard and reinstitute the shutdown. Governor Olson called it "direct defiance of . . . military order."[71] He instructed the Guard to surround union headquarters. At four in the morning, eight hundred troops backed by fifty army trucks and six large machine guns moved in and occupied the building. Union leaders, including Vince Dunne, were led out onto 8th Street in handcuffs.[72]

But if the idea was to end the strike, it didn't work. "Instead of beheading the movement," as one commentator put it, "[the arrests] infused it, at least temporarily, with a daemonic fury."[73] Angry strikers tipped over parked trucks, and school kids, books in hand, grinned at the mayhem. "Everybody was an organizer," as one worker put it, "everybody!"[74]

The next day, the Governor seemed to shift sides. Or straddle sides. He released the union leaders and now ordered the Guard to raid Citizens' Alliance headquarters. There, they confiscated evidence that the businessmen had been negotiating in bad faith, had never considered recognizing the union.[75] Now the Governor threatened to use the Guard to stop all truck deliveries unless companies signed an agreement.

President Roosevelt wanted the strike over before the November midterms, considered a referendum on his handling of the Depression.[76] As part of his administration's economic efforts, the federal Reconstruction Finance Corps had loaned Minneapolis banks some $23 million. Governor Olson saw these loans as leverage over big business; he persuaded the feds to threaten withdrawing the funds if "employer resistance" continued.[77] Two weeks later, the Employers' Committee agreed to recognize the local union, to authorize better pay, to improve working conditions.

Local 574 had "won everything."[78] The banner headline on the union newsletter read "VICTORY!"[79] It was, to believers, a victory for fundamental equality. "The strike had challenged and broken dictatorship."[80] It was a local victory first, fought and won on the streets of Minneapolis by immigrants and the sons and daughters of immigrants. But beyond that, the strike was hailed as a model of what could happen nationally, "[a] burst of originality in theory [and] action . . . a laboratory of social experiment for a future America."[81] Here, finally, was the new world coming.

. 28 .

WITH THE TRUCKERS' VICTORY, Minneapolis was no longer an open shop. The city's painters and decorators negotiated a wage increase from eighty-seven-and-a-half cents an hour to a dollar, and painters working for the public-school system demanded the same.[1] In July, 1934, the ornamental ironworkers struck; in August, so did hosiery workers, the majority of them Scandinavian women.[2] In September 1935, the Association of Machinists tried to unionize one of the city's iron works.[3] The company's owner, a leader of the Citizens' Alliance, brought in nonunion replacement workers from Chicago. Protests swelled. Some five thousand strikers faced police squadrons armed with guns and tear gas. By the end of the confrontation, twenty-eight had been injured, including bystanders, and two were dead.[4] But the machinists won their demands. Minneapolis was becoming a Union Town.

A major strike at one of the city's knitting mills stretched on for seven months before the union won.[5] Through 1935 and 1936, there were actions by electrical workers, furniture makers, and others. The national Wagner-Connery Labor Relations Act guaranteed unions the right to organize. Pressure to create activist, broad-based locals like 574 forced the AF of L to form a Committee for Industrial Organization. The more radical CIO would split from the parent union in the summer of 1936.[6]

Anticommunism continued to be the main rhetorical weapon against unions. The day after the truckers' strike was settled, the Mayor of Minneapolis declared he was "serving notice here and now that our fight on Communism has just begun. . . . It will be a fight to the finish. . . ."[7] The national Teamsters Union saw Local 574's brand of on-the-street confrontation as dangerous and counterproductive; even in victory, it refused to recognize the triumphant local and would go on to revoke its charter.[8] The strategy was national. In 1934, when New York City's painters' union picketed for better work conditions, the Brotherhood of Painters, Paper-hangers and Decorators District Council declared 40 percent of the five-hundred-member local were Reds and revoked its charter. "The Communists," said the district secretary, "were never interested in union matters as such [but in] . . . disrupting the morale."[9]

Governor Olson started to talk about an alternative "cooperative common-wealth wherein the government will stifle as much as possible the greed and avarice of the private profit system. . . ."[10] It would be a new democracy, one that redefined equality. Working with a conservative Legislature, Olson pushed for a minimum wage, unemployment insurance, a progressive income tax, social security for the elderly, environmental conservation laws, and a law calling for equal pay for women. He also solidified the right to collective bargaining and broke the hiring ban against Jews in state jobs.[11] By June of 1937, Pillsbury and some of the city's other big mills would sign contracts with the AF of L agreeing for the first time to recognize unions.[12]

The Governor extended his "cooperative commonwealth" campaign by run-ning for Senate in 1936. To succeed him as governor, the Farmer-Labor Party put up the equally outspoken Elmer Benson. Benson's main concern was "the con-centration of wealth," and he was open about his politics: "I am what I want to be, a radical." He would take the governorship by the largest voting margin in state history.

With the possibility of both state and national leadership, the Farmer-Labor's vision of the future seemed attainable.[13] But Governor Olson died suddenly of can-cer. And after Roosevelt's reelection, the federal government backed off expendi-tures on relief and public work. Sales dropped; hard times returned. By the spring of 1938, unemployment—down to almost 14 percent a year earlier—had jumped back up to 20 percent in what became known as the Roosevelt Recession.[14]

Large companies turned to advertising to try and rally consumers. Sherwin-Williams, in their 1934 catalogue called "The Joys of Colorful Living," had insisted: "Years of Lasting Happiness can be achieved with Sherwin-Williams Quality Paint. Painting offers the most natural way in the world to escape the drabness of dingy surroundings."[15] The system wasn't broke; it was drab. Troubles could be covered over. Happiness was as close as a coat of paint.

Her family's firm took out an ad reminding its customers, "TO FINANCE that painting job, long postponed, loans are now available under the NATIONAL HOUS-ING ACT."[16] But people had more pressing needs than paint. As demand continued to drop, the firm's sales fell, dividends stopped arriving, her stock remittances trickled down to nothing. Across the country, "[m]iddle and smaller firms faced actual bankruptcy."[17]

At the same time, the city's anti-Semitism seemed to increase. Of 464,000 Minneapolis residents, some 16,000 were Jews, but in 1935, the local Jewish Free Employment Bureau was only able to place some two hundred in permanent jobs." It is felt," a citywide study carefully concluded, "that discrimination exists. . . ."[18]

To those who knew Minneapolis, it was the equivalent of a family secret: obvious, of long standing, unspoken. The embarrassment would come when a national investigation by Carey McWilliams, a prominent liberal journalist, named Minneapolis "the capitol of anti-Semitism in the United States."[19] McWilliams went on to say, "Fascists use patterns like this as bait, organize them and bring them to the surface. And, if we ever get mass fascism in the United States, there will be a whale of a lot of people besides Jews and Negroes who will feel the pinch."[20]

In the mid-1930s the Silver Shirts—a White supremacist group founded in the South—began recruiting members in the Twin Cities. They were convinced state government had been taken over by "Commie Jews."[21] According to a report in the *Minneapolis Journal*, the group had 300,000 members nationwide and 6,000 in Minneapolis.[22] Soon, the Silver Shirts were holding public rallies that attracted school board members and leaders of local industry.

As President Roosevelt ran for reelection, some of his opponents accused him of pandering to Jews, calling his New Deal the "Jew Deal" and spreading doggerel that had him saying to his wife, "You kiss the nigger / I'll kiss the Jew / We'll stay in the White House / As long as we choose."[23] As the ugliness spread, Roosevelt defended his actions, but he also brushed aside calls for dramatic action against the Nazis and, even with the number of escaping German immigrants rising, supported immigration quotas, effectively closing the nation's doors.[24] As Minnesota Senator Thomas Schall put it, "To hell with Europe and the rest of those nations!"[25]

The Jewish community in Minneapolis reacted to hard times by looking after its own. As the executive secretary of the Jewish Family Welfare Association put it, the agency's "natural" response was to "turn its attention to the effects of the prolonged crisis upon the economic structure of our community." A committee was formed to see how widespread Jewish unemployment was.[26] Researchers went out to survey the Eastern European community, the "dark" Jews.

Among them was the forty-eight-year-old Wellesley graduate and mother of three. It was low paid work and temporary, but it brought in a little supplemental income, something she'd never done before. And it took the diary keeper out of the house, connecting her with another side of the city, people barely managing to survive. Over the course of several months, she interviewed more than five hundred Jewish families, five and six families a day. And she was good at it. The director gave her a glowing recommendation letter "for any position in this field."

But she didn't enter the field. She stayed with her writing and the traditional woman's role at home, dealing with family. She tried, as she wrote in her diary, "to keep up some of a relationship with Mother because I loved her, because I wanted not to hurt her, and yet a stubborn will to logic in me knew Mother had been unfair, and I stuck to it and blamed her." On top of that break—between mother and daughter—there was the distance between the daughter and her own children.

The younger son graduated from Dartmouth in the spring of 1935 and headed for law school; by the mid-1930s, Jews made up almost a quarter of the nation's law students.[27] The older son had found work in sales, continuing a family tradition. Both stayed East, leaving their little sister to enter her teens alone at home with her middle-aged parents. The family sent her east during the summer of her fourteenth year. She stayed with her grandmother on her father's side: the Pekin girl, now in her seventies, who'd attended finishing school in New York City. They toured the major sights, stopping in Atlantic City before the daughter returned home. But travel didn't make adolescence any easier.

"Those years," her mother wrote in her diary, "like a dark murky miasma. It seems to me like a swamp." Out her sunroom window, the green public space across the street disappeared down the hill. "I think of the low marsh over in the park, submerged, hiding dirty shiny life of negation in its depths. . . . I wonder now if much of [my daughter's] life and her impulses were not higher and cleaner than I thought then. She kept everything secret; she told, explained nothing. So I surmised the worst."

Young women in their circle were supposed to see respectable boys and girls— boys and girls, that is, from within that circle. But her daughter's high school social life was a mystery. "Why didn't I insist on knowing? Why didn't I say, 'I trust you. I am sure where you are and what you are doing is all right but tell me in a general way so I don't worry.'" Instead, the mother "surmised," guessing where her daughter went, what she did and with whom. And assumed it was improper. Or feared—generations repeating—that it would be perceived of as improper.

According to the diary, the adolescent "shut up like a clam. She got loud and angry if I asked, so I stopped asking. Was I afraid of her? What was I afraid of?" The mother blamed herself. She kept tracing the trouble back to when her husband was let go, the child listening to that "long, explosive harangue" with the St. Paul uncle. "It affected her. I know [it did;] those years of my agony and helplessness and hate of family."

Her older sister, now in her late fifties, had lived with Mother her whole life, infatuated for three decades with a married man. When the man's wife died from her long and debilitating skin disease, the dutiful friend attended the service at temple. During the mourning period, she and the widowed husband were together constantly. "She was his consoler, his companion. . . . He took her often to [his first wife's] grave, where a headstone next to [the wife's] was ready for him with his name inscribed already."

He'd been a successful furniture manufacturer, throwing a lavish wedding for his daughter at the Nicollet Hotel. But he'd sold the business in 1932 with the economy in ruins. Now, he claimed he wanted to marry the elder sister but couldn't afford to. "[And] wouldn't live in her mother's home, where the family came and went and would see him unoccupied." The only sign of his trying to make a living was a patent he filed for "an extremely simple and highly efficient egg weighing scale."[28]

Finally, they eloped—the unemployed groom approaching seventy, the long-single bride near sixty. When they returned, the family "didn't give presents or congratulate them." The marriage, according to the diary, was strained. The new husband "tormented her with recriminations. . . . If a sister or brother didn't please him, he forbade her to speak with that person. . . . He cut her off from all her family." And she, according to her younger sister, "obeyed him. She let him completely rule her. . . . [She] hadn't the sense or the strength to resist his will or his self-adoration. . . ." On the wall of their bedroom were pictures of the first wife and their children, and they continued to visit her grave. "[O]utwardly," the diarist wrote, "[my sister] worshipped at [the] shrine. 'He's an angel,' she would say. She didn't even realize his conceit, his cruelty. . . ."

The summer of 1938, a large ad appeared in the *Minneapolis Star Tribune:* "Last Chance / Last Call . . . CLOSING FOR GOOD AND FOREVER. Building will be vacated by midnight JULY 30TH!" After fifty-eight years in Minneapolis, the family business was selling all the machinery, furniture, and paint at discount, as it "Bid[] Goodbye to its Thousands of Customers."[29]

It left her big brother, in his midfifties, no longer owner or manager. Instead, he went back to something like peddler, a "salesman and jobber" for a "retail paint and wallpaper" business. His wife and seventeen-year-old daughter chipped in by working at a local radio station; the nineteen-year-old daughter became a sales-clerk at a furniture store. They lived in a rented house south of the city center, taking in lodgers to help pay the rent.

Her youngest sister, the former pianist, continued to be the least affected by the business failure. Her husband supported her and their two children, one of whom went off to Harvard, the other to Wellesley.

But the youngest brother had no other source of income. The World War I veteran had always worked for the family and depended on his shares in the business to get by. As the firm went under, he'd briefly become president, a largely symbolic title. He lived in a rented apartment in St. Paul with his wife and four children under ten. On a morning in May 1938, the man who'd once dreamed of having a pet bear, drove west along the banks of the Mississippi river. He was almost forty-seven-years-old. Instead of going to work, he pulled off the public highway, connected a garden hose to his exhaust pipe, fed it back into the car, and waited.

In her diary, she recalled her little brother as "a poet . . . lacking self-confidence . . . abashed by the heaviness of life." As she put it, "he slipped out, under the gentle, deadly odorless fumes of carbon-monoxide."

Their mother was inconsolable. He'd been her youngest, her last, the child who'd kept the house lively as his siblings grew up and left. In her sorrow, the mother fell back on the Torah, repeating some of the psalms she'd learned by heart. "Yet, tho she knew much of [the verse], held them in her mind as in a cup," the middle daughter wrote in her diary, "I don't believe they comforted her at the end. I wish," she went on, "I had recited the 23rd Psalm with her—it might have brought her comfort. . . ."

The LORD is my shepherd; I shall not want. He maketh me to lie down in green pastures; He leadeth me beside the still waters.[30]

They both knew the words. But the daughter didn't believe them, didn't believe there was a shepherd, didn't believe she was being led. The pastures and still waters were metaphor—poetry, not fact—and the poetry had lost its ability to reach her.

"When [my little brother] lay in his coffin, and [Mother] didn't want to leave him, I said, 'Come away, he knows you love him.' She moved at once, like a child. 'Do you think he does know?' she asked, and she left him and came with me.

"I wish I had talked to her about death. She wanted to talk. I couldn't because I had no faith."

. 29 .

IT WAS, BY NOW, AN OLD STORY. The way to stop the "cooperative commonwealth" was the way immigrants were isolated, Jim Crow was upheld, and women were kept in their place: by narrowing the definition of who was and was not an American.

When Governor Benson ran for reelection in 1938, his opponents distributed an editorial cartoon, "The Three Jehu Drivers," that depicted the progressive governor as a horse ridden by three of his Jewish advisors.[1] They also issued a sixty-page pamphlet, "Are They Communists or Catspaws?" insinuating that Jews were *Aliens* out to overthrow the republic.[2] Benson called the anti-Semitism of the time "rampant. . . . It was like the way the feeling against black people used to be—in some instance, even more so."[3] The pamphlet—funded by the president of the Citizens' Alliance, the chairman of General Mills, the president of Hormel, and other prominent Minnesota businessmen—also attacked Benson for being sympathetic to Negro poet Langston Hughes. It cited Hughes's "Goodbye Christ," which begins: "Listen, Christ/ You did alright in your day, I reckon/ But that day's gone now."[4]

Benson lost in a landslide. The statewide defeat of all but one of the Farmer-Labor candidates marked the end of the third-party's viability. In response to the "Jew-bating campaign," Jewish leaders in the Twin Cities and Duluth formed the Anti-Defamation Council, soon to become the tristate Jewish Community Relations Council.[5] As the influence of the Silver Shirts kept growing, Local 574 established a six-hundred-man, armed "defense guard."[6] Extremism increased. One of Benson's triumphant opponents wrote, "Hitler has shown us the only practical way to crush the labor movement, strikes and Jew Communism."[7]

Hitler's Germany took over Czechoslovakia, including Bohemia, after the 1938 Munich Pact. This western part of Czechoslovakia quickly turned virulently pro-Nazi; its shops were plastered with signs: "Don't buy from the Jews." Mobs smashed windows, and 17,000 of the region's 27,000 Jews fled. As one Jewish observer wrote, "A man would devour his fellow man out of sheer despair, and for the simple fact that we had been abandoned."[8]

By November 1938, after the wave of violence known as *Kristallnacht* (the Night of Broken Glass), Jews in Bohemia were barred from "all forms of commerce and liberal professions."[9] They were among the first to be subjected to what the Nazis called their "dejudization campaign."[10] Doctors were thrown out of hospitals, journalists fired, professors dismissed from universities.[11] Within six months, all Jews were registered, their ration books stamped with a J.[12] Soon, daily deportation trains were leaving the region, taking Jews to "vocational retraining camps."[13]

The Jews of Bohemia had never fully assimilated. Instead, they'd followed the Talmudic injunction that "the law of the land is the law," surviving through adjustments, compromises, unspoken agreements. Now the Nazis appointed a *Judenrat*, a council of Jewish leaders, to help implement dejudization. "Step by step, they were made tractable," is how one contemporary saw it. As their community was backed into a deadly corner, the council kept trying to find a way out, to discuss the issues, to behave rationally. "Finally, the Nazis asked for life itself. For this, it was the task of the Judenrat to decide who would go first, who later. The road the Judenrat took was torturous and led nearly always to the abyss."[14]

As early as 1933, popular American magazines like *Time, Cosmopolitan, Newsweek* had written about the German persecution of Jews. In 1935, her Minneapolis branch of the Council of Jewish Women had declared it "[the] topic . . . uppermost in our minds. . . ."[15] A columnist warned members that the Nazis wanted to reimpose "Medieval conditions" on the Jews, declaring that "[m]ost German Jews of the present time consider themselves happy and fortunate to be ignored."[16] In 1936, the Council had assisted some four thousand Jews fleeing the Nazis. Two years later, Vince Dunne, leader of Local 544, was talking about "refugees from Fascist terrors" and how it was the workers' obligation to "fight on an international scale against the blacklist, the frame-up, the torture and murder methods of 'democratic' as well as Fascist reaction."[17] By the late Thirties, a poll found 94% of Americans claimed to "disapprove" of Nazi anti-Semitism. But over 70% opposed letting any more Jewish refugees into the United States.[18]

By the end of 1939, the *London Times* recognized the German vocational camps for what they were in an article titled, "The Nazi Plan: A Stony Road to Extermination."[19] And during the summer of 1941, Yiddish papers in New York began carrying stories about the Nazis' final solution. But the *New York Times* didn't pick up the story until that fall, just before Pearl Harbor. And it wasn't until the spring of 1942 that mainstream media began discussing mass extermination.[20]

America would maintain its closed-door policy toward refugees fleeing the Nazis.[21] In early 1944, President Roosevelt would receive a report from his treasury department on "the Acquiescence of the Government in the Murder of the Jews."[22] It asserted that US State Department officials "have not only failed to use the government machinery at their disposal to rescue Jews from Hitler, but have even gone so far as to use this Governmental machinery to prevent the rescue of these Jews."[23] By the end of World War II, there would be about 14,000 Jews left alive in Czechoslovakia. Of the approximately 82,000 Jews in the Protectorate of Bohemia and Moravia, 71,000 would be murdered.[24]

Her worst fears had come true: persecution, rampant tribalism, her nation at war, both her sons in the military. The diary entry for February 20, 1944, noted the US Air Force's massive attacks on the German aviation industry. "4000 killed. 8000 missing. 50,000 more or less wounded." The Big Week, as it would come to be called, tested her pacifism. "Lord, let me not triumph & rejoice. Berlin bombed. Leipzig on fire. Lord let me not gloat. . . . Lord, let me not accept this sadistic apathy with indifference. I never want to become so callous that I hear it all without a sense of horror."

From her sunroom, she could see an end to the war. "The time is now, if ever," she wrote to the local paper, "to turn all logical far-sighted thinking towards averting future wars." But in her diary, her hopes were muted. "The unpossessed millions will probably not get much after this war in India or Europe or here. They are dying and leaving their homes and their work and speakers & writers and statesmen-politicians are mouthing phrases but I doubt if after the war the millions will have any more leisure or peace or beauty or time—time filled with happy, creative life."

"The few will—yes. The few who lobby against taxes, who hate the leaders who plan to bring abundance to those who aren't shrewd enuf to get it for themselves." She saw the plunderers, not the people, benefitting yet again.

In the patriotic run-up to the war, Congress had passed the Alien Registration Act, calling for all "non-Citizens'" to be registered and fingerprinted. Shaped and signed by the Roosevelt administration, the law authorized fines and prison terms for anyone who "knowingly or willfully advocates, abets, advises or teaches the duty, necessity, desirability, or propriety of overthrowing or destroying the government of the United States. . . ." That included organizing "any society, group, or assembly of persons" that was deemed to be seditious.[25] Through the act, nearly five million *Aliens* were processed, providing information on their race, their relatives in the United States, their membership in any clubs and organizations.[26]

The AF of L telegrammed FDR that Local 574 was one such suspect group, accusing them of trying to set up a socialist state. Its leaders were targeted; the FBI and Justice Department raided the Twin Cities' Socialist Workers Party in June 1941.[27] With the support of Minnesota's new Republican governor, the raid led to the arrest and indictment of twenty-nine party members, including Carl Skoglund and the Dunne brothers.[28] Their arrests were the "first peacetime sedition indictments in more than 140 years."[29]

Among those who believed the indictments were unconstitutional—breaking the American promise—were the American Civil Liberties Union and the NAACP.[30] Supporting the indictments, on the other hand, were most state and local politicians, who saw the arrests as a fitting and patriotic response to the Socialist Workers Party's antiwar position. The trial would eventually be recognized "as the test case of civil liberties in World War II."[31]

The day before the proceedings began, Grant Dunne, brother of codefendants Vincent and Miles, put a .22 bullet through his head. He left a wife and two sons. In his eulogy, he was described as "caught up in the vortex of this whirlpool of persecution" and "a victim of this witch-hunt, because he was against Roosevelt's war program. . . . Let us bury him with the honor of a soldier in the liberation war of the workers."[32]

The trial took place in Minneapolis from late October through November 1941. Germany's invasion of Russia had neared Moscow, and the Japanese were refusing the United States's call to leave China. FDR had made his position clear: the nation was preparing for war, and workers' rights were secondary. He'd come down hard on a national coal miner's strike and sent troops to bust a labor stoppage in an airplane manufacturing plant.[33]

The lawyer for Skoglund and the Dunnes quoted Justice Brandeis's 1925 opinion that people were free to express any and all ideas unless they presented "a clear and present danger." On the other side, the prosecution argued that Local 574's "defense guard" (formed to counter the Silver Shirts) amounted to support of armed revolution.[34]

On December 1st, the jury found eighteen of the defendants guilty of advocating for the violent overthrow of the US government. Six days later, the Japanese attacked Pearl Harbor. The day after Pearl Harbor, the defendants received sentences ranging from a year and a day to eighteen months in federal prison.[35]

Seventeen men and one woman entered the appeal process. Meanwhile, their "liberation war of workers," the Labor War, had all but disappeared under the momentum of the United States entry into World War II. By late spring of 1942, the radical wing of what had been Local 574 dissolved, declaring there was "no longer any realistic basis on which to continue the trade union struggle."[36]

The indicted members of the Socialist Workers Party took some hope from a 1943 US Supreme Court ruling. The court had declared a Russian immigrant couldn't lose his US citizenship simply because he belonged to the Communist Party: "[T]he constitutional fathers, fresh from a revolution, did not forge a political straightjacket for generations to come."[37] But the Supreme Court rejected a petition along those grounds from the Minneapolis case. It ruled, instead, that the Alien Registration Act was constitutional.[38]

That ended their last chance for an appeal. On December 28, 1943, two hundred and fifty people attended a farewell banquet in Minneapolis, offered toasts and speeches, sang "Solidarity Forever." Three days later, the former leaders of Local 574 marched two abreast down the streets of Minneapolis to the Federal Courthouse, where they surrendered.

Vince Dunne and other strike leaders spent sixteen months in a federal prison in Sandstone, Minnesota. As felons, they lost the power to vote and other "unalienable" rights. The federal government tried to deport Carl Skoglund. He would die, after a half century in America, with his citizenship still being attacked. Not since the Alien and Sedition Act of 1798 had there been this kind of legal precedent: being an American depended on what you did and didn't say, who your friends were, what clubs you belonged to. A citizen's rights were transitory, liable to interpretation and censorship. It was as if you could never become an American—not permanently anyway.

A total of a hundred and forty-five citizens would eventually be indicted under the Alien Registration Act. The Minneapolis case was the basis for the internment of Japanese Americans in early 1943; McCarthy and House Un-American Activities Committee hearings in the '50s; counterintelligence or COINTELPRO files kept on activists in the 1960s; and continuing border-closing, deportation, and anti-immigration rulings into the twenty-first century.[39]

In Minneapolis, the postwar permutation of the Citizens' Alliance would help write new labor relations laws that prohibited mass picketing, wildcat strikes, solidarity actions by union members. The Minneapolis law became the model for the national Taft Hartley Act, which, among other things, declared all closed union shops illegal. It was sometimes referred to as "the slave labor act."[40]

The diary of the middle-aged woman sitting in Minneapolis mentioned none of this. It focused mainly on family matters. In 1939, not long after Germany's invasion of Poland, her younger son had married a Jewish girl with family in St. Paul. Almost a year after Pearl Harbor, they'd had a baby, the first grandchild. Surely this child—the fifth generation of her family to live in the United States, the third to be born there—qualified as a full-fledged American with equal rights under the law? But it was a girl. And the amendment guaranteeing her rights had spent two decades in Congress and was no closer to being passed.[41]

By the time she decided to keep a diary, it had been fifteen years since her husband was fired. Back in 1939, the family had rallied to celebrate her mother's eighty-first birthday. The Council had sponsored a "pageant-drama" at the temple, and the siblings had put aside differences to take part. Her big brother's wife played the "pioneer woman;" her younger sister arranged the music; both her big sister and her little brother's wife attended, and the diarist acted as narrator.[42]

But she was still angry, unforgiving, hadn't spoken to her big brother. "What havoc he wrought! How much misery he caused—reaching on to [my little brother']s death. I wonder has he ever felt it or realized it under his egotism, his stoical restraint & self-blindness."

She had tried "to keep up some sort of a relationship with mother because I loved her, because I wanted not to hurt her." At a Council meeting, she'd praise her mother's "[u]nflagging enthusiasm, warmth, tenderness—from these came the fruits of her hand and heart."[43] But her own "stubborn will to logic [knew] Mother had been unfair, and I stuck to it and blamed her."

The child who had seen the bombing of Fort Sumpter was now in her mid-80s. Her eyes had gone bad, "and she had little else but a game now and then." The game she loved was anagrams. "She was smart, keen, quick-seeing with words." So, the daughter would go over to her apartment and play: the middle-aged woman and her ancient, fading mother rearranging letters, turning *iceman* into *cinema*, *Minnesota* into *nominates*. "She always beat me," the daughter confessed. And added, in her diary, "I couldn't bear to play with her."

It wasn't getting beaten that bothered her; it was the old rift. Mostly, they didn't discuss it. If the daughter did bring it up, trying to understand it, to heal, "[my mother] said her heart was bad and she mustn't get emotional. [Or] she said she hadn't a business head; she didn't grasp the business details." It was hard for her daughter to believe. "I saw where she had sense, keen sense, for anagrams and none for what was being done, even when accountants and lawyers pointed things out to her."

No, it hadn't been lacking business sense. It had been her sense of propriety and family loyalty. "[And] it was her pity, her pride," the daughter wrote. "She let [my older brother] disadvantage [my husband], grab for himself, make [my husband] the goat, because she was sorry for [my older brother] . . . as her son, she gave him her vote. She never stopped him."

The two would play games, exchange local news, make small talk, and all the time the younger woman thought how her mother was "wrong . . . unfair. I was mad. I boiled inside. Every game brought it back, and it ate into me so I thought it was better to play no more. . . . I finally quit."

The visits a dutiful daughter paid to her aging mother—that both knew were meant to show an end-of-life mercy and charity—simply stopped. "From this time on I couldn't go to her."

She blamed herself. "I know my spirit was wrong, hard, unforgiving . . . [It was] logic not love. . . . I should have set myself aside and have taken it. Because she was so good, because of all my years of love. I should have understood her motives and have kept warm and tender. . . . I knew she was dying but even then, inside, I was hard." There was no movement of love.

The diary was an attempt to make peace with all that, with the past. "Oh that even now that she is dead, I could in some way bridge the gap that grew between us. . . . She was unfair, but she had been the best of mothers. I knew she loved me: whether less than she did him I don't know."

She wrote this sitting in her once-modern house in Minneapolis. She was about to turn fifty-seven, her children grown, her days of being a "club woman" winding down. "I have disciplined myself—gone out among people tho in my heart of hearts I didn't want to; tho peace, happiness come only when I am alone."

Trying to set up that "happy, creative life" she'd imagined for so long, she worked out a schedule.

1 Day—read at Library
1 Day—". . ." home (novels & stories . . .)
1 Day—Mend, Clean
1 Day—company for lunch-dinner
Mornings—write

Mornings—every morning—write. That was the ideal. She sketched story ideas. One was about a woman who was "restless, longing for something . . . dissatisfied on account of her marriage" and comes to the "gradual realization that all is within her. Show her childhood by back flash, then on to her adult problems and difficulties and frustrations."

Many of her story ideas never got written. Those that did she submitted to monthly magazines, only to have them rejected. Her professor at Wellesley had said she would be heard from someday. Almost four decades later, the gray-haired woman wrote in her diary, "She was entirely mistaken; nobody has heard of me except the few in the Minneapolis Writers Workshop."

Not only was there no literary career but also the therapeutic side of writing—the cure she yearned for—didn't seem to work. "Thoughts and feelings—so many, so intense, but unexpressed, bottled up until they become enmeshed like nerve ganglia that can't be disentangled for utterance." She wrote poems about not being heard.

My soul cries out and calls in vain.
Stone silence answers, that is all.
'Come back,' I cry, 'Oh, come again.'
Time, empty time, answers my call.

She looked for help, went to a therapist. "Dr. A. says forget. She says don't think back at all if in doing so you think of the painful memories." But how to do that? How to not think back? The past was right there, every day, in the portraits on the mantle, the furniture, her children, her aged hands. She couldn't figure out how to forget and start over, how to forgive herself or her big brother or her mother.

By now, her husband had found advertising work with a string of medical journals. It was the beginning of a boom time for his profession, with revenues climbing exponentially.[44] But his wasn't a high-powered, well-paying job. He was loyal, well-liked, satisfied; he'd never be rich.

They kept the house, though it was mostly empty, the kids' rooms cleaned out and maintained for occasional guests. With the war ending, her sons would soon return—not here but back to the east coast—her eldest to his sales job, the younger to his law firm. They would both prosper. Her daughter had graduated the same high school the boys had, then—like her mother and in a continuation of the family dream—gone off to college in the East. But she didn't make it through freshman year, suffering a breakdown and returning home. Her mother called her a disappointment and blamed herself. "I don't know," she wrote in her diary, "but what letting oneself be unhappy is a crime, one of the greatest."

In her careful handwriting, she outlined another story idea. "A woman who couldn't get along with people. Started out all right as a little girl. Wanted perfect—disappointed again and again. Lost all admiration and respect for human beings. Wanted to be alone. One after another drops off. . . ."

She found herself doing something she'd never done before. Alone, "cryingly alone" in the empty house, the white-haired woman would slip out of her chair from time to time and kneel. When she did, "the door to my inner self seems to open better, I become more sensitive, more conscious and concentrated, when I kneel on the floor and bend over a bed or a sofa. It may be this position relaxes certain nerve-centers."

She went back over her history—the old hurts, like war wounds—and then, as if to clear her mind, "I kneel, relax in this position for a few seconds. I find myself breathing deeply. Things clear. . . ."

She knew what it looked like; it was a familiar, an ancient position. But she was a modern woman. "The experience isn't exactly prayer. . . ." It was hard to define. "[T]he longer I sit, the deeper my spirit penetrates, the more placid and at peace I become, and the more definite what I wish for. . . . People laugh at 'in tune with the Infinite' but that is what it is. . . ."

Like prayer, then, but not prayer.

And in that position, she asked a higher power to grant her one thing. "God give me love again. Let me love even without thought of its being returned, as I had it long ago."

POSTLUDE

The advertising man died in 1972. His daughter, married but childless, preceded him by four years.

The diary keeper died in 1978.

Their eldest son died in 1985 without having fathered children.

The middle son died in 2011. At the time of his death, he had three children, seven grandchildren, and four great-grandchildren. All born in the United States, all therefore and presumably Americans.

Notes

PRELUDE

1. All quotes from the diary and other papers from the central character's family are in the private collection of the author. Descriptions of people and places are based on family documents and photographs.

2. "Expulsion of Jews from Czech Cities Resumed by Nazis; Pilsen Made 'judenrein,'" *Jewish Telegraphic Agency,* January 27, 1942. http://www .jta.org/1942/01/27/archive/expulsion-of-jews -from-czech-cities-resumed-by-nazis-pilsen -made-judenrein.

CHAPTER 1

1. See Alexandra M. Wyatt, "Birthright Citizenship and Children Born in the United States to Alien Parents: An Overview of the Legal Debate," Congressional Research Service, October 28, 2015, p. 3. https://hgp.fas.org/crs /misc/R44251.pdf.

2. Ibid., 4.

3. Robert N. Rosen, *Confederate Charleston: An Illustrated History of the City and the People During the Civil War* (Columbia: University of South Carolina Press, 1994), 14.

4. Dred Scott *v.* Sandford, https://www.oyez .org/cases/1850-1900/60us393; and DECLARATION OF THE IMMEDIATE CAUSES WHICH INDUCE AND JUSTIFY THE SECESSION OF SOUTH CAROLINA FROM THE FEDERAL UNION, December 20, 1860, http://teachingamericanhistory.org/library /document/south-carolina-declaration-of-causes -of-secession/.

5. E. Milbury Burton, *The Siege of Charleston, 1861–1865* (Columbia: University of South Carolina Press, 1970), 42–49.

6. John Marszalek, ed., *The Diary of Emma Holmes, 1861–1866* (Baton Rouge: Louisiana State University Press, 1979). http://mrthompson.org /tb/16-1.pdf.

7. Burton, *Siege,* 55.

8. Mêsto Strakonice, http://www.strakonice .eu/en/content/town-history.

9. Marilyn J. Chiat and Chester Proshan, "German Jews in Minnesota: 1845–1910," in *A Heritage Fulfilled: German-Americans,* Clarence A. Glasrud, editor (Moorhead, MN: Concordia College, 1984), 169.

10. Olivia Remy Constable, *Trade and Traders in Muslim Spain: The Commercial Realignment of the Iberian Peninsula, 900–1500* (Cambridge: Cambridge University Press, 1996), 203–4.

11. *Encyclopedia Judaica:* "Bohemia, Czech Republic," http://www.jewishvirtuallibrary.org /jsource/judaica/ejud_0002_0004_0_03252 .html.

12. Livia Rothkincher, *The Jews of Bohemia and Moravia: Facing the Holocaust* (Lincoln: University of Nebraska Press, 2012), 8–9.

13. Rabbi Dr. Max Hoch, *The History of the Jews in Pilsen,* translated by Jan O. Hellmann, edited in English by Rob Pearman, from *Die Juden und Judengemeinde Bohems in Vergangenheit un Gegenwart (The Jews and Jewish Communities of Bohemia in the past and present),* edited by Hugo Gold (Brunn-Prague: Judischer Buch-und Kunst Verlag, 1934); http://www.jewishgen.org/yizkor /bohemia/boh479.html.

14. Joseph Havrda, "The History of the Jews in Strakonice," http://www.jewishgen.org/yizkor /bohemia/boh613.html.

15. Rothkincher, *Jews of Bohemia,* 10.

16. Hoch, *The History of the Jews.*

17. Wilma Abélés Iggers, ed., *The Jews of Bohemia and Moravia: A Historical Reader* (Detroit, MI: Wayne State University Press, 1992), 17–18.

18. Ibid., 30.

19. Ibid., 31.

20. Hasia R. Diner, *A Time of Gathering: The Second Migration 1820–1880* (Baltimore, MD: Johns Hopkins University Press, 1992), 45, and "Familianten Gesetz, Gotthard Deutsch," *Jewish*

Encyclopedia, http://jewishencyclopedia.com /articles/6005-familianten-gesetz.

21. Frederich Karl, *Franz Kafka: Representative Man* (Boston: Ticknor and Fields, 1991), 18.

22. Hoch, *History of the Jews in Pilsen.*

23. Diner, *A Time,* 5–21.

24. *History of Minneapolis, Gateway to the Northwest* (S. J. Clarke Publishing, Chicago-Minneapolis, 1923), vol. 2: 556–57, https://books .google.com/books/about/History_of_Minne apolis.html?id=nSgUAAAAYAAJ.

25. Chiat and Proshan, "German Jews," 169.

26. Max B. May, *Isaac Mayer Wise: The Founder of American Judaism, A Biography* (New York: G. P. Putnam's Sons, 1916). http:// collections.americanjewisharchives.org/wise /attachment/5365/IMWise_max_may.pdf.

27. Mêsto Strakonice, http://www.strakonice .eu/en/content/town-history.

28. Derek Penslar, *Shylock's Children: Economics and Jewish Identity in Modern Europe* (Berkeley: University of California Press, 2001), 19–20.

29. Iggers, *Jews of Bohemia,* 567; Penslar, *Shylock's Children,* 19.

30. Sefton Temkin, "Isaac Mayer Wise: A Biographical Sketch," Collection of the Jewish American Archives, http://collections.american jewisharchives.org/wise/attachment/5288/Isaac MayerWise_temkin.pdf p. 8.

31. Iggers, *Jews of Bohemia,* 78.

32. Ibid., 109.

33. May, *Isaac Mayer Wise,* 11–12.

34. "Dobrzany," Virtual Shtetl, http://www .sztetl.org.pl/en/article/dobrzany/5,history/.

35. Chiat and Proshan, "German Jews," 168.

36. Temkin, "Isaac Mayer Wise," 10.

37. Chiat and Proshan, "German Jews," 169.

38. Iggers, *Jews of Bohemia,* 135.

39. Ibid., 134.

40. Chiat and Proshan, "German Jews," 169.

41. Oscar Handlin, *The Uprooted: The Epic Story of the Great Migrations that Made the American People,* 2nd ed. (Boston: Little Brown and Co., 1973), 36.

42. Oscar Handlin, ed., *Immigration as a Factor in American History* (Upper Saddle River, NJ: Prentice-Hall, Inc., 1959), 24.

43. Diner, *A Time,* 46.

44. Robert N. Rosen, *The Jewish Confederates* (Columbia: University of South Carolina Press, 2000), 9, quoting Charles Mailert.

45. Handlin, *Immigration,* 17.

46. Theodore Rosengarten and Dale Rosengarten, eds., *A Portion of the People: Three*

Hundred Years of Southern Jewish Life (Columbia: University of South Carolina Press, 2002), 90.

47. Henry Steele Commager, ed., *Living Ideas in American* (New York: Harper & Brother, 1951), 138.

48. Guido Kisch, *In Search of Freedom: A History of American Jews from Czechoslovakia* (London: Edward Goldston and Son, 1949), 260.

49. Handlin, *Immigration,* 45.

50. This and subsequent diary quotes from Stuart E. Rosenbaum, ed., *A Voyage to America Ninety Years Ago* (San Bernardino, CA: The Borgo Press, 1995).

51. Handlin, *Uprooted,* 46.

52. Emma Lazarus, *The New Colossus.* https:// www.nps.gov/stli/learn/historyculture/colossus .htm.

53. Edwin G. Burrows and Mike Wallace, *Gotham: A History of New York City to 1898* (Oxford, England: Oxford University Press, 1999), 737; Annie Pollard and Daniel Soyer, *Emerging Metropolis: New York Jews in the Age of Immigration, 1840–1920* (New York: New York University Press, 2012), 2.

54. Matthew Frye Jacobsen, *Whiteness of a Different Color: European Immigrants and the Alchemy of Race* (Cambridge, MA: Harvard University Press, 2003), 215–16.

55. Tacitus.nu/historical-atlas/population /Germany.htm.

56. Notes on the State of Virginia, Thomas Jefferson, http://xroads.virginia.edu/~hyper /jefferson/ch19.html.

57. William Cobbett, quoted in Verlyn Klinkenborg, "Green and Pleasant Land," *New York Review of Books* 65, no. 14 (September 27, 2018).

58. US Census, 1810, FamilySearch.

59. Roger Daniels, *Guarding the Golden Door: American Immigrations Policy and Immigrants since 1882* (New York: Hill and Wang, 2004), 7.

60. "A Century of Law-Making for a New Nation: US Congressional Documents and Debates, 1774–1875," Library of Congress, Naturalization Act of 1790, 1st Cong., 2nd Sess.Ch. 3, loc.gov.

61. Africans in America: Race-based legislation in the North, 1807–1850, pbs/wgbh/aia /part4/4p2957.html.

62. Alien and Sedition Acts (1798) | National Archives, http://www.ushistory.org/us/19e.asp.

63. *Property Ownership and the Right to Vote: The Compelling State Interest Test,* R. Bradley Lewis, Louisiana Law Review, Vol. 30, #2, 1970

64. Federalist, no. 10 (James Madison), quoted in Jeffrey Sklansky, *The Soul's Economy: Market Society and Selfhood in American Thought, 1820–1920* (Chapel Hill: University of North Carolina Press, 2002), 25.

65. Daniels, *Golden Door*, 8.

66. J. Hector St. John de Crèvecoeur, *Letters from an American Farmer*, quoted in Handlin, *Immigrants*, 149.

67. St. John de Crevecoeur, *Letters from an American Farmer*, Letter III, 1782, http://xroads .virginia.edu/~hyper/crev/home.html.

68. 'Immigrant Name Changes,' US Citizenship and Immigration Services, https://www .uscis.gov/records/genealogy/genealogy-note book/immigrant-name-changes.

69. Miloslav Rechcígl Jr., "Bohemian and Czech Jews in American History," http://www .jewishgen.org/austriaczech/MilaRechcigl.html.

70. US Declaration of Independence.

CHAPTER 2

1. See Herbert G. Gutman, *Work, Culture and Society in Industrializing America* (New York: Vintage, 1977).

2. Ernest Ludlow Bogart, *Economic History of the American People* (New York: Longmans, Green and Co., 1937), 275.

3. "City of New York & Boroughs: Population & Population Density from 1790," data from decennial US Census, demographia.com/dm-nyc .htm.

4. Howard B. Rock, *Haven of Liberty: New York Jews in the New World, 1654–1865* (New York: New York University Press, 2012), 167.

5. "Cholera in 1849," http://www.virtualny .cuny.edu/cholera/1849/cholera_1849_set.html.

6. David Ward, *Poverty, Ethnicity, and the American City, 1840–1925: Changing Conceptions of the Slum and the Ghetto* (Cambridge: Cambridge University Press, 1989), 29.

7. Burrows and Wallace, *Gotham*, 735.

8. Daniels, *Golden Door*, 9–10.

9. Herbert Asbury, "The Abolitionist Riot of 1834," *New Yorker*, November 5, 1932, pp. 52–57.

10. See Taylor Anbinder, *Five Points: The 19th-Century New York City Neighborhood That Invented Tap Dance, Stole Elections, and Became the World's Most Notorious Slum* (New York: The Free Press, 2001).

11. Development of Kleindeutschland or Little Germany, Dr. Richard Haberstroh, Lower East Side Preservation Initiaitive, http://www.lespi -nyc.org/history

/kleindeutschland-little-germany-in-the-lower -east-side.html; and Rock, *Haven*, 154.

12. Deborah Dash Moore, Howard B. Rock, Annie Polland, Daniel Soyer, Jeffrey S. Gurock, *City of Promise: A History of the Jews of New York* (New York: New York University Press, 2012); and Hasia R. Diner, "German Jews and Peddling in America" (Immigrant Entrepreneurship, German Historical Institute, 2014) at http:// www.immigrantentrepreneurship.org/entry .php?rec=191.

13. Moore et al., *City of Promise*, 18; and Noel Ignatiev, *How the Irish Became White* (Abingdon-on-Thames: Rutledge Classics, 1995), 49.

14. Eric Foner, *Gateway to Freedom: The Hidden History of the Underground Railroad* (New York: W. W. Norton and Co., 2015).

15. Leslie M. Harris, *In the Shadow of Slavery: African Americans in New York City, 1626–1863* (Chicago: University of Chicago Press, 2003).

16. Foner, *Gateway*, 118, 119, 270; Harris, *In the Shadow*, 260, 265.

17. Fredrick Douglass, *Narrative of the Life of Frederick Douglass, an American Slave* (Boston: Boston Anti-Slavery Office, 1849), 107–8.

18. Ignatiev, *How the Irish*, 127.

19. Ward, *Poverty, Ethnicity, and the American City*, 14–15.

20. Moore et al., *City of Promise*, 18.

21. Burrows and Wallace, *Gotham*, 742.

22. Moore et al., *City of Promise*, 11–12, quoting Rabbi Isaac Mayer.

23. Jackson Lears, *Fables of Abundance: A Cultural History of Advertising in America* (New York: Basic Books, 1994), 55.

24. Hasia R. Diner, "German Immigrant Period in the United States," Jewish Women's Archives Encyclopedia, http://jwa.org/encyclo pedia/article/german-immigrant-period-in -united-states.

25. Bogart, *Economic History*, 352–54.

26. Lears, *Fables*, 65.

27. See Hasia R. Diner, *Roads Taken: The Great Jewish Migrations to the New World and the Peddlers Who Forged the Way* (New Haven, CT: Yale University Press, 2015), especially p. 66.

28. Moore et al., *City of Promise*, 23.

29. Ibid.

30. Diner, "Peddling."

31. Lears, *Fables*, 65, 69.

32. Ibid., 80, 86.

33. From *Some Adventures of Captain Simon Suggs* (1845), as quoted in Alfred Bendixen, *A*

Companion to the American Novel (Hoboken, NJ: John Wiley and Sons, 2012).

34. Moore et al., *City of Promise*, 22.

35. Rosenbaum, *A Voyage*, 69.

36. Gary M. Walton and Hugh Rockoff, *History of the American Economy*, 9th ed. (Boston: Thomson Learning Inc., 2002), 259.

37. Handlin, *Immigration*, 49, quoting Abraham Kohn.

38. Hasia Diner, "Entering the Mainstream of Modern Jewish History: Peddlers and the American Jewish South," in Marcie Cohen Ferris and Mark I. Greenberg, eds., *A New History* (Waltham, MA: Brandeis University Press, 2006), 97.

39. Ibid, 91.

40. See Henry Feingold, *Zion in America: The Jewish Experience from Colonial Times to the Present* (New York: Hippocrene Books, Inc., 1974), 74–75.

41. Anshe Slonim Synagogue, Landmarks Preservation Commission, 2/10/87, http://www.neighborhoodpreservationcenter.org/db/bb_files/87-anshe-slonim.pdf.

42. Ibid.

43. Rock, *Haven*, 206.

44. Diner, *A Time*, 43–44.

45. Roger W. Moss, ed., *Paint in America: The Colors of Historic Buildings* (Washington, DC: National Trust for Historic Preservation, 1994), 21.

46. *Paint, Oil and Chemical Review* 19 (1895): 19.

CHAPTER 3

1. Wilbert L. Jenkins, *Seizing the New Day: African Americans in Post–Civil War Charleston* (Bloomington: Indiana University Press, 1998), xi.

2. "City of Charleston, South Carolina, looking across Cooper's River," G. Cooke, https://www.loc.gov/resource/pga.00199/.

3. Gerda Lerner, *The Grimké Sisters from South Carolina: Rebels Against Slavery* (Boston: Houghton Mifflin, 1967), 69.

4. John H. Tibbetts, "Rise and Fall and Rise: South Carolina's Maritime History," *Coastal Heritage* 17, no. 2, http://www.scseagrant.org/content/?cid=189.

5. Rosen, *The Jewish Confederates*, 37, quoting Bruce Catton.

6. This letter, in the author's collection, was translated from the German by Abigail Taplin.

7. Rosen, *The Jewish Confederates*, 40.

8. Cynthia M. Kennedy, *Braided Relations, Entwined Lives: The Women of Charleston's Urban Slave Society* (Bloomington: Indiana University Press, 2005), 130.

9. Lerner, *The Grimké Sisters*, 30–31.

10. Robert Alston Jones, *Common Blood: The Life and Times of an Immigrant Family in Charleston, South Carolina* (Bloomington, IN: Xlibris Corporation, 2012), 19.

11. Jones, *Common Blood*, 105.

12. Frederic Bancroft, *Slave Trading in the Old South* (Baltimore, MD: J. H. Furst and Co., 1931), 165. https://books.google.com/books/about/Slave_Trading_in_the_Old_South.html?id=czx3AAAAMAAJ p. 165.

13. Lerner, *The Grimké Sisters*, 68–69.

14. "Total and Foreign-born Population New York City, 1790–2000," New York City Department of City Planning, Population Division, census data, https://www1.nyc.gov/assets/planning/download/pdf/data-maps/nyc-population/historical-population/1790-2000_nyc_total_foreign_birth.pdf.

15. Paul Starobin, *Madness Rules the Hour: Charleston, 1860 and the Mania for War* (New York: Public Affairs, 2017), 20 and 101.

16. Bancroft, *Slave Trading*, 165.

17. Wilbert L. Jenkins, *Seizing the New Day: African Americans in Post–Civil War Charleston* (Bloomington: Indiana University Press, 1998), xi.

18. Rosengarten and Rosengarten, *A Portion of the People*, xvii.

19. Nell Porter Brown, "A Portion of the People," *Harvard Magazine*, January–February 2003. http://harvardmagazine.com/2003/01/a-portion-of-the-people.html.

20. Rosengarten and Rosengarten, *A Portion of the People*, xvi.

21. Chiat and Proshan, "German Jews," 170.

22. Rosengarten and Rosengarten, *A Portion of the People*, 2.

23. Deborah Dash Moore, "Freedom's Fruits: The Americanization of an Old-time Religion," 13, in Rosengarten and Rosengarten, *A Portion of the People*; Rosen, *The Jewish Confederates*, 281; Charles Reznikoff, *The Jews of Charleston* (Philadelphia, PA: Jewish Publication Society of America, 1950), 103.

24. Rosen, *The Jewish Confederates*, 149.

25. Sara B. Chase, "Painting Historic Interiors," Brief 28, Technical Preservation Services,

National Park Service, US Department of the
Interior, https://www.nps.gov/tps/how-to-pre
serve/briefs/28-painting-interiors.htm#history.

26. Martin Guertin, "How Paint Ended up in
a Can," http://digipubcloud.com/article/how
+paint+ended+up+in+a+can/1804431/0
/article.html; Chase, 'Painting Historic Interiors,'
http://www.nps.gov/tps/how-to-preserve/briefs
/28-painting-interiors.htm.

27. Guertin, "How Paint Ended up in a Can."

28. Jessica Parker Dockery, "Pre-1850 Paint
in Historic Properties: Treatment Options
and Processes," thesis, University of Georgia,
2005, https://getd.libs.uga.edu/pdfs/dockery
_jessica_p_200505_mhp.pdf pp. 26–29.

29. *The American Grainers' Hand-Book: A
Popular and Practical Treatise on the Art of
Imitating Colored and Fancy Woods* (New York:
John W. Masury and Son, 1872), 7.

30. Dockery, "Pre-1850 Paint," 26–29.

31. Michael Gold, *Jews Without Money* (New
York: Carroll & Graf Publishers, Inc., 1930/1984),
111.

32. Bogart, *Economic History*, 397.

33. Jenna Weissman Joselit, "Land of Promise:
The Eastern European Jewish Experience in
South Carolina," in Rosengarten and Rosengar-
ten, *A Portion of the People*, 25.

34. Rabbi Rachel M. Solomin, "Sephardic,
Ashkenazic, Mizrahlic and Ethiopian Jews,"
https://www.myjewishlearning.com/article
/sephardic-ashkenazic-mizrahi-jews-jewish
-ethnic-diversity/.

35. Reznikoff, *The Jews of Charleston*, 117;
Allan Tarshish, "The Charleston Organ Case,"
American Jewish Historical Quarterly 54, no. 4
(June 1965).

36. Solomon Breibart, *Explorations in Charleston's Jewish History* (West Columbia, SC: History
Press, Arcadia Publishing, 2005), 117.

37. Bertram Wallace Korn, *Jews and Negro
Slavery in the Old South, 1789–1865* (Elkins Park,
PA: American Jewish Historical Society, 1961),
xli.

38. Moore. "Freedom's Fruits: The Americanization of an Old-time Religion," in Rosengarten
and Rosengarten, *A Portion of the People*, 15.

39. Hagy, *This Happy Land*, 256.

40. Tarshish, "The Charleston Organ Case," 415.

41. Breibart, *Explorations*, 156.

42. Moore, "Freedom's Fruits." 15.

43. Breibart, *Explorations*, 118.

44. Reznikoff, *The Jews of Charleston*, 127–34.

45. Reznikoff, *The Jews of Charleston*, 138;
and Marcie Cohen and Mark I. Greenberg, eds.,
Jewish Roots in Southern Soil: A New History
(Waltham, MA: Brandeis University Press,
2006), 6.

46. Feingold, *Zion in America*, 109–10.

47. Breibart, *Explorations*, 43, quoting Penina
Moïse.

48. Hagy, *This Happy Land*, 240.

49. Moore, "Freedom's Fruits," 18–19.

50. Hagy, *This Happy Land*, 253.

51. Feingold, *Zion in America*, 109–10.

52. Tarshish, "The Charleston Organ Case," 445.

CHAPTER 4

1. Stephanie Coontz, *Marriage, A History:
from Obedience to Intimacy or How Love Conquered Marriage* (New York: Viking, 2005), 6.

2. Wilma Abeles Iggers, ed., *The Jews of Bohemia and Moravia: A Historical Reader* (Detroit,
MI: Wayne State University Press, 1992), 61.

3. Iggers, *The Jews of Bohemia and Moravia*,
72, quoting Peter Beer.

4. Christine A. Lunardini, *Women's Rights,
Social Issues in American History* (Phoenix, AZ:
Oryx Press, 1996), 72.

5. Hasia R. Diner, *The Jews of the United
States*, (Oakland: University of California Press,
2004), 83.

6. Jefferey Sklansky, *The Soul's Economy: Market Society and Selfhood in American Thought,
1820–1920* (Chapel Hill: University of North
Carolina Press, 2002), 63.

7. Rock, *Haven*, 173.

8. Elizabeth Cady Stanton, "Declaration of
Sentiments" (Rochester, NY: Printed by John
Dick, office of Frederick Douglas,) 1848. Manu-
script Division, Library of Congress (007.00.00).

9. Korn, *Jews and Negro Slavery*, 1.

10. Bogart, *Economic History*, 420; Daniels,
Golden Door, 5.

11. Ralph Waldo Emerson, "Thy Young
Americans," quoted in Sacvan Bercovitch, *The
Rites of Ascent: Transformation in the Symbolic
Construction of America* (Abingdon, UK: Rout-
ledge, 1993), 289.

12. Herman Melville, *White Jacket*, quoted in
Bercovitch, *The Rites of Ascent*, 290.

13. See David Roediger, *The Wages of Whiteness: Race and the Making of the American Working Class* (New York: Verso, 1991), especially p.
95.

14. Coontz, *Marriage, A History*, 148.

15. Robert A. Baker, "Cazenovia Convention: A Meeting of Minds to Abolish Slavery," *Post Standard* (Syracuse), February 4, 2005, https://www.syracuse.com/news/2005/02/cazenovia_convention.html.

16. Ward, *Poverty. Ethnicity, and the American City*, 26.

17. Bogart, *Economic History*, 433; Burrows and Wallace, *Gotham*, 743; Lunardini, *Women's Rights*, 45; Eleanor Flexner, *Century of Struggle: The Woman's Rights Movement in the United States* (New York: Atheneum, 1970), 178.

18. Lunardini, *Women's Rights*, 81.

19. Shari Rabin, "You Are Where You Live: Jews, Religion, and the New York Boarding House," December 22, 2015, The Gotham Center for New York History, http://www.gothamcenter.org/blog/you-are-where-you-live-jews-religion-and-the-new-york-boardinghouse.

20. Rabin, 'You Are Where You Live."

21. Burrows and Wallace, *Gotham,* 642–44.

22. ANSHE SLONIM SYNAGOGUE, Landmarks Preservation Commission, 2/10/1987, http://www.neighborhoodpreservationcenter.org/db/bb_files/87-anshe-slonim.pdf; and Rock, *Haven,* 187.

23. Rock, *Haven,* 206.

24. Ibid., 214.

25. Ibid., 218.

26. Ibid., 215.

27. ANSHE SLONIM SYNAGOGUE, Landmarks Preservation Commission, 2/10/1987.

28. Rock, *Haven,* 186.

29. Ibid., 157.

30. Reznikoff, *The Jews of Charleston*, 148.

31. May, *Isaac Mayer Wise*, 97.

32. Ibid.

33. Rosengarten and Rosengarten, *A Portion of the People*, p. xv.

34. George Consider Hale, *History of the World's Greatest Fires* (Kansas City, MO: F. Hudson Publishing Co., 1905), https://books.google.com/books?id=1dsrAQAAMAAJ&printsec=frontcover&source=gbs_ge_summary_r&cad=0#v=onepage&q&f=true (Charleston, SC: The College of Charleston, May 2009); http://nationalregister.sc.gov/SurveyReports/HC10005.pdf, p. 2; Moore, "Freedom's Fruits," 11.

35. Directory of the City of Charleston, 1851 (Charleston, SC: J. H. Bagget, 1851), 133.

Chapter 5

1. James Glen, "A Description of South Carolina," in *Colonial South Carolina: Two Contemporary Descriptions by Governor James Glen and Doctor George Milligen-Johnston,* edited by Chapman J. Millings (South Carolina Sesquicentennial Series, no. 1 [Columbia, SC: 1951], sect. 2, reprinted in Merrill Jensen, ed., *English Historical Documents: Ame,rican Colonial Documents to 1776* (New York: Oxford University Press, 1955), volume 9, p. 3, 32–34.

2. Damon Fordham, "A Port of Entry for Enslaved Africans," *Charleston Chronicle*, March 4, 2016.

3. Ned and Constance Sublette, *The American Slave Coast: A History of the Slave-Breeding Industry* (Chicago, IL: Lawrence Hill Books, 2016), 70.

4. Victoria Proctor, "Rice and Indigo in South Carolina," 2014, https://www.sciway3.net/proctor/sc_rice.html; and Wilbert L. Jenkins, *Seizing the New Day: African Americans in Post-Civil War Charleston* (Bloomington: Indiana University Press 1998), 3.

5. Sublette and Sublette, *American Slave Coast,* 171.

6. Proctor, "Rice and Indigo."

7. Fordham, "Port of Entry."

8. Korn, *Jews and Negro Slavery, 16*

9. Moore, "Freedom's Fruits," 13.

10. Jenna Weissman Joselit, "Land of Promise: The Eastern Jewish Experience in South Carolina," in Rosengarten and Rosengarten, *A Portion of the People*, 25.

11. See Edward E. Baptist, *The Half Has Never Been Told: Slavery and the Making of American Capitalism* (New York: Basic Books, 2014).

12. Stephanie E. Yuhl, "Hidden in Plain Sight: Centering the Domestic Slave Trade in American Public History," *Journal of Southern History* 79, no. 3 (August 2013).

13. Bancroft, *Slave Trading*, 178.

14. George C. Rogers Jr. and C. James Taylor, *A South Carolina Chronology 1497–1992* (Columbia: University of South Carolina Press, 1994).

15. US Census Bureau, 1850, FamilySearch.

16. Christopher Dickey, *Our Man in Charleston: Britain's Secret Agent in the Civil War South* (New York: Broadway Books, 2015), 9.

17. Jones, *Common Blood*, 58.

18. Kennedy, *Braided Relations*, 79.

19. Jones, *Common Blood*, 58.

20. J. K. Cardozo, *Reminiscences of Charleston* (Charleston, SC: Joseph Walker, 1866), 9.

21. Sklansky, *The Soul's Economy*, 29.

22. Kennedy, *A Nation of Immigrants*, 92; US Census Bureau, 1850; and Bernard E. Powers,

Black Charlestonians: A Social History, 1822–1883 (Fayetteville: University of Arkansas Press, 1994), 37. A Nation of Immigrants, John Fitzgerald Kennedy (Boston: Harper and Row, 1964), 92.

23. Chestnut, *Diary*, 29.

24. Powers, *Black Charlestonians*, 41, 269.

25. Thomas Holt, *Black over White: Negro Political Leadership in South Carolina during Reconstruction* (Champaign: University of Illinois Press, 1977), 65.

26. Powers, *Black Charlestonians*, 48.

27. See Baptist, *The Half Has Never Been Told*; Sublette and Sublette, *American Slave Coast*.

28. Jenkins, *Seizing the New Day*, 5.

29. Ibid.

30. George Fitzhugh, 1854, quoted in Sklansky, *The Soul's Economy*, 96.

31. "Denmark Vesy," *People of Faith*, Public Broadcasting System, http://www.pbs.org /thisfarbyfaith/people/denmark_vesey.html . supplementary information for the PBS series, "This Far by Faith," 2003.

32. See Lacy Ford, "An Interpretation of Denmark Vesey's Insurrection Scare," *The Proceedings of the South Carolina Historical Association* (Charleston: South Carolina Historical Association, 2012).

33. Rosen, *The Jewish Confederates*, 135.

34. Frederick Law Olmstead quoted in Jones, *Common Blood*, 77.

35. Dickey, *Our Man in Charleston*, 35.

36. Jenkins, *Seizing the New Day*, 10, 19.

37. Robert N. Rosen, "Jewish Confederates," in Ferris and Greenberg, 110.

38. Ibid.

39. Korn, *Jews and Negro Slavery*, 45.

40. Rosengarten and Rosengarten, *A Portion of the People*, 11; Bertram W. Korn, *American Jewry and the Civil War* (New York: Atheneum, 1970), xxviii.

41. US Census Bureau,1860.

Chapter 6

1. Daniels, *Golden Door*, 11.

2. Kennedy, *A Nation of Immigrants*, 70.

3. Daniels, *Golden Door*, 11.

4. Abraham Lincoln, Letter to Joshua Speed, August 24, 1855, https://www.nps.gov/liho/learn /historyculture/knownothingparty.htm.

5. Kenneth M. Stampp, *America in 1857: A Nation on the Brink* (Oxford, England: Oxford University Press, 1990), 36.

6. Bogart, *Economic History*, 420.

7. Ivan D. Steen, "Charleston in the 1850s: As Described by British Travelers," *South Carolina Historical Magazine* 71, no. 1 (January 1970): 36–45.

8. Kennedy, *A Nation of Immigrants*, 194.

9. T. Lloyd Benson, *The Caning of Senator Sumner* (Boston: Cengage Learning, 2003), 2–7.

10. *Mercury* (Charleston, SC), May 28, 1856, http://history.furman.edu/editorials/see.py? sequence=sumenu&location=Sumner+Caning &ecode=sccmsu560528a.

11. Harriet Beecher Stowe, *Uncle Tom's Cabin* (Boston, MA: John P. Jewett, 1852), 181.

12. Rosengarten and Rosengarten, *A Portion of the People*, 85.

13. Lerner, *The Grimké Sisters*, 33.

14. Chestnut, *Diary*, li and xlix.

15. Stephen R. Wise, *Lifeline of the Confederacy: Blockade Running During the Civil War* (Columbia: University of South Carolina Press, 1988), 11.

16. Rock, *Haven*, 228–29.

17. Bogart, *Economic History*, 435–36.

18. Sublette and Sublette, *American Slave Coast*, 609; and Phillip S. Foner, *Business and Slavery: The New York Merchants and the Irrepressible Conflict* (New York: Russell and Russell, 1941), 139–44.

19. Rock, *Haven*, 239.

20. Dickey, *Our Man in Charleston*, 99.

21. Burrows and Wallace, *Gotham*, 864.

22. Rock, *Haven*, 233–34.

23. Korn, *Jews and Negro Slavery*, 17.

24. Harry Golden, *Our Southern Landsmen* (New York: G. P. Putnam's Sons, 1974), 110.

25. Ibid., 113.

26. Dickey, *Our Man in Charleston*, 85, 125.

27. See US Census Bureau, 1860, http:// docsouth.unc.edu/imls/census/census.html.

28. Rosengarten and Rosengarten, *A Portion of the People*, 85.

29. US Census Bureau,1860.

30. Diner, "Entering the Mainstream," 99.

31. Clive Webb, "Jewish Merchants and Black Customers in the Age of Jim Crow," *Southern Jewish History* 2 (1999): 55–80.

32. Powers, *Black Charlestonians*, 46.

33. Ibid., 45.

34. Breibart, *Explorations*, 160.

35. *Eleventh Annual Report of the Board of State Charities of Massachusetts* (Boston: Wright and Potter State Printers, 1875), 106.

36. Rosengarten and Rosengarten, *A Portion of the People*, 95 and 97; Reznikoff, *The Jews of Charleston*, 148–50.

37. Thomas J. Tobias, "The Hebrew Benevolent Society of Charleston, S.C. Founded 1784: The Oldest Jewish Charitable Society in the United States, An Historical Sketch" (Charleston, SC: Hebrew Benevolent Society, 1965).

38. Hagy, *This Happy Land*, 55.

39. Rosengarten and Rosengarten, *A Portion of the People*, 65, 78.

40. Ibid., 78.

41. Margaret C. Jacob, *The Origins of Freemasonry: Facts and Fiction* (Philadelphia: University of Pennsylvania Press, 2002), 13.

42. Lynn Dumenil, *Freemasonry and American Culture: 1880–1930* (Princeton, NJ: Princeton University Press, 1984), 55–56.

43. Jacob, *The Origins of Freemasonry*, 15–22; Mark C. Carnes, *Secret Ritual and Manhood in Victorian America* (New Haven, CT: Yale University Press, 1989), 22.

44. "Minneapolis Lodge Number 19, A.F & A.M., Minneapolis, Mn." (Mahn and Harmon Company, Printers, 1910), 77. https://www.mn-masons.org/sites/mn-masons.org/files/Minneapolis%2019%20early%20history.pdf.

45. Carnes, *Secret Ritual and Manhood*, 28.

46. Ibid., 125.

47. Ibid., 131.

48. Barrett Abraham Elzas, *The Jews of South Carolina: From the Earliest Times to the Present Day* (Philadelphia, PA: J. P. Lippincott Company, 1905), 144.

CHAPTER 7

1. Dickey, *Our Man in Charleston*, 176.

2. National Republican platform. Adopted by the National Republican Convention, held in Chicago, May 17, 1860. The Alfred Whital Stern Collection of Lincolniana, Library of Congress (Chicago, IL: Chicago Press and Tribune Office, 1860).

3. Stampp, *America in 1857*, 133; Lincoln's 1st Inaugural Address, The Avalon Project, Yale Law School, https://avalon.law.yale.edu/19th_century/lincoln1.asp.

4. Foner, *Business and Slavery*, 207.

5. Harris, *In the Shadow of Slavery*, 279

6. Rock, *Haven*, 240.

7. Stampp, *America in 1857*, 113.

8. Roediger, *The Wages of Whiteness*, 56.

9. "Resolution to Call the Election of Abraham Lincoln as U.S. President a Hostile Act, 9 November 1860," Resolutions of the General Assembly, 1779–1879. S165018. South Carolina Department of Archives and History, Columbia, SC. https://digital.scetv.org/teachingAmerhistory/tTrove/ResolutiontocalltheelectionofAbrahamLincolnaHostileActNovember1860.html.

10. "Resolution to Call the Election of Abraham Lincoln as U.S. President a Hostile Act and to Communicate to Other Southern States South Carolina's Desire to Secede from the Union. 9 November 1860" Resolutions of the General Assembly, 1779–1879. S165018. South Carolina Department of Archives and History, Columbia, SC; Jones, *Common Blood*, 74.

11. Bogart, *Economic History*, 583.

12. Joseph Kelly, *America's Longest Siege: Charleston, Slavery, and the Slow March Towards Civil War* (New York: The Overlook Press, 2013), 282.

13. Ben Ames Williams, ed., *A Diary from Dixie by Mary Chesnut Boykin* (Cambridge, MA: Harvard University Press, 1980), 19–20.

14. Cardozo, *Reminiscences*, 6.

15. E. Milby Burton, *The Siege of Charleston, 1861–1865* (Columbia: University of South Carolina Press, 1970), 62.

16. Ibid., 76–77.

17. Rosen, *The Jewish Confederates*, 86.

18. Jones, *Common Blood*, 139.

19. Rosen, *The Jewish Confederates*, 81.

20. *Charleston Mercury*, November 4, 1861, 3, in Vicki Betts, "Charleston Mercury, July 1860–December, 1862," Scholar Works at UT Tyler Civil War Newspapers, 2016.

21. Ethan J. Kytle and Blain Roberts, *Denmark Vesey's Garden: Slavery and Memory in the Cradle of the Confederacy* (New York: The New Press, 2018).

22. Dickey, *Our Man in Charleston*, 299; Robert N. Rosen, *Confederate Charleston: An Illustrated History of the City and the People During the Civil War* (Columbia: University of South Carolina Press, 1994), 87.

23. Rosen, *The Jewish Confederates*, 237.

24. Dickey, *Our Man in Charleston*, 299.

25. Rosengarten and Rosengarten, *A Portion of the People*, 129.

26. Marszalek, *The Diary of Emma Holmes*, 110.

27. Jones, *Common Blood*, 141.

28. Jeff Wilkinson, "From the archives: 150 years ago: The Siege of Charleston," *The State*, July 9, 2013, http://www.thestate.com/news/special-reports/article14436602.html.

29. Jones, *Common Blood*, 129.

30. Burton, *The Siege of Charleston*, 244.

31. Rosengarten and Rosengarten, *A Portion of the People*, 128–29.

32. Betts, *The Charleston Mercury*, October 15, 1862, 2.

33. "Circular of the Free Market of Charleston," *Charleston Mercury*, July 30, 1862, http://www.cw-chronicles.com/blog/circular-of-the-free-market-of-charleston/.

34. Kelly, *America's Longest Siege*, 293; Rosen, *The Jewish Confederates*, 237.

35. Rosen, *The Jewish Confederates*, 88.

36. Wilkinson, "From the archives: 150 years ago"; Burton, *The Siege of Charleston*, 97.

37. Rosen, *The Jewish Confederates*, 89.

38. Betts, "Charleston in War Times—As Seen by a Yankee Lady," *Charleston Mercury*, September 30, 1862, 1.

39. Rosen, *The Jewish Confederates*, 237.

40. W. E. B. Du Bois, *Black Reconstruction*, vol. 2, in *The Seventh Son: The Thoughts and Writings of W. E. B. Du Bois* (New York: Random House, 1971), 470.

41. Burton, *The Siege of Charleston*, 134.

42. *Encyclopedia of Southern Jewish Communities—Sumter, South Carolina*, http://www.isjl.org/south-carolina-sumter-encyclopedia.html; Jacob Radar Marcus, *The American Jewish Woman: A Documentary History* (New York: KTAV Publishing, 1981).

43. Tobias, "The Hebrew Benevolent Society of Charleston," 18.

44. Rosen, *The Jewish Confederates*, 37, quoting Rabbi Bertman Wallace Korn.

45. Kelly, *America's Longest Siege*, 300.

46. Burton, *The Siege of Charleston*, 136.

47. Rosen, *The Jewish Confederates*, 121; Kelly, *America's Longest Siege*, 303.

48. Wise, *Lifeline of the Confederacy*, 124; Rosen, *The Jewish Confederates*, 236; Kelly, *America's Longest Siege*, 303.

49. Marszalek, *The Diary of Emma Holmes*, 192.

50. Korn, *Jews and Negro Slavery*, 122.

51. Ibid., 132.

52. Ibid., 186–87

53. Burton, *The Siege of Charleston*, 265.

54. Ibid., 247.

55. Bombardment of Charleston, 1863–65, 1/28/2014, https://lowcountrywalkingtours.com/2014/01/28/bombardment-of-charleston-1863-65/.

56. Herman Melville, "The Swamp Angel," in *Battle Pieces and Aspects of War* (Amherst: University of Massachusetts Press, 1972), 107; Kelly, *America's Longest Siege*, 307–8.

57. Rosen, *The Jewish Confederates*, 237, and Burton, *The Siege of Charleston*, 155.

58. Rosen, *Confederate Charleston*, 125.

59. Burton, *The Siege of Charleston*, 311.

60. Jenkins, *Seizing the New Day*, 30.

61. Korn, *Jews and Negro Slavery*, 53.

62. Sublette and Sublette, *American Slave Coast*, 651.

63. Jenkins, *Seizing the New Day*, 31, quoting the *Boston Journal*.

64. Rosen *Confederate Charleston*, 142.

65. Dickey, *Our Man in Charleston*, 325.

66. Powers, *Black Charlestonians*, 68.

67. Eric Foner, *Reconstruction: America's Unfinished Revolution 1863–1877* (New York: Harper & Row, 1988), 72; Powers, *Black Charlestonians*, 69.

68. Jenkins, *Seizing the New Day*, 35–36; Sidney Andrews in the *Boston Advertiser*, quoted in Rosen, *The Jewish Confederates*, 309.

69. Letter from Major General W. T. Sherman to General John A. Rawlins, May 9, 1865, in *The War of the Rebellion: A Compilation of the Official Records of the Union and Confederate Armies*, Part 1: Report (Washington, DC: Government Printing Office, 1895), 38.

CHAPTER 8

1. Korn, *Jews and Negro Slavery*, 211.

2. Jacob R. Marcus, *The American Jewish Woman, 1654–1980* (New York and Cincinnati: KTAV Publishing/American Jewish Archives, 1981), 31.

3. Rosen, *The Jewish Confederates*, 335.

4. Jenkins, *Seizing the New Day*, 46.

5. Ibid., 47.

6. James H. Tuten, *Lowcountry Time and Tide: The Fall of the South Carolina Rice Kingdom* (Columbia: University of South Carolina Press, 2012), 26.

7. Ibid.

8. Korn, *Jews and Negro Slavery*, 54.

9. Rosen, *The Jewish Confederates*, 337.

10. Reznikoff, *The Jews of Charleston*, 162–63; Breibart, *Explorations*, 149.

11. Quoted in Rosen, *The Jewish Confederates*, 310.

12. Korn, *Jews and Negro Slavery*, 46.

13. Foner, *Reconstruction*, 71; Tuten, *Lowcountry Time and Tide*, 29.

14. Foner, *Reconstruction*, 403.

15. Jenkins, *Seizing the New Day*, 48.

16. Ibid., 41.

17. Powers, *Black Charlestonians*, 227.

18. Foner, *Reconstruction*, 90.

19. see David W. Blight, *Race and Reunion: The Civil War in American Memory*, Belknap Press, 2002.

20. Rosen, *The Jewish Confederates*, 142.

21. *Charleston Daily News*, November 2, 1865.

22. Jenkins, *Seizing the New Day*, 41.

23. Robert J. Zalimas, "A disturbance in the City: Black and White Soldiers in Postwar Charleston," in *Black Soldiers in Blue: African American Troops in the Civil War Era*, ed. John David Smith, 361–91 (Chapel Hill: University of North Carolina Press, 2004).

24. Powers, *Black Charlestonians*, 76; Jenkins, *Seizing the New Day*, 141.

25. Powers, *Black Charlestonians*, 76.

26. Jenkins, *Seizing the New Day*, 44.

27. Cardozo, *Reminiscences*, 10.

28. Foner, *Reconstruction*, 200.

29. Michael Trinkley, "South Carolina African Americans—Major Events in Reconstruction Politics," http://www.sciway.net/afam/reconstruction/majorevents.html.

30. Jenkins, *Seizing the New Day*, 55.

31. Ibid., 143.

32. Holt, *Black Over White*, 35.

33. *South Carolina Encyclopedia*, "Whipper, William J. 1834–1907," scencyclopedia.org/see/entries/whipper-william-j/.

34. See Steve Estes, Charleston in *Black and White: Race and Power in the South after the Civil Rights Movement* (Chapel Hill: University of North Carolina Press, 2015), and Powers, *Black Charlestonians*, 97.

35. Foner, *Reconstruction*, 305–6.

36. Marcus, *The American Jewish Woman*, 6.

37. Peggy Lamson, *The Glorious Failure: Black Congressman Robert Brown Elliot and the Reconstruction in the South* (New York: W. W. Norton and Co., 1973), 44.

38. John D. Hedrick, *Harriet Beecher Stowe: A Life* (Oxford, England: Oxford University Press, 1994), 355.

39. Flexner, *Century of Struggle*, 144.

40. Rosen, *The Jewish Confederates*, 336; Bertram W. Korn, *American Jewry and the Civil War* (New York: Meridian Books, 1956), 53; Gary Phillip Zola, "The Ascendency of Reform Judaism in the American South During the Nineteenth Century," in Ferris and Greenberg, *Jewish Roots*, 164; and Reznikoff, *The Jews of Charleston*, 168.

41. Reznikoff, *The Jews of Charleston*, 179.

42. Ibid.

43. Tobias, "The Hebrew Benevolent Society of Charleston," 41.

44. Ibid., 24.

45. Ibid., 19–20.

46. Newspaper reports 1867–71 in various Charleston papers (see *Charleston Daily News* for April 28, 1866; March 20, 1870; April 14, 1870).

47. "John W. Masury and Son, Paint Manufacturer," www.colorantshistory.org/MasuryPaint.html.

48. *Charleston Daily News*, March 26, 1870.

49. *Charleston Daily News*, February 4, 1867.

50. "C.R.C." 'Woman' in J. S. Burgess, *Southern Literary Journal and Monthly Magazine* 3 (1837): 180–83.

51. Bogart, *Economic History*, 589; Breibart, *Explorations*, 42; Kennedy, *A Nation of Immigrants*, 81.

52. Breibart, *Explorations*, 42.

53. Ibid., 81.

54. *Charleston Daily News*, January 21, 1869, p. 3.

55. Jenkins, *Seizing the New Day*, 72–87.

56. Powers, *Black Charlestonians*, 107.

57. Ibid., 98

58. Jenkins, *Seizing the New Day*, 65–66.

59. Powers, *Black Charlestonians*, 128–29; "Persecution for Opinion's Sake," *Charleston Daily News*, October 29, 1869, p. 2.

60. Bogart, *Economic History*, 590.

61. Roediger, *The Wages of Whiteness*, 71–74.

62. Bogart, *Economic History*, 594.

63. Ibid., 591.

64. "The Charleston Strike," *Charleston Daily News*, October 30, 1869, p. 3.

65. Powers, *Black Charlestonians*, 112.

66. Ibid., 127.

67. *Charleston Daily Courier*, October 26, 1869, p. 1.

68. *Charleston Daily News*, October 28, 1869.

69. "The Charleston Strike," *Charleston Daily News*, October 30, 1869, p. 3.

70. Jenkins, *Seizing the New Day*, 67.

Chapter 9

1. "Table 1: Population of the United States (By States and Territories)," in *Ninth Census, Volume 1: The Statistics of the Population of the United States* (Washington, DC: Government Printing Office, 1872).

2. Jeffrey G. Strickland, "Ethnicity and Race in the Urban South: German Immigrants and African-Americans in Charleston South Carolina During Reconstruction," PhD diss., Florida

State University, Department of History, 2003, 23. http://diginole.lib.fsu.edu/islandora/object /fsu:176051/datastream/PDF/view.

3. Michale Freund, "Fundamentally Freund: What American Jewry Can Learn from Emperor Joseph," *Jerusalem Post*, November 23, 2016. http://www.jpost.com/Opinion/Fundamentally -Freund-What-American-Jewry-can-learn -from-Emperor-Franz-Joseph-473487#/.

4. Louis Begley, *Franz Kafka: The Tremendous World I Have Inside My Head* (New York: Atlas and Co., 2009), 10–11.

5. see Robert S. Wistrich, *Austrians and Jews in the Twentieth Century* (New York: Springer, 1992).

6. CESKE BUDEJOVICE: Bohemia, International Jewish Cemetery Project, International Association of Jewish Genealogical Societies, https://iajgscemetery.org/eastern-europe/czech -republic/ceske-budejovice.

7. "Button Making": http://www.bohemia historicalsocietyny.org/button-making .html.

8. Jenkins, *Seizing the New Day*, 88.

9. quoting Stephen Powers, from Strickland, 'Ethnicity and Race.' 1.

10. "United States Census, 1870," database with images, *FamilySearch* (https://familysearch .org/ark:/61903/1:1:M8R4-4WX : accessed 10 May 2016).

11. Lunardini, *Women's Rights*, 38.

12. By the summer of 1867, there were 54 freedmen schools in South Carolina, serving some 5,000 students a day. See Martin Abbot, *The Freedmen's Bureau in South Carolina, 1865–1872* (Chapel Hill: University of North Carolina Press, 1967), 85–98.

13. Powers, *Black Charlestonians*, 136–41.

14. Geo. H. Chapin, *Health Resorts of the South* (Boston: Geo. H. Chapin, 1894), 204.

15. Flexner, *Century of Struggle*, 94.

16. "Academies and Seminaries," Women's Education Home Page, *Women's Education Evolves, 1790–1890—Selected Primary Works from the W. L. Clements Library*, University of Michigan, http://clements.umich.edu/exhibits /online/womened/Institutions.html.

17. Arthur Mazyck, compiler, *Guide to Charleston, Illustrated* (Charleston, SC: Walker, Evans and Cogswell, 1875).

18. US Bureau of the Census, 1870.

19. Foner, *Reconstruction*, 395; US Bureau of the Census, 1870.

20. Arthur Aryeh Goren, "1870–1920,"

Encyclopedia Judaica: New York City, http:// www.jewishvirtuallibrary.org/jsource/judaica /ejud_0002_0015_0_14806.html#_1870-1920.

21. Ward, *Poverty. Ethnicity, and the American City*, 45.

22. Roediger, *The Wages of Whiteness*, 145.

23. Laura Robertson-Lorant, *Melville: A Biography* (Amherst: University of Massachusetts Press, 1996), 461–62; Melville, "The House-top," *Battle Pieces*, 87.

24. *New York Times*, July 16, 1873, quoted in Matthew Frye Jacobson, *Whiteness of a Different Color: European Immigrants and the Alchemy of Race* (Cambridge, MA: Harvard University Press, 1998), 19.

25. Robertson-Lorant, *Melville: A Biography*, 463.

26. John Higham, *Strangers in the Land: Patterns of American Nativism, 1860–1925* (New York: Atheneum, 1963), 16.

27. Ward, *Poverty, Ethnicity, and the American City*, 39.

28. Robert Hendrickson, *The Grand Emporiums: The Illustrated History of America's Great Department Stores* (New York: Stein and Day, 1979), 32.

29. Hendrickson, *The Grand Emporiums*, 66; Cyrus Adler and Joseph Jacobs, "Strauss" in *Jewish Encyclopedia* (1906). http://www.jewish encyclopedia.com/articles/14072-straus.

30. Cyrus Adler, Max J. Kohler, Cyrus L. Sulzberger, D. M. Hermalin, "New York," in *Jewish Encyclopedia* (1906). http://www.jewish encyclopedia.com/articles/11501-new-york.

31. Hendrickson, *The Grand Emporiums*, 74.

32. Jan Toporowski, "Kalecki and Steindl in the Transition to Monopoly Capital," *Monthly Review*, 68, no. 3 (July–August 2016).

33. See Kuhn, Loeb and Co., *Investment Banking through Four Generations* New York: Kuhn, Loeb and Co., 1955).

34. James Ford Rhodes, *History of the United States from the Compromise of 1850, Vol. 7* (New York: MacMillan, 1906), 41.

35. "New York City," *Encyclopedia Judaica*, Jewish Virtual Library, https://www.jewish virtuallibrary.org/new-york-city.

36. Ward, *Poverty, Ethnicity, and the American City*, 39.

CHAPTER 10

1. "Population of St. Augustine, Fl," Historical population, https://population.us/Fl/st -augustine/.

2. Virginia Edwards, "Stories of Old St. Augustine," http://augustine.com/history/old-st-augustine/augustine-life.php.

3. Harriet Beecher Stowe, *Palmetto Leaves* (Boston: James R. Osgood and Co., 1873), 206.

4. Gutman, *Work, Culture and Society*, 52.

5. Jenkins, *Seizing the New Day*, 159.

6. C. S. Monaco, *Moses Levy of Florida: Jewish Utopian and Antebellum Reformer* (Baton Rouge: Louisiana State University Press, 2005), 43.

7. "David Levy Yulee (1810–1886)," Jewish Virtual Library, http://www.jewishvirtuallibrary.org/jsource/biography/yulee.html; and James M. Denham, "Florida's Forgotten Visionary: Moses Elias Levy," H-Net, March 2006, reviewing C. S. Monaco, *Moses Levy of Florida: Jewish Utopian and Antebellum Reformer* (Baton Rouge: Louisiana State University Press, 2005), http://www.h-net.org/reviews/showrev.php?id=11530.

8. Monaco, *Moses Levy*, 44 and 43.

9. Denham, "Florida's Forgotten Visionary," quoting Monaco, 9, and Monaco, *Moses Levy*, 49–50.

10. "Downtown History," Downtown Jacksonville, http://www.downtownjacksonville.org/Media/HistoryofDowntown.aspx.

11. Monaco, *Moses Levy*, 105.

12. Charlton W. Tebeau, *A History of Florida, Third Edition* (Coral Gables, FL: University of Miami Press, 1971/1999), 158.

13. Monaco, *Moses Levy*, 143.

14. Denham, "Florida's Forgotten Visionary."

15. James Weldon Johnson, *Along This Way: The Autobiography of James Weldon Johnson* (New York: Viking Press, 1933), 6.

16. Stowe, *Palmetto Leaves*, 14–15.

17. "Population of Jacksonville, Fl," Historical population, https://population.us/Fl/jacksonville/.

18. Johnson, *Along This Way*, 6.

19. See "History of Jacksonville," Thomas Frederick Davis (Jacksonville, FL: H & W. B. Drew Co., 1911), and "Historical population of Jacksonville city for period 1850–2014," population.us/fl/Jacksonville.

20. Stowe, *Palmetto Leaves*, 36.

21. Ibid., 38.

22. Foner, *Reconstruction*, 189.

23. Gilmore Academy-Jackson County Training School Alumni Association, Inc., *Jackson County Florida* (Mount Pleasant, SC: Arcadia Publishing, 2000), introduction.

24. Testimony Taken by the Joint Select Committee to inquire into The Condition of Affairs in the Late Insurrectionary States: Florida; 42nd Congress, 2nd Session, 82 (United States Congress, Senate, 1872), 9.

25. Stowe, *Palmetto Leaves*, 14.

26. "Historical population of Jacksonville city for period 1850–2014," population.us/fl/Jacksonville.

27. Hedrick, *Harriet Beecher Stowe*, 328.

28. Ibid., 340.

29. Ibid., 359.

30. Stowe, *Palmetto Leaves*, 289.

31. Hedrick, *Harriet Beecher Stowe*, 341.

32. Dr. Wayne Wood, "Jacksonville: Florida's Tourist Mecca and Its Grand Hotels: 1869 to 1926," Jacksonville Historical Society, http://www.jaxhistory.org/jacksonville-floridas-tourist-mecca-and-its-grand-hotels-1869-to-1926/.

33. Bogart, *Economic History*, 592–93.

34. "Historical population of Jacksonville city for period 1850–2014," population.us/fl/Jacksonville.

35. Johnson, *Along This Way*, 31.

36. Diner, *A Time*, 92–93.

37. "Jewish Jacksonville," http://exhibits.uflib.ufl.edu/jewishjacksonville/; Diner, *A Time for Gathering*, 95; and "Index to Florida Jewish History in the American Israelite, 1850–1900," George A. Smathers Libraries, University of Florida, http://ufdc.ufl.eduUF00015495/00001/1j, p. 1.

38. Gilmore Academy-Jackson County Training School, *Jackson County Florida*, 172; Stephen Robertson, "Age of Consent Laws," Children and Youth in History, http://chnm.gmu.edu/cyh/teaching-modules/230.

39. Holt, *Black Over White*, 51.

40. Abdulbari Bener, Elnour E. Dafeeah, and Nancy Samson, "Does Consanguinity Increase the Risk of Schizophrenia? Study Based on Primary Health Care Centre Visits," *Mental Health in Family Medicine* 9, no. 4 (December 2012): 241–48; and "Marriage between First Cousins Doubles Risk of Birth Defects, Say Researchers," *The Guardian*, July 4, 2013, https://www.theguardian.com/science/2013/jul/04/marriage-first-cousins-birth-defects.

41. "List of coupled cousins," Wikipedia, https://en-wikipedia.org/wiki/List_of_coupled_cousins.

CHAPTER 11

1. "The Revised Statutes of the State of South Carolina" Title VII, (Columbia, SC: Republican Printing Co., 1873), 481.

2. *Encyclopedia of Southern Jewish Communities*—Savannah, Georgia; http://www.isjl.org/georgia-savannah-encyclopedia.html.

3. "Jewish Marriage Notices FROM THE NEWSPAPER PRESS of Charleston, S. C. (1775–1906)," compiled by Barnett A. Elizas (New York: Bloch Publishing, 1917). https://archive.org/stream/jewishmarriagenoooelza/jewishmarriage noooelza_djvu.txt.

4. Ella Teague De Berard, *Steamboats in the Hyacinths* (New York: College Publishing Company, 1956), 13.

5. "Supplement for Florida," United States Census, 1910, https://www2.census.gov/prod2/decennial/documents/41033935v9-14ch01.pdf; and Johnson, *Along This Way*, 6.

6. *Webb's Jacksonville City Directory* (W. H. Webb and Company, 1876), 140, http://jpl.coj.net/dlc/florida/rbmp/cd/1876/index.html.

7. De Berard, *Steamboats in the Hyacinths*, 14, 15. It was actually Johnston's Kalsomine.

8. Moss, *Paint in America*, 27, 38.

9. "John W. Masury and Son: Paint Manufacturers," ColorantsHistory.org, http://www.colorantshistory.org/MasuryPaint.html.

10. Moss, *Paint in America*, 56.

11. Johnson, *Along This Way*, 6.

12. "Birdseye view of Jacksonville, Fla." (Alvord, Kellog & Campbell, 1876). https://www.loc.gov/resource/g3934j.pm001130/.

13. "Our History," Congregation Ahavath Chesed, https://thetemplejacksonville.org/history/.

14. *Index to Florida Jewish History in the American Israelite* (University of Florida, George A. Smathers Library), 20, https://ufdc.ufl.edu/UF00015495/00001.

15. Coontz, *Marriage, A History*, 153–56, 165.

16. *Jewish Marriage Notices from the Newspaper Press of Charleston, South Carolina, 1775–1906* (Charleston, SC: Bloch Publishing Co., 1917), 39; *Webb's Historical, Industrial, and Biographical, Florida* (New York: W. S. Webb Co., 1888), 157.

17. "Supplement for Florida," US Census 1910, https://www2.census.gov/prod2/decennial/documents/41033935v9-14ch01.pdf.

18. *Webb's Jacksonville Directory 1876–77* (New York: W. S. Webb and Company, 1876). http://www.latinamericanstudies.org/19-century/Jacksonville-1876.pdf.

19. "Downtown History," Downtown Jacksonville, http://www.downtownjacksonville.org/Media/HistoryofDowntown.aspx.

20. *Webb's Jacksonville Directory, 1878–79* (New York: W. S. Webb and Co., 1878), 187.

21. Johnson, *Along This Way*, 6.

22. Julia Brock and Daniel Vivian, *Leisure, Plantations, and the Making of a New South: The Sporting Plantations of the South Carolina Low Country and Red Hills Region, 1900–1940* (Lanham, MD: Lexington Books, 2015), 156.

23. Foner, *Reconstruction*, 281.

24. Johnson, *Along This Way*, 45.

25. Stowe, *Palmetto Leaves*, 317.

26. Hedrick, *Harriet Beecher Stowe*, 341.

27. Stowe, *Palmetto Leaves*, 317.

28. *Charleston Daily News*, July 22, 1871.

29. Flexner, *Century of Struggle*, 169.

30. Douglas R. Egerston, *The Wars of Reconstruction: The Brief, Violent History of America's Most Progressive Era* (New York: Bloomsbury Books, 2014), 312.

31. Foner, *Reconstruction*, 567.

32. M. Stolp-Smith, "The Hamburg Massacre (1876)," 2011, BlackPast.org, http://www.blackpast.org/aah/hamburg-massacre-1876; and N. R. Kleinfeld, "Counting the Vote: The History; President Tilden? No, but Almost, in Another Vote That Dragged On," *New York Times*, November 12, 2000.

33. Jerrell H. Shofner, "Florida in the Balance: The Electoral Count of 1876," *Florida Historical Quarterly* (October 1968): 124.

34. Lamson, *The Glorious Failure*, 247–51.

35. Foner, *Reconstruction*, 581.

36. W. E. B. Du Bois, "The Propaganda of History," from *Black Reconstruction in America* (New York: Free Press, 1998), 726–28. Originally published in 1935.

37. Philip S. Foner, *The Great Labor Uprising* (New York: Monad Press, 1977), 20, 24.

38. Ibid., 18.

39. Ibid., 232–24.

40. Ibid., 189.

41. Ibid., 37–38.

42. Ibid., 217.

43. Higham, *Strangers in a Strange Land*, 31.

44. Foner, *The Great Labor Uprising*, 8–9.

45. Ibid.,122.

46. Ibid., 237.

47. Ibid.

48. Ibid., 204.

49. Gutman, *Work, Culture and Society,* 50.

50. "Contributions to St. Luke's Hospital Jacksonville, Fl 11"; on the whiteway Corners website, Current Events and Historical Content, http://www.whitewayrealty.com.

51. "Jewish Cemetery," A list of those buried in the Hebrew Section, Old City Cemetery, Jacksonville, FL; read and transcribed by: Jon R. Ferguson and Michael E. Lawson; Duval County Florida GenWeb, http://fl-genweb.org/duval/dcems/jewish.html.

CHAPTER 12

1. Federal Writers' Project, *The WPA Guide to Minnesota* (St. Paul: Minnesota Historical Society Press, 1985, copyright 1938), 16; Leif Enger, "A History of Timbering in Minnesota," November 16, 1998. http://news.minnesota.publicradio.org/features/199811/16_engeri_history-m/.

2. Rhoda R. Gilman, "Territorial Imperative: How Minnesota Became the 32nd State," in *The North State: A Minnesota History Reader,* edited by Anne J. Aby, (St. Paul: Minnesota Historical Society Press, 2002), 52–53.

3. Federal Writers' Project, *The WPA Guide to Minnesota,* 51.

4. Martin Ridge, *Ignatius Donnelly: Portrait of a Politician* (St. Paul: Minnesota Historical Society Press, 1962).

5. Ridge, *Ignatius Donnelly,* 17.

6. Matt Reicher, "Nininger," *MNopedia,* http://www.mnopedia.org/place/nininger.

7. Brainard, Dudley S. "Nininger, a Boom Town of the Fifties." *Minnesota History* 13, no. 2 (1932): 127–51. http://www.jstor.org/stable/20160970.

8. Federal Writers' Project, *The WPA Guide to Minnesota,* 52.

9. Michael G. Rapp, "Samuel N. Deinard and the Unification of Jews in Minneapolis," *Minnesota History* (Summer 1973): 214.

10. Ridge, *Ignatius Donnelly,* 35.

11. Federal Writers' Project, *The WPA Guide to Minnesota,* 57.

12. Ibid.

13. Enger, "A History of Timbering in Minnesota,"

14. Federal Writers' Project, *The WPA Guide to Minnesota,* 69.

15. Ibid., 75.

16. Lincoln Steffens, "The Shame of Minneapolis: The Ruin and Redemption of a City

that was Sold Out," McClure's Magazine, January, 1903, http://minnesotalegalhistoryproject.org/assets/Steffens-%20of%20Shame%20of%20Mpls.pdf.

17. Federal Writers' Project, *The WPA Guide to Minnesota,* 159.

18. "Flour Milling," St. Anthony Falls Heritage Board, mnhs.org/places/safhb/history_four.php.

19. Hyman Berman and Linda Mack Schloff, *Jews in Minnesota* (St. Paul: Minnesota Historical Society, 2002), 8.

20. Lucile M. Kane, *The Falls of St. Anthony: The Waterfall that Built Minneapolis* (St. Paul: Minnesota Historical Society Press, 1987), 104.

21. David Paul Nord, "Minneapolis and Pragmatic Socialism of Thomas Van Lear," *Minnesota History* (Spring 1976).

22. Steffens, "The Shame of Minneapolis,"

23. Laura E. Weber, "'Gentiles Preferred' Minneapolis Jews and Employment 1920–1950," *Minnesota History* (Spring 1991): 166–82. http://collections.mnhs.org/MNHistoryMagazine/articles/52/v52i05p166-182.pdf.

24. William D. Green, "Race and Segregation in St. Paul's Public Schools: 1846–1869," in Anne J. Aby, ed., *The North State: A Minnesota History Reader,* 338 http://collections.mnhs.org/MNHistoryMagazine/articles/55/v55i04p138-149.pdf.

25. Weber, "Gentiles Preferred."

26. Berman and Schloff, "Jews in Minnesota," 3 and Chiat and Proshan, "German Jews," 174.

27. Berman and Schloff, "Jews in Minnesota," 9.

28. "Minneapolis, Minnesota: Population History, 1880–2018" Biggest U.S. Cities, http://www.biggestuscities.com/city/minneapolis-minnesota.

29. Berman and Schloff, "Jews in Minnesota," 9 and 5.

30. Michael G. Rapp, "Samuel N. Deinard and the Unification of Jews in Minneapolis," *Minnesota History* (Summer 1973): 214.

31. Map Monday: "To Elevate the Moral Standard of the Drama" The Historyapolis Project, History Department, Augsburg University, http://historyapolis.com/blog/2014/10/20/map-monday-elevate-moral-standard-drama/.

32. *Minneapolis Star Tribune,* April 2, 1872.

33. *Minneapolis Star Tribune,* June 15, 1882.

34. "Regular Paint Store," *Minneapolis Star Tribune,* September 11, 1880, p. 2.

35. "History of Sherwin-Williams," http://excellence.sherwin.com/history_timeline.html.

36. *Minneapolis Journal,* December 1923.

37. Jan Toporowski, "Kalecki and Steindl in the Transition to Monopoly Capital," *Monthly Review* (July–August 2016).

38. Berman and Schloff, "Jews in Minnesota," and Amos S. Deinard interview, Minnesota Oral History Project, December 10, 1978, http://collections.mnhs.org/cms/web5/media .php?pdf=1&irn=10065654.

39. Rhoda Lewin, *Reform Jews of Minneapolis* (Charleston, SC: Arcadia Publishing, 2004), introduction and p. 15.

40. "Reform Judaism: The Origins of Reform Judaism," Jewish Virtual Library, http://www .jewishvirtuallibrary.org/jsource/Judaism/The _Origins_of_Reform_Judaism.html.

41. Berman and Schloff, "Jews in Minnesota," 21.

42. Ibid., 8–9, 48.

43. Ibid., 7.

44. Elizabeth Ann Lorenz-Meyer, "Gender, Ethnicity and Space: Jews in Minneapolis and St. Paul, 1900–1930," thesis, Graduate School of the University of Minnesota, 2006, Gunther Plant, 31.

45. Weber, "Gentiles Preferred."

46. Berman and Schloff, "Jews in Minnesota," 7.

47. Lorenz-Meyer, "Gender, Ethnicity and Space," 31.

48. Rapp, "Samuel N. Deinard," 215.

49. Ira Nathanson, *Minneapolis in the Twentieth Century: The Growth of an American City* (Minneapolis: Minnesota Historical Society, 2010), 44; Rapp, "Samuel N. Deinard," 214; Berman and Schloff, "Jews in Minnesota," 12.

50. Amos S. Deinard interview, Minnesota's Immigrants, 1978, https://immigrants.mndigital .org/items/show/228.

51. *Shole's Directory of the City of Charleston* (Charleston, SC: A. E. Sholes, 1882).

52. Muriel B. Christison, "Leroy S. Buffington and the Minneapolis Boom of the 1880's," http:// collections.mnhs.org/MNHistoryMagazine /articles/23/v23i03p219-232.pdf.

53. Christison, "Leroy S. Buffington" and *Minneapolis Journal*, May 1, 1902.

54. Moss, *Paint in America*, 22–38.

55. Perseus Shearer, "Benjamin Moore Paint, a brief history," 2011, http://www.shearerpaint ing.com/blog/resources/history-of-benjamin -moore-paint/.

CHAPTER 13

1. Gutman, *Work, Culture*, 33.

2. "The Pillsbury Company History," from *International Directory of Company Histories*, Vol. 62, (St. James Press, 2004) http://www .fundinguniverse.com/company-histories /the-pillsbury-company-history/.

3. Hull House report in Ward, *Poverty, Ethnicity, and the American City*, 86.

4. Meridel LeSueur, *Ripening: Selected Work* (New York: Feminist Press, 1990), 64.

5. "From Shop and Mill," *St. Paul Globe*, May 3, 1885, 7.

6. Marcus, *The American Jewish Woman*, 45.

7. Daniels, *Golden Door*, 28.

8. George B. Engberg, "The Knights of Labor in Minnesota," *Minnesota History Magazine*, Minnesota Historical Society, 22, no. 4 (December 1941), 376, http://collections.mnhs.org/MN HistoryMagazine/articles/22/v22i04p367-390 .pdf.

9. Dave Riehle, "The Knights of Labor: the Nation's First Labor Movement," *Workaday Minnesota*, http://www.workdayminnesota.org /articles/knights-labor-nations-first-real-labor -movement.

10. Louis Adamic, "The Knights of Labor, 1869–1885," from *Dynamite: The Story of Class Violence in America* (Chico, CA: AK Press, 2008).

11. Jeremy Brecher, *Strike!* (San Francisco, CA: Straight Arrow Books, 1972), 29.

12. Bogart, *Economic History*, 593.

13. Flexner, *Century of Struggle*, 200, quoting Leonara Barry.

14. Brecher, *Strike!*, 28.

15. Minnesota Federations of Labor, *Official Yearbook*, 1917, 31.

16. Riehle, "The Knights of Labor."

17. Dave Riehle, "The Knights of Labor: The Nation's first real labor movement," Workaday Minnesota, https://workdayminnesota.org /the-knights-of-labor-the-nations-first-real -labor-movement/, speech given March 2, 1886.

18. Donald F. Warner, "Prelude to Populism," *Minnesota History* 32, no. 3 (September 1951): 129–30.

19. LeSueur, *Ripening*, 57.

20. Lunardini, *Women's Rights*, 85.

21. Richard M. Valelly, *Radicalism in the States: The Minnesota Farmer-Labor Party and the American Political Economy* (Chicago: University of Chicago Press, 1989), 8; Martin Ridge, *Ignatius Donnelly: Portrait of a Politician* (St. Paul: Minnesota Historical Society Press, 1962), 245.

22. Ridge, *Ignatius Donnelly,* 31.

23. Ibid., 137.

24. Allan M. Axelrod, "Ideology and Utopia in the Works of Ignatius Donnelly," *American Studies* 12, no. 2 (1971): 47–65.

25. Ridge, *Ignatius Donnelly,* 245.

26. Dorfman, *Thorstein Veblen,* 15.

27. Ridge, *Ignatius Donnelly,* 134.

28. Ibid., 245–52.

29. Minnesota Federations of Labor, Official Yearbook (Minnesota State Federation of Labor, 1917), 31.

30. *Saint Paul Globe,* May 18, 1890, 20.

31. Higham, *Strangers in a Strange Land,* 138.

32. Hannah Arendt, "Lawlessness Is Inherent in the Uprooted," *New York Times Magazine* (April 28, 1968): 24–25.

33. Daniels, *Golden Door,* 29–31.

34. *Saint Paul Globe,* May 18, 1890, 20.

35. Jay Driskell, "Florida's 'Second Reconstruction': The Knights of Labor and Interracial Politics in Jacksonville, Florida, 1887–1889." Paper delivered at the American Historical Association Annual Meeting, Washington, DC, 3 Jan 2014.

36. Ibid.

37. James Fallows, "The Two Great Classes—Tramps and Millionaires," *Atlantic,* June 25, 2012.

CHAPTER 14

1. Michael Haines, "Fertility and Mortality in the United States," The Economic History Association, undated, https://eh.net/encyclopedia/fertility-and-mortality-in-the-united-states/.

2. *Minneapolis Star Tribune,* May 20, 1899.

3. *Minneapolis Star Tribune,* March 24, 1891.

4. *Minneapolis Star Tribune,* May 2, 1890, 8.

5. *St. Paul Globe,* September 3, 1889; and *St. Paul Globe,* May 2, 1884.

6. Lorenz-Meyer, *Gender, Ethnicity,* 171.

7. *St. Paul Globe,* June 3, 1892.

8. Lunardini, *Women's Rights,* 106–8.

9. Lunardini, *Women's Rights,* 106.

10. Lunardini, *Women's Rights,* 99; Flexner, *Century of Struggle,* 179.

11. Originally called the Council of Jewish Women.

12. Susan B. Anthony, "Organization among Women as an Instrument in Promoting the Interests of Political Liberty," to the World's Congress of Representative Women, May 20, 1893; http://ecssba.rutgers.edu/docs/sbaexpo.html.

13. Melissa R. Klapper, *Ballots, Babies and Banners of Peace: American Jewish Women's Activism, 1890–1940* (New York: New York University Press, 2013), 8; Hasia R. Diner, *The Jews of the United States* (Berkeley: University of California Press, 2004), 193; *St. Paul Globe,* August 15, 1894; Faith Rogow, *Gone to Another Meeting: The National Council of Jewish Women, 1893–1993* (Tuscaloosa: University of Alabama Press, 1993), 34.

14. Rogow, *Gone to Another Meeting,* 2.

15. Diner, *The Jews of the United States,* 192; Marcus, *The American Jewish Woman,* 86–87.

16. Klapper, *Ballots,* 21.

17. Marcus, *The American Jewish Woman,* 91.

18. Lorenz-Meyer, *Gender, Ethnicity,* 265.

19. Daniels, *Golden Door,* 31.

20. Diner, *The Jews of the United States,* 193; *St. Paul Globe,* August 15, 1894; Berman and Schloff, *Jews in Minnesota,* 33.

21. United States Immigration Commission (1907–10), "Statements and recommendations submitted by societies and organizations interested in the subject of immigration," (Washington, DC: Government Printing Office, 1911).

22. Rogow, *Gone to Another Meeting,* 42 *Church of the Holy Trinity v. U.S.* 143 U.S. 457 (1892).

23. Rogow, *Gone to Another Meeting,* 47.

24. *St. Paul Globe,* April 10, 1889, p. 3.

25. *Minneapolis Junior Journal,* September 1904.

26. *Minneapolis Journal,* August 2, 1901.

27. Rapp, *Samuel N. Deinard,* 215.

28. Cyrus Adler, Henriette Szold, *American Jewish Year Book: Directory of Local Organizations* (American Jewish Committee, 1899), 167; Karla Goldman, "Reform Judaism in the United States," Jewish Women's Archive Encyclopedia, https://jwa.org/encyclopedia/article/reform-judaism-in-united-states.

29. "Minneapolis, Minnesota Population History 1880–2020, http://www.biggestuscities.com/city/minneapolis-minnesota.

30. *Minneapolis Journal,* May 1, 1902.

31. *Minneapolis Star Tribune,* May 19, 1898.

CHAPTER 15

1. *Minneapolis Journal,* August 17, 1901.

2. See "Lost Minneapolis Mansions, Part II," 1889 Victorian House Restoration, http://1889victorianrestoration.blogspot.com/2012_06_25_archive.html?view=classic.

3. *Minneapolis Journal,* April 8, 1901.

4. Judge Charles E. Flandreau, *Encyclopedia of Biography of Minnesota: History of Minnesota,*

Vol. 1 (Chicago: Century Publishing and Engraving Company, 1900), 149–151.

5. *Minneapolis Journal*, August 6, 1901.

6. *Minneapolis Journal* September 28, 1901.

7. *Minneapolis Journal* February 27, 1904.

8. *Minneapolis Star Tribune*, November 21, 1908.

9. "$49,000 Awarded by Court," *New Ulm Review* (New Ulm, MN), December 18, 1912, p. 4.

10. *Minneapolis Journal*, September 10, 1901.

11. Gutman, *Work, Culture, and Society*, 13.

12. Bogart, *Economic History*, 606.

13. Official Yearbook, Minnesota Federations of Labor, 1917.

14. *Minneapolis Journal*, May 21, 1901 and April 14, 1905.

15. "YERXA," *Minneapolis Journal*, May 8, 1901. http://chroniclingamerica.loc.gov/lccn /sn83045366/1901-05-08/ed-1/seq-7/ocr.txt.

16. *Seventh Biennial Report, Bureau of Labor for the State of Minneapolis* (St. Paul, MN: Pioneer Press Company: 1901).

17. Ibid.

18. Iric Nathanson, "Dr. Samuel Deinard," Jewish Historical Society of the Midwest, 2012 http://www.jhsum.org/2012/09/dr-samuel -deinard/.

19. Berman and Schloff, *Jews in Minnesota*, 23.

20. "Intermarriage Is Opposed by Rabbi," *Star Tribune* (Minneapolis), November 21, 1908, p. 8.

21. Eli Lederhendler, *American Jewery: A New History* (Cambridge, England: Cambridge University Press, 2017), 79–80.

22. Lorenz-Meyer, *Gender, Ethnicity*, 106.

23. See Deborah Y. Bachrach, "Samuel N. Deinard: An Unsung Zionist Leader," American Jewish Archives, Vol LXVII, #1. http://american jewisharchives.org/publications/journal/PDF /2015_67_01_00_bachrach.pdf.

24. *American Jewish World* 2, no. 1 (July 30, 1915): 17.

25. Lorenz-Meyer, *Gender, Ethnicity*, 209–12.

26. A lodge Jew paid more attention to his lodge—Masonic, Elks—than temple. Rapp, *Samuel N. Deinard*, 219.

27. Nathanson, "Dr. Samuel Deinard."

28. John E. Haynes, "A Frustrated Voice of Socialism, 1910–1919", *The New Times*, Spring 1991, http://collections.mnhs.org/MNHistory Magazine/articles/52/v52i05p183-194.pdf.

29. Deboarh Y. Barach, "Samuel N. Deinard: An Unsung Zionist Leader," *The American Jewish Archives Journal*, Vol. LXVII, #1, 2015, pgs 1–26.

30. Ibid.

31. William Millikan, *A Union Against Unions: The Minneapolis Citizens Alliance and Its Fight Against Organized Labor, 1903–1947* (St. Paul: Minneapolis Historical Society Press, 2001), 5.

32. Ridge, *Ignatius Donnelly*, 383, 399.

33. Lunardini, *Women's Rights*, 88.

34. Thomas K. Backerud, "Progressive Era in Minnesota," MNopedia, Minnesota Historical Society, November 30, 2018, http://www.mnopedia.org/event/progressive-era -minnesota-1899-1920.

35. Millikan, *A Union Against Unions*, 3.

36. Ibid., 6.

37. Ibid., 8–12.

38. Ibid., 22.

39. Ibid., 15.

40. Ibid., 24.

41. Ibid., 25.

42. Ibid., 35.

43. Phillips Korth, *Minneapolis Teamsters Strike of 1934* (East Lansing: Michigan State University Press, 1995), 14–15.

44. Isaac Atwater, ed., *History of the City of Minneapolis*, vol. 2 (New York: Munsell and Company, 1893), 556–57.

45. Lewin, *Reform Jews of Minneapolis*, 19.

46. Ibid., 20.

47. *Minneapolis Journal*, June 4, 1904.

48. Flexner, *Century of Struggle*, 232.

49. Ibid., 231.

CHAPTER 16

1. Marcus, *The American Jewish Woman*, 68.

2. *Davison's Minneapolis City Directory*, Vol. XXXI (Minneapolis Directory Company, 1903), 1879 https://box2.nmtvault.com/Henne pin2/jsp/RcWebImageViewer.jsp?doc_id=096 c15a1-2813-4856-a7c9-6a72aa07236b/mnmhc loo/20130429/00000011&pg_seq=25&search _doc=.

3. "A Brief History of Wellesley College," web .wellesely.edu/PublicAffaris/About/briefhistory .html.

4. Josh Dorin, "College Hall," https://welles leyhistory.wordpress.com/2013/06/04/college -hall-wellesley-college/.

5. Wellesley College, "Wellesley College Calendar 1903–1904" (1903). *The Wellesley College Catalogs*. Book 5. http://repository.wellesley.edu /catalogs/5.

6. Rosengartens and Rosengartens, *A Portion of the People*, 142.

7. "A Brief History of Wellesley College," Office of Public Affairs, August 6, 2007, web

.wellesley.edu/PublicAffairs/About/briefhistory
.html and Dorin "College Hall".

8. *A Record of the Exercises Attending the Inauguration of Caroline Hazard, LITT. D, as President of Wellesley College, III October MDCCCXCIX*, Wellesley College (Riverside Press, 1899).

9. Florence Converse, *The Story of Wellesley* (University of Michigan Library, January 1, 1915) http://www.fullbooks.com/The-Story-of-Wellesley2.html.

10. Helen Farrell Allen, "An Article for Wellesley, on their President Caroline Hazard, 1899–1910, of Rhode Island," http://www.tempusfugitri.com/2010/04/article-for-wellesley-on-their.html and Esther Kim, "On A Hazardous Woman," *Counterpoint: The Wellesley Journal of Campus Life*, http://counterpointmagazine.tumblr.com/post/29975930207/wlsy-370-first-chapter-on-a-hazardouswoman.

11. Converse, *The Story of Wellesley*.

12. Kim, "Hazardous."

13. Converse, *The Story of Wellesley*.

14. Kim, "Hazardous."

15. See Helen Lefkowitz Horowitz, ALMA MATER: Design and Experience in the Women's Colleges from Their Nineteenth Century Beginnings to the 1930's (Amherst: University of Massachusetts Press, 1984).

16. *Wellesley College News*, October 20, 1904.

17. "Wellesley College was founded in 1870 by Henry and Pauline Durant, who were passionate about the higher education of women" My Wellesley http://www.wellesley.edu/about/collegehistory.

18. Wellesley College Calendar 1903–04 https://repository.wellesley.edu/cgi/viewcontent.cgi?article=1000&context=catalogs.

19. "Wellesley College was founded in 1870 by Henry and Pauline Durant, who were passionate about the higher education of women" My Wellesley http://www.wellesley.edu/about/collegehistory.

20. Wellesley College Calendar 1903–04 https://repository.wellesley.edu/cgi/viewcontent.cgi?article=1000&context=catalogs.

21. Flexner, *Century of Struggle*, 129.

22. *Wellesley College News*, November 2, 1904. https://repository.wellesley.edu/news/105/?utm_source=repository.wellesley.edu%2Fnews%2F105&utm_medium=PDF&utm_campaign=PDFCoverPages.

23. *Wellesley College News*, November 1, 1905.

https://repository.wellesley.edu/cgi/viewcontent.cgi?article=1138&context=news.

24. Wellesley College Calendar 1903–4. https://repository.wellesley.edu/cgi/viewcontent.cgi?article=1000&context=catalogs.

25. Lawrence Harmon, "Wellesley College Can't Tiptoe Around Anti-Semitism," *Boston Globe*, December 12, 2014.

26. Poet Katherine Lee Bates quoted in Kim, "Hazardous."

CHAPTER 17

1. Stephen Edgell, *Veblen in Perspective: His Life and Thought* (Rutledge, Abington and New York, 2015), 8 and Joseph Dorfman, *Thorstein Veblen and His America* (New York: Augustus M. Kelley, 1934, (1966)), 176 and 352.

2. Dorfman, *Thorstein Veblen*, 10.

3. Ibid., 294.

4. Ibid., 17, 55–56, 58.

5. Thorstein Veblen, *The Theory of Business Enterprise* (New York: Cosimo Classics, 2005), 7.

6. Veblen, *The Theory of Business Enterprise*, 30 and 7.

7. *Minneapolis Journal*, January 6, 1904.

8. Veblen, *The Theory of Business Enterprise*, 31.

9. Ibid., 31 and 7.

10. Ibid., 7.

11. George B. Hechel, "Growth of the Paint Manufacturing Industry," *The Book-Keeper: The Business Man's Magazine* 20, no. 11 (May 1908): 381.

12. *Minneapolis Star Tribune*, May 19, 1907.

13. Veblen, *The Theory of Business Enterprise*, 8.

14. *Minneapolis Star Tribune*, May 19, 1907.

15. Veblen, *The Theory of Business Enterprise*, 8.

16. Ibid., 126.

17. Farrell Dobbs, *Teamster Rebellion* (New York: Pathfinder, London, 1974, 2004), 42.

18. Nord, "Thomas Van Lear."

19. Elizabeth Faue, *Community, Suffering and Struggle: Women, Men, and the Labor Movement in Minneapolis, 1915–1945* (Chapel Hill: University of North Carolina Press, 1991), 23.

20. LeSueur, *Ripening*, 67.

21. David Stevenson, "Europe before 1914," British Library, 2014, https://www.bl.uk/world-war-one/articles/europe-before-1914.

22. Klapper, *Ballots*, 109.

23. Warren F. Kuehl and Gary P. Ostrower, "Internationalism," *Encyclopedia of American*

Foreign Policy (Charles Scribners Sons, 2002) https://www.encyclopedia.com/social-sciences -and-law/political-science-and-government /military-affairs-nonnaval/internationalism.

24. Coontz, *Marriage, A History,* 207.

25. Tim Brady, "A Difference in Tone," *Minnesota Magazine,* http://web.archive.org /web/20070808194323/http://alumni.umn.edu /A_Difference_in_Tone.html.

26. Brady, "A Difference in Tone."

27. Ibid.

28. Ibid.

29. Ibid.

30. Linda Schloff, "Fanny Fligelman Brin," *Jewish Woman's Archive Encyclopedia,* https:// jwa.org/people/brin-fanny.

31. Thorstein Veblen, "The Economic Theory of Woman's Dress," *Popular Science Monthly,* Vol. 46, New York, 1894, 204.

32. Veblen, *The Theory of Business Enterprise,* 127.

33. Veblen, "The Economic Theory of Woman's Dress," 199.

34. Ibid., 203.

35. Dorfman, *Thorstein Veblen,* 176–79; Veblen, "The Economic Theory of Woman's Dress," 199.

CHAPTER 18

1. *St. Paul Globe,* November 17, 1885.

2. Alan Levinson, "The Posen Factor," *Shofar* 17, no. 1 (Fall 1998): 72.

3. "Virtual Jewish World: Prussia," *Jewish Virtual Library,* from *Encyclopaedia Judaica,* http://www.jewishvirtuallibrary.org/jsource /vjw/Prussia.html.

4. Jonathan Bauch, "Public German, Private Jews: The Secret Identity of Berthold Lindau in Howell's A Hazard of New Fortunes," *American Literary Realism* 41, no. 1 (Fall 2008): 22.

5. Christopher Clark, "Why Should We Think about the Revolution of 1848 Now?" *London Review of Books,* March 7, 2019.

6. Sharfman, "Jewish Emancipation,"

7. Iggers, *The Jews of Bohemia,* 139.

8. Kisch, *In Search,* 32–33 and 37; Ezra Mendelsohn, *The Jews of East Central Europe Between the World Wars* (Bloomington: Indiana University Press 1987), 136.

9. Kisch, *In Search,* 42.

10. Higham, *Strangers in a Strange Land,* 8.

11. *Mobile Daily Advertiser,* 1844: November 13, December 11, May 16.

12. United States Census, Virginia: (NARA Series M653, Roll 1380).

13. Bancroft, *Slave Trading,* 24–26.

14. See "History," Fredericksburg Masonic Lodge #4, Masoniclodge4.org/history-of -lodge-4.

15. *Report on Population of the United States at the Eleventh Census,* 1890, Part 1 (United States. Census Office Washington, DC, 1895), 57 and Vernon Watson, "Burnt Corn, Alabama," 2019, http://www.burntcorn.com/.

16. *United States Census, 1860,* https://www .familysearch.org/ark:/61903/1:1:MHDX-XDH.

17. *Richmond Dispatch* (Richmond, VA), July 29, 1862, p. 2.

18. Wise, *Lifeline of the Confederacy,* 20.

19. "Civil War Times," Mobile Bay Civil War Trail, 2018, https://battleofmobilebay.com /civil-war-times.

20. Rosen, *Jewish Confederates,* quoting Howard M. Sacher, 31.

21. Robert Rosen, "Jewish Confederates," in Ferris and Greenberg, *Jewish Roots in Southern Soil,* 109 Some six thousand Jews fought on the Union side. Morris U. Schappes, *Documentary History of the Jews in the United States, 1654–1875,* (The Citadel Press, New York, 1950).

22. Rosengartens, *A Portion of the People,* 126.

23. "Confederate Alabama Troops, 2nd Regiment, Alabama Infantry," National Park Service, https://www.nps.gov/civilwar/search-battle -units-detail.htm?battleUnitCode=CAL0002RI.

24. *Richmond Dispatch,* April 9, 1861.

25. Sublette and Sublette, *American Slave Coast,* 476.

26. "Interesting Decision Under the Sequestration Act," *Richmond Dispatch,* January 11, 1862, p. 3.

27. Zola in Ferris and Greenberg, *Jewish Roots in Southern Soil* p. 168 and Rosen in Ferris and Greenberg, *Jewish Roots in Southern Soil,* 111.

28. Susanna Michele Lee, "Refugees during the Civil War," *Encyclopedia Virginia. Virginia Humanities, March 27, 2017. Web June 1, 2020.*

29. *Richmond Dispatch,* October 18, 1862.

30. John K. Trammell, "Travelers to wartime Richmond had a wide choice of luxurious hotels, inns and taverns," http://www.historynet.com /travelers-to-wartime-richmond-sept-96-ameri cas-civil-war-feature.htm.

31. Chris Mackowski and Kristopher D. White, "Before the Slaughter," *Hallowed Ground Magazine* (Winter 2012).

32. Reid Mitchell, *The American Civil War, 1861–1865* (Routledge, 2013), "Chronology".

33. See "History," Fredericksburg Masonic Lodge #4, Masoniclodge4.org/history-of -lodge-4.

34. Georgeanna Woolsey, *Letters of a Family During the Civil War* (Big Byte Books, 2001), Fredericksburg, May 19.

35. Laura Smith Haviland, A Woman's Life Work: Labors and Experiences of Laura S. Haviland (Walden and Stowe, 1882), Library of Congress https://memory.loc.gov/service/gdc /lhbum/24792/24792.pdf.

36. Zola in Ferris and Greenberg, *Jewish Roots in Southern Soil,* 178.

37. Herman Eliasoff, "The Jews of Illinois: Their Religious and Civic Life, Their Charity and Industry, Their Patriotism and Loyalty to American institutions, from their earliest settlement in the State unto the present time," Lawrence J. Gutter Collection of Chicagoana (University of Illinois at Chicago) 1901, https://archive.org /stream/jewsofillinoisthooelia/jewsofillinois thooelia_djvu.txt.

38. *Chicago Tribune,* November 8, 1868, 2.

39. United States Census, 1870, Chicago, 10th Ward, (NARA Series M593, Roll 205), 308.

40. United States Census, Chicago, 1860–1870.

41. United States Census, 1870, Chicago, 10th Ward, (NARA Series M593, Roll 205), 308.

42. *The American Hatter,* Vol. 27, 1897, 58.

43. United States Census, 1870, Chicago, 3rd Ward, (NARA Series M593, Roll 199), 389.

44. Lorenz-Meyer, *Gender, Ethnicity,* 4.

45. see Elias Colbert and Everett Chamberlin, *Chicago and the Great Conflagration* (Cincinnati: C. F. Vent, J. S. Goodman & Co., 1871), 298.

46. Eli Lederhendler, *American Jewery: A New History* (Cambridge, England: Cambridge University Press, 2017), 67.

47. Daniel A. Graff, "Socialist Parties," *Encyclopedia of Chicago.* http://www.encyclopedia .chicagohistory.org/pages/1161.html.

48. Alice Maggio, "Chicago Burns Again: The Second Great Fire," *Gapers Block,* February 9, 2006. http://gapersblock.com/airbags/archives /chicago_burns_again_the_second_great_fire/.

49. *The InterOcean* (Chicago), February 22, 1877, p. 5.

CHAPTER 19

1. *The Inter Ocean,* February 22, 1877.

2. *The Inter Ocean,* February 22, 1877; *Chicago Daily Tribune,* November 23, 1884.

3. *Chicago Tribune,* March 28, 1880, p. 11.

4. *Chicago Tribune,* November 9, 1884.

5. Ibid.

6. *The Inter Ocean,* November 16, 1884.

7. *Chicago Tribune,* November 15, 1884, 6.

8. *The Inter Ocean,* November 16, 1884.

9. *Chicago Tribune,* November 23, 1884, 2.

10. *Saint Paul Globe,* March 31, 1888, 8.

11. *Minneapolis Star Tribune,* May 16, 1899, 10.

12. *Minneapolis Star Tribune,* May 16, 1899, 10.

13. *Minneapolis Journal,* June 4, 1902, 7.

14. Paul Gustafson, "Archaeology of the Ritz Block: Part IV, A Minneapolis Palace," Hennepin County Library, http://hclib.tumblr.com /post/109700671628/archaeology-of-the-ritz -block-part-iv-a.

15. Ibid.

16. "Palace Clothing, High Art Clothiers, Minneapolis, Minnesota," Minnesota Reflections; Hennepin County Library, James K. Hosmer Special Collections Library, https://reflections .mndigital.org/catalog/mpls:23261?pn=false# /image/0?searchtext&viewer=os.

17. Veblen, *The Theory of Business,* 36.

18. Ibid.,

19. *Minneapolis Journal,* August 5, 1904, 10.

20. *American Journalism from the Practical Side* (New York: Holmes Publishing Co., 1897), 203 https://archive.org/stream /cu31924027456031/cu31924027456031_djvu .txt.

21. Palace Clothing Ad, *Marketing Communications,* 1908.

22. "Minnesota," *Men's Wear* [semimonthly] vol. 18 (1905): 79.

23. *Minneapolis Journal,* June, 23, 1904.

24. Ibid.

25. "Maurice Rothchild to Establish Foreign Office," *Men's Wear: The Retailer's Newspaper,* July 6, 1910, p. 86.

26. handbook, 4.

27. Jacob, 18 and Dumenil, *Freemasonry* 11.

28. Dumenil, *Freemasonry,* 55–6, xiii, and handbook, 77.

29. Dumenil, *Freemasonry,* 225.

30. handbook, 82.

31. Carnes, *Secret Ritual,* 131.

32. Dumenil, *Freemasonry,* xi, xxxi, 6, 49; Carnes, *Secret Ritual,* 31.

CHAPTER 20

1. Lewin, *Reform Jews,* 15 and Lorenz-Meyer, *Gender, Ethnicity,* 194.

2. Laura E. Weber, "Gentiles Preferred":

Minneapolis Jews and Employment, 1920–1950, *Minnesota History*, Spring, 1991.

3. Weber, "Gentiles"; Faue, *Community, Suffering and Struggle,* 195.

4. John Bodnar, *The Transplanted: A History of Immigrants in Urban America,* (Bloomington: Indiana University Press 1955), xix.

5. Daniels, *Golden Door,* 45.

6. David Paul Nord, "Minneapolis and the Pragmatic Socialism of Thomas Van Lear," *Minnesota History* (Spring, 1996): 1–10.

7. Nord, "Minneapolis and the Pragmatic Socialism."

8. Gerald D. Anderson (Illustrious Potentate), *A Century of Progress and Pictorial History of Zuhrah Temple, 1886–1992* (Minneapolis: Zuhrah Temple, 1992), 18.

9. Anderson, *A Century of Progress,* 23.

10. Dumenil, *Freemasonry,* 206; Anderson, *A Century of Progress,* 22.

11. Noah S. Bucher, "Minneapolis Valley Scottish Rite Temple, 17," 2011, http://mpls19.org /scottish-rite-temple/.

12. Jackson Lears, *Fables of Abundance: A Cultural History of Advertising in America* (New York: Basic Books, 1994), 55.

13. Lears, *Fables,* 217, 160.

14. Lears, *Fables,* 55 and 1, quoting Marshall McLuhan.

15. *Minneapolis Star Tribune,* March 26, 1911, and November 28, 1908.

16. *Minneapolis Star Tribune,* April 5, 1914.

17. *Minneapolis Star Tribune,* November 30, 1912.

18. See Richard Ellison Ritz, "Purcell, William Gray," *Architects of Oregon: A Biographical Dictionary of Architects Deceased—19th and 20th Centuries* (Portland, OR: Lair Hill Publishing, 2002), 325–26.

19. William Gray Purcell letter, 1910, William Gray Purcell Papers, Northwest Architectural Archives, University of Minnesota, [AR:B4D1.6 http://www.organica.org/pejn174_1.htm.

20. John Milton Cooper, *Woodrow Wilson: A Biography* (Alfred E. Knopf, New York, 2009), 126 and Dorfman, *Thorstein Veblen,* 303.

21. August Heckscher, *Woodrow Wilson: A Biography* (New York: Charles Scribner's Sons, 1991), 260.

22. Heckscher, *Woodrow Wilson,* 27, 12, and 2.

23. Lunardini, *Women's Rights,* 100.

24. Flexner, *Century of Struggle,* 264.

25. Burton A. Boxerman, "Adolph Joachim Sabath in Congress: The Early Years, 1907–1932."

Journal of the Illinois State Historical Society (1908–1984) 66, no. 3 (1973): 327–40. www.jstor .org/stable/40190589.

26. "First Inaugural Address of Woodrow Wilson," March 4, 1913, Lillian Goldman Law Library, Yale Law School https://avalon.law.yale .edu/20th_century/wilson1.asp.

27. Frank E. Smitha, "Macrahistory and World Timeline: The Taft Years," http://www.fsmitha .com/h2/ch03-9.htm.

28. *The Painter and Decorator,* Vol. XXVIII, 759.

29. *Minneapolis Star Tribune,* June 16, 1899.

30. Rogow, *Gone to Another Meeting,* 134.

31. Ibid., 132.

32. Sarah Imhoff, *Masculinity and the Making of American Judaism* (Bloomington: Indiana University Press, 2017), 228.

33. C. Vann Woodward, *Tom Watson: Agrarian Rebel* (Savannah, GA: The Beehive Press, 2nd edition, 1973), 379–80.

34. Tom Watson, "The Official Record in the Case of Leo Frank, a Jew Pervert," *Watson's Magazine* 21, no. 5 (September 1915). https:// theamericanmercury.org/2014/03/the-official -record-in-the-case-of-leo-frank-a-jew -pervert/.

35. Higham, *Strangers in a Strange Land,* 92.

36. William Faulkner, *The Sound and The Fury* (New York: Random House, 1956), 149.

37. Watson, "The Official Record".

38. Vann Woodward, *Tom Watson,* 379.

39. Watson, "The Official Record".

40. Steve Oney, *And the Dead Shall Rise: The Murder of Mary Phagan and the Lynching of Leo Frank* (New York: Pantheon Books, 2003), 606.

41. *American Jewish Weekly* Vol. II, #2, 9/10/15, lead editorial.

42. Heckscher, *Woodrow Wilson* pp. 335–37.

43. Klapper, *Ballots,* 107.

44. Lorenz-Meyer, *Gender, Ethnicity,* 270; Angela Jabour, "Why Women's Peace Activism in World War I Matters Now," *The Conversation,* April 2, 2017, rawstory.com.

45. Heckscher, *Woodrow Wilson,* 199 and 490.

46. Richard M. Valelly, *Radicalism in the States: The Minnesota Farmer-Labor Party and the American Political Economy* (Chicago: University of Chicago Press, 1989), 17.

47. Ibid., 24.

48. Ibid., 20.

49. Nord, "Minneapolis and the Pragmatic Socialism" and Valelly, *Radicalism,* 22.

50. Millikan, *A Union Against Unions*, 50–52; Nord, "Minneapolis and the Pragmatic Socialism" and Valelly, *Radicalism*, 23.

51. Nord, "Minneapolis and the Pragmatic Socialism".

52. Millikan, *A Union Against Unions*, 55.

53. "Minneapolis Mayor," General Election, "Our Campaigns," http://www.ourcampaigns .com/RaceDetail.html?RaceID=719567.

54. *American Jewish Weekly*, Vol. VII, #2, 89, editorial.

55. Flexner, *Century of Struggle*, 265–66.

56. See Melvin I. Urofksy, *Louis D. Brandeis: A Life* (New York: Pantheon Books, 2009), especially 3–20.

57. Urofsky, *Louis D. Brandeis*, 20 and 32; Flexner, *Century of Struggle*, 5.

58. Klapper, *Ballots*, 55.

59. *American Jewish Weekly*, Vol II, #3, 9/24/15, editorial.

60. Heckscher, *Woodrow Wilson* pp. 199, 440, and 490.

CHAPTER 21

1. *WPA Guide to Minnesota*, 62.

2. Kathryn R. Goetz, "Women on the WW I Home Front," MNopedia, Minnesota Historical Society, http://www.mnopedia.org/women -world-war-i-home-front.

3. Dorfman, *Thorstein Veblen*, 382.

4. Lederhendler, *American Jewry*, 222 and H. C. Peterson and Gilbert C. Fife, *Opponents of War, 1917–1918.* (Madison: University of Wisconsin Press, 1957), 76–77.

5. Geoffrey Wawro, "How 'Half-Americans' Won World War I," *New York Times*, September 13, 2018.

6. Millikan, *A Union Against Unions*, 119.

7. Karen Brodkin, *How Jews Became White Folks and What that Say about Race in America* (New Brunswick, NJ: Rutgers University Press, 1998), 28 & 30.

8. Millikan, *A Union Against Unions*, 102–18 and *Minneapolis Star Tribune* October 24, 1918.

9. "Minneapolis, Minnesota Population History," 2020, http://www.biggestuscities.com/city /minneapolis-minnesota.

10. "Expert Who Urges Insurance Publicity," *Minneapolis Tribune*, February 25, 1917; Speech delivered before The Minneapolis Association of Life Underwriters by Charles L. MacGregor.

11. Berman and Schloff, *Jews in Minnesota*, 42.

12. Sadye A. Kantrowitz, "Report of the Minneapolis Section, Official Report of the National Council of Jewish Women Triennial Convention: 1920–1923," vol. 9, 337–39.

13. "National Council of Jewish Women," 1954 report; Minneapolis Section, 1893–1954; p. 5.

14. Klapper, *Ballots*, 125 and 114.

15. Natasha Karunaratne, "The Anti-German Sentiment of World War I' Re-Imagining Migration, https://reimaginingmigration.org/the-anti -german-sentiment-of-world-war-i/.

16. Adam Hochschild, "When Dissent Became Treason," *New York Review of Books*, September 28, 2017, 82.

17. Dorfman, *Thorstein Veblen*, 319.

18. Korth, *Minneapolis Teamsters Strike*, 37–40; and Thomas Gerald O'Connell, "Toward the Cooperative Commonwealth: An Introductory History of The Farmer-Labor Movement in Minnesota (1917–1948)," PhD thesis, Union Graduate School, 1979, http://justcomm.org /fla-hist.htm.

19. "Meints v. Huntington," *The Federal Reporter*, Vol. 276, January–March 1922 (St. Paul, MN: West Publishing, 1922), 247.

20. Rogan, *Gone to Another* Meeting, 178–80.

21. Lorenz-Meyer, *Gender, Ethnicity,* 86.

22. Heckscher, *Woodrow Wilson,* 261.

23. Woodrow Wilson, speech in support of the League of Nations, September 25, 1919, Pueblo, Col. http://www.firstworldwar.com /source/wilsonspeech_league.htm.

24. Heckscher, *Woodrow Wilson,* 534, 551.

25. "A New Year of Work for the Council of Jewish Women," *American Jewish Weekly*, Vol. VII, #1, New Year's Edition, 1918, 6.

26. Bethanee Bemis, "Mr. President, How Long Must Women Wait for Liberty?" *Smithsonian Magazine*, Jan 12, 2017, https:// www.smithsonianmag.com/smithsonian -institution/scrap-suffrage-history-180961780/.

27. Cooper, *Woodrow Wilson,* 414.

28. Berman and Schloff, *Jews in Minnesota,* 42.

29. Cameron McWhirter, *Red Summer: The Summer of 1991 and the Awakening of Black America,* (New York: Griffin, 2012), 19.

30. McWhirter, *Red Summer,* 16.

31. Equal Justice Initiative, "Lynching in America: Targeting Black Veterans," 2017, eji.org /reports/lynching-in-america-targeting-black -veterans.

32. McWhirter, *Red Summer,* 41–46.

33. Mike Royko, *Boss Daley*, quoted in McWhirter, *Red Summer,* 116.

34. McWhirter, *Red Summer,* 147.

35. Ibid., 183.

36. Dorfman, *Thorstein Veblen,* 434–45.

37. Higham, *Strangers in a Strange Land,* 265.

38. Hochschild, "When Dissent Became Treason," 84.

39. McWhirter, *Red Summer,* 20.

40. Alan Greenspan and Adrian Woolridge, *Capitalism in America: An Economic History of the United States* (London: Penguin Books, 2018), 193.

41. Guide to Declarations of Martial Law in the United States | Brennan Center for Justice, August 20, 2020.

42. Valelly, *Radicalism in the States,* 34; and William Milliken, "Where's the Working Class at the Mill City Museum?", Minnesota History Net, http://www.minnesotahistory.net/wptest/?p=3431.

43. Ann Lonstein, "'We must not seek to modify war but to outlaw it.'" The History apolis Project, March 21, 2014, Augsburg College, http://historyapolis.com/blog/tag/reform-and-activism/.

44. "Jewish Women Urge Disarming," *Minneapolis Star,* May 9, 1921, pg. 7.

45. *Minneapolis Star Tribune,* April 16 and August 29, 1919.

46. *Minneapolis Star Tribune,* May 1, 1918.

47. Marion Daniel Shutter, *History of Minneapolis, Gateway to the Northwest* (Chicago: S. J. Clarke Publishing Co., 1923), Vol II, 556–57 and *Advertising and Selling,* June 7, 1919.

CHAPTER 22

1. See Daniels, *Golden Door,* 46.

2. Daniels, *Golden Door,* 46–47.

3. Ibid., 47–48.

4. Higham, *Strangers in a Strange Land,* 284.

5. Ibid., 278.

6. Leonard Dinnerstein, *Anti-Semitism in American* (Oxford, England: Oxford University Press, 1994), 80.

7. William Gray Purcell Papers, Northwest Architectural Archives, University of Minnesota, [AR:B4D1.6].

8. Ibid.

9. Dorfman, *Thorstein Veblen,* 379.

10. *Musical America,* Vol. 22, 1915; and *The American Hebrew,* February 15, 1918.

11. *American Jewish Weekly,* Vol VII, #28, pg. 462.

12. Shutter, *History of Minneapolis,* 556–57.

13. *Brainerd Daily Dispatch,* May 12, 1917.

14. "War Records Commission: Minneapolis Civic & Commerce Association,' An Inventory of Its Records at the Minnesota Historical Society, 1916–1919.

15. Temple Israel Ledger & Composition Book, 1903-09-06–1923-03-08, Berman Archives, letter from President Weil, 1922.

16. June Stern, "Interview with Rabbi Albert G. Minda," July–November, 1968, Minneapolis, MN, Jews in Minnesota Oral History Project, Minnesota Historical Society, http://collections.mnhs.org/cms/web5/media.php?pdf=1&irn=10235284.

17. *Historical Statistics of the United States, Colonial Times to 1970,* Bicentennial Edition (US Census Bureau, Washington, DC), 1970, series A6.

18. *The Equal Rights Amendment: A Brief History,* the Alice Paul Institute, https://www.alicepaul.org/wp-content/uploads/2019/05/ERA-A-History.pdf.

19. Flexner, *Century of Struggle,* 295–300.

20. Ibid., 325.

21. George B. Heckel, "Growth of the Paint Manufacturing Industry," in *The Book-Keeper: The Business Man's Magazine,* Vol. XX, #11, May 1908, 380.

22. "Paint, Oil and Drug Review," Vol. 73, April 12, 1922, 13.

23. John Kenneth Galbraith, *The Great Crash* (Boston: Houghton Mifflin, 1954), 9, 11.

24. Greenspan and Wooldridge, *Capitalism,* 208.

25. Bob Leonard, "FLORIDA IN THE 1920'S: THE GREAT FLORIDA LAND BOOM," Florida History Internet Center, http://floridahistory.org/landboom.htm.

26. McElvaine, *The Great Depression,* 43.

27. Bogart, *Economic History,* 579.

28. Dorfman, *Thorstein Veblen,* 283.

29. Britt Arnold, "Foshay built utilities empire and Minneapolis' tallest building, but lost it all," MNopedia, December 10, 2013.

30. Foshay v. United States, 68F .2d 205 (8th Cir. 1934) dhttps://casetext.com/case/foshay-v-united-states-2.

31. Sklansky, *The Soul's Economy,* 207.

32. Ibid., 179.

33. Debbie Crossland, "Hotel Albert featured in Fairview Festival Button," Sidney Herald (Montana), July 16, 2013.

CHAPTER 23

1. Sinclair Lewis, *Main Street: The Story of Carol Kennicott* (Harcourt Brace Jovanovich, 1920; The Library of America, 1992), 5.

2. Ibid., 42.

3. Ibid., prologue.

4. Ibid., 653.

5. Ibid., 288, 13, 29.

6. *Minneapolis Star Tribune*, March 8, 1926.

7. Linda A. Cameron, "Agricultural Depression, 1920–1934," MNopedia, Minnesota Historical Society, 2018.

8. Ibid.

9. *WPA Guide to Minnesota*, 69.

10. Valelly, *Radicalism in the States,* 72.

11. Cameron, "Agricultural Depression, 1920–1934."

12. Valelly, *Radicalism in the States,* 72.

13. Bogart, *Economic History*, 697.

14. Lewis, *Main Street,* 55.

15. Charles Rumford Walker, *American City: A Rank and File History of Minneapolis* (Minneapolis: University of Minnesota Press, 1965), 72.

16. Valelly, *Radicalism in the States,* 41.

17. Weber, "Gentiles Preferred."

18. Millikan, *A Union Against Unions*, 219.

19. Bryan D. Palmer, *Revolutionary Teamsters: The Minneapolis Truckers' Strike of 1934* (Chicago: Haymarket Books, 2014), 274.

20. Milliken, "Where's the Working Class."

21. Faue, *Community, Suffering and Struggle,* 29.

22. Daniels, *Golden Door,* 55.

23. Daniels, *Golden Door,* 53 and 56.

24. Higham, *Strangers in a Strange Land,* 287, 289, 296; Marilyn J. Chiat, "Jewish Community Relations Council, Anti-Defamation League," 1/11/85, manuscript in Box 0020-002 Berman Archives.

25. Michael Novack, *Unmeltable Ethnics: Politics and Culture in American Life* (London: Routledge, 2018).

26. Dobbs, *Teamster Rebellion,* 48.

27. Lewis, *Main Street,* 57.

28. John Higham's "Strangers in the Land," quoted in Weber, "'Gentiles Preferred."

29. FREEMASONRY, Jewish Virtual Library, from Encyclopaedia Hebraica, https://www.jewishvirtuallibrary.org/Freemasons.

30. Jerome Karabell, *The Chosen: The Hidden History of Admission and Exclusion at Harvard, Yale and Princeton* (Boston: Houghton Mifflin, 2005), 585, note 113.

31. Weber, "'Gentiles Preferred."

32. Berman and Schloff, *Jews in Minnesota*, 48.

33. Daniels, *Guarding the Golden Door*, 147.

34. Lorenz-Meyer, *Gender, Ethnicity,* 194–95.

35. Lewin, *Reform Jews,* 24.

36. Karabell, *The Chosen*, 86.

37. Ibid., 584 note 94.

38. Ibid., 585, note 115.

39. Ibid., 134.

40. Ibid., 601, note 75.

41. Valelly, *Radicalism in the States,* 71, quoting Lincoln Steffens.

42. Gordon Lloyd, *The Two Faces of Liberalism: How the Hoover-Roosevelt Debate Shapes the 21st Century* (M & M Scrivner Press, 2006), 27.

43. Milton Meltzer, *Brother, Can You Spare a Dime?: The Great Depression 1929–1933* (New York: Facts on File, Knopf, 1969), 6, 8.

44. Walton and Rockoff, *History of the American Economy*, 485; Meltzer, *Brother, Can You Spare a Dime?*, 6, 7.

45. Greenspan and Wooldridge, *Capitalism*, 207.

46. Valelly, *Radicalism in the States,* 70.

47. Robert S. McElvaine, *The Great Depression: America, 1929–1944* (New York: Times Books, 1984/1993), 38.

48. Lewis, *Main Street,* 13.

49. *New York Times*, October 25, 1929.

50. Herbert Hoover, "Message Regarding 'Black Thursday,'" October 25, 1929, transcript via Miller Center, University of Virginia, https://millercenter.org/the-presidency/presidential-speeches/october-25-1929-message-regarding-black-thursday.

51. Gary Richardson, Alejandro Komai, Michael Gou, Daniel Park, "Stock Market Crash of 1929," Federal Reserve History, 2013, https://www.federalreservehistory.org/essays/stock_market_crash_of_1929.

52. Gordon Parks, *Voices on the Mirror* (New York: Doubleday, 1990), 26 and Gordon Parks, *A Choice of Weapons* (Minnesota Historical Society, 2010), 55.

53. Millikan, *A Union Against Unions*, 240.

54. Arnold, "Foshay."

55. Richardson, Komai, etc., "Stock Market Crash of 1929."

56. Lewin, *Reform Jews,* 18.

CHAPTER 24

1. Deuteronomy 7:3, *The Holy Scriptures*, Jewish Publication Society, Tanakh 1917 edition (Philadelphia, 1917).

2. Gold, *Jews Without Money,* 135.

3. Isaac Atwater, *History of the City of Minneapolis, Minnesota*, Part 1 (New York: Munsell and Company, 1893), 157.

CHAPTER 25

1. Aristotle. *Poetics*. Trans. Gerald F. Else (Ann Arbor: University of Michigan Press, 1967), 25–27.

2. Aristotle. *Aristotle in 23 Volumes*, Vol. 23, translated by W. H. Fyfe. (Cambridge, MA: Harvard University Press; London: William Heinemann Ltd. 1932), Section 1452a, http://www.perseus.tufts.edu/hopper/text?doc=Perseus:abo:tlg,0086,034:1452a.

3. Meltzer, *Brother, Can You Spare a Dime?*, 11, 16.

4. Ibid., 30.

5. Lorenz-Meyer, *Gender, Ethnicity*, 3.

6. Weber, "'Gentiles Preferred.'"

7. Beth S. Wenger, *New York Jews and the Great Depression: Uncertain Promise* (New Haven, CT: Yale University Press, 1996), 200.

8. Weber, "'Gentiles Preferred.'"

9. Ibid.

10. Weber, "'Gentiles Preferred,'" quoting Edward P. Schwartz.

11. Wenger, *New York Jews*, 5.

12. United States census, April 1, 1930.

13. Raymond L. Koch, "Politics and Relief in Minneapolis During the 1930's," *Minnesota Historical Magazine*, Winter 1968, 156.

14. Palmer, *Revolutionary Teamsters*, 33.

15. George H. Mayer, *The Political Career of Floyd B. Olson* (St. Paul: Minnesota Historical Society Press, 1987), 7.

16. Mayer, *Olson*, 15.

17. Mayer, *Olson*, 26.

18. "REDS STORM GATEWAY STORE," *Star Tribune* (Minneapolis), February 26, 1931, 1.

19. Raymond L. Koch, "Politics and Relief in Minneapolis in the 1930's," *Minnesota History*, Winter 1968.

CHAPTER 26

1. FDR campaign speech October 13, 1932, from *The Public Papers and Addresses of Franklin D. Roosevelt*, compiled by Samuel P. Rosenman, 1938–1950, 13 vols. http://89888433.weebly.com/fdrs-philosophy.html.

2. Faue, *Community, Suffering and Struggle*, 59.

3. Raymond L. Koch, "Politics and Relief in Minneapolis During the 1930's," *Minnesota Historical Magazine* (Winter 1968): 156.

4. Dorfman, *Thorstein Veblen*, 176.

5. Mayer, *Olson*, 86–87.

6. Mayer, *Olson*, 78, 102.

7. LeSueur, *Ripening*, 138.

8. Mayer, *Olson*, 106–8.

9. Korth, *Minneapolis Teamsters Strike of 1934*, 2 and Galbraith, *The Great Crash*, 173.

10. Millikan, *A Union Against Unions*, 249.

11. Palmer, *Revolutionary Teamsters*, 36.

12. Mayer, *Olson*, 108.

13. Wenger, *New York Jews*, 142, 149.

14. Patricia Clavin, "The Great Depression in Europe, 1929–39, *History Review* 37 (September 2000): http://www.historytoday.com/patricia-clavin/great-depression-europe-1929-3.

15. John Bellamy Foster, "Neofascism in the White House," *Monthly Review* 68, no. 1 (April 2017): 7.

16. Karabell, *The Chosen*, 584, note 94.

17. *Minneapolis Star Tribune*, November 11, 1932.

18. Walker, *American City*, 85.

19. LeSueur, *Ripening*, 144.

20. See Winifred D. Wandersee Bolin, "The Economics of Middle-Income Family Life: Working Women During the Great Depression," *Journal of American History* 65, no. 1 (June 1978): 60–74; and "Population: the Labor Force," the Sixteenth Census of the United States, 1940.

21. Walker, *American City*, 87.

22. Korth, *Minneapolis Teamsters Strike*, 28.

23. "Carl Skoglund," *International Socialist Review* 22, no.1 (Winter 1961): 2. https://www.marxists.org/history/etol/newspape/isr/vol22/no01/carls.htm.

24. see Lila Johnson Goff, "Oral history interview with Vincent Raymond Dunne," April 27, 1969, Minnesota Historical Society, http://collections.mnhs.org/cms/display.php?irn=10446082.

25. Dobbs, *Teamster Rebellion*, 48–51; Donna T. Harverty-Stacke, *Trotyskyists on Trial: Free Speech and Political Persecution Since the Age of FDR* (New York: New York University Press, 2016), 11–12; Harry Ring, "Vincent R. Dunne, Interview with a Twentieth Century Pioneer" www.marxists.org/history/etol/writers/dunne/interview.htm; see also Palmer, *Revolutionary Teamsters*.

26. Kristoffer Smemo, "The Politics of Labor Militancy in Minneapolis, 1934–1938," Master's thesis, University of Massachusetts, February 2014, http://scholarworks.umass.edu/theses/719.

27. Smemo, "The Politics of Labor Militancy," 24.

28. Millikan, *A Union Against Unions*, 268.

29. Ibid., 266.

30. Brecher, *Strike!*, 161, and Mayer, *Olson*, 188.

31. Walker, *American City*, 90; and Korth, *Minneapolis Teamsters Strike*, 60.

32. Dobbs, *Teamster Rebellion*, 35; and Walker, *American City*, 97.

33. Palmer, *Revolutionary Teamsters*, 58.

34. Walker, *American City*, 106.

35. Korth, *Minneapolis Teamsters Strike*, 66.

36. Walker, *American City*, 94–5.

37. Korth, *Minneapolis Teamsters Strike*, 75.

38. Palmer, *Revolutionary Teamsters*, 62.

39. Dobbs, *Teamster Rebellion*, 91.

40. Korth, *Minneapolis Teamsters Strike*, 81.

41. Ibid., 85–90.

CHAPTER 27

1. Walker, *American City*, xiv.

2. Ibid., 98.

3. Ibid., 101.

4. *Dunkirk Evening Observer*, May 18, 1934.

5. Brecher, *Strike!*, 162.

6. Palmer, *Revolutionary Teamsters*, 75–76.

7. Dobbs, *Teamster Rebellion*, 99.

8. Palmer, *Revolutionary Teamsters*, 77; "The Secret of Local 574," James P. Cannon, Daily Strike Bulletin, August 18, 1934 (marxists .org).

9. Walker, *American City*, chap. 7.

10. Ibid.

11. Dobbs, *Teamster Rebellion*, 37.

12. Korth, *Minneapolis Teamsters Strike*, 90, 93; Brecher, *Strike!*, 163.

13. Korth, *Minneapolis Teamsters Strike*, 49.

14. Dorfman, *Thorstein Veblen*, 183.

15. Palmer, *Revolutionary Teamsters*, 93.

16. Dobbs, *Teamster Rebellion*, 114.

17. Brecher, *Strike!*, 163.

18. Walker, *American City*, chap. 7.

19. Ibid., 113.

20. Korth, *Minneapolis Teamsters Strike*, 98; Brecher, *Strike!*, 164.

21. Walker, *American City*, chap. 8.

22. Korth, *Minneapolis Teamsters Strike*, 113–14.

23. Millikan, *A Union Against Unions*, 273.

24. Mayer, *Olson*, 198.

25. "Learn from Minneapolis!" James P. Cannon, Strike Bulleting, May 1934. James P. Cannon: Learn from Minneapolis! (May 1934) (marxists.org).

26. Korth, *Minneapolis Teamsters Strike*, 118.

27. Walker, *American City*, 116.

28. *Minneapolis Star Tribune*, June 4, 1934, 3.

29. Dobbs, *Teamster Rebellion*, 121.

30. Smemo, "The Politics of Labor Militancy," 32.

31. Korth, *Minneapolis Teamsters Strike*, 126.

32. Cannon, "The Secret of Local 574."

33. Ibid., 122.

34. Walker, *American City*, 157.

35. Ibid., chap. 10.

36. Ibid.

37. Nathanson, *Minneapolis in the Twentieth Century*, 77.

38. Mayer, *Olson*, 203.

39. Dobbs, *Teamster Rebellion*, 147.

40. Ibid., 148–49.

41. Palmer, *Revolutionary Teamsters*, 130.

42. Dobbs, *Teamster Rebellion*, 155.

43. Meridel Le Sueur, "I Was Marching," in *Ripening: Selected Works*, 2nd ed. (New York: The Feminist Press, 1990), 160.

44. Palmer, *Revolutionary Teamsters*, 145.

45. LeSueur, *Ripening*, 158.

46. Ibid., 57.

47. Ibid., 158.

48. Ibid., 159, 163.

49. Ibid., 159.

50. Ibid., 163.

51. Millikan, *A Union Against Unions*, 279.

52. Mayer, *Olson*, 208.

53. Palmer, *Revolutionary Teamsters*, 162.

54. Ibid., 163.

55. *Minneapolis Star*, July 25, 1934.

56. Brecher, *Strike!*, 165.

57. Walker, *American City*, chap. 10.

58. *The Organizer*, July 25, 1934, Georgianna E. Herman Library, Carlson School of Management, http://cdm16022.contentdm.oclc.org/cdm /compoundobject/collection/p16022coll43/id/41 /rec/2.

59. Walker, *American City*, chap. 10.

60. LeSueur, *Ripening*, 163.

61. Palmer, *Revolutionary Teamsters*, 168.

62. LeSueur, *Ripening*, 164.

63. Korth, *Minneapolis Teamsters Strike*, 152.

64. Palmer, *Revolutionary Teamsters*, 179.

65. Valelly, *Radicalism in the States*, 111.

66. Mayer, *Olson*, 211.

67. Palmer, *Revolutionary Teamsters*, 181.

68. *The Organizer*, July 28, 1934, Georgianna E. Herman Library, Carlson School of Management, http://cdm16022.contentdm.oclc.org/cdm /compoundobject/collection/p16022coll43/id/50 /rec/6.

69. *The Organizer*, July 31, 1934, Georgianna E. Herman Library, Carlson School of Management, http://cdm16022.contentdm.oclc.org/cdm

/compoundobject/collection/p16022coll43/id/59/rec/9.

70. Walker, *American City*, 213.

71. Palmer, *Revolutionary Teamsters*, 188.

72. Ibid.

73. Walker, *American City*, 211.

74. Korth, *Minneapolis Teamsters Strike*, 110.

75. Mayer, *Olson*, 215 and Millikan, *A Union Against Unions*, 281.

76. Palmer, *Revolutionary Teamsters*, 213.

77. Mayer, *Olson*, 221.

78. Korth, *Minneapolis Teamsters Strike*, 162; Valelly, 114.

79. *The Organizer*, August 22, 1934, Georgianna E. Herman Library, Carlson School of Management, https://reflections.mndigital.org/catalog/p16022coll43:120#/image/0.

80. Walker, *American City*, 219.

81. Ibid., 271–72.

CHAPTER 28

1. *Minneapolis Star*, July 27 and August 17, 1934.

2. Faue, *Community, Suffering and Struggle*, 100–101.

3. Dobbs, *Teamster Power*, 134–37.

4. Ibid.

5. Mayer, *Olson*, 277.

6. Dobbs, *Teamster Rebellion*, 116, 188.

7. Ibid., 33.

8. Brecher, *Strike!*, 163–66; Dobbs, *Teamster Rebellion*, 91.

9. "Painters Purge Union of Reds, Disband Local," *Jewish Telegraphic Agency*, August 7, 1934. http://www.jta.org/1934/08/07/archive/painters-purge-union-of-reds-disband-local.

10. Mayer, *Olson*, 171.

11. Mayer, *Olson*, 122–23, 259; and Weber, "Gentiles Preferred," p. 171.

12. Millikan, *A Union Against Unions*, 311.

13. Martin J. MacGowan, "Interview with Elmer A. Benson," 1981 and 83, for Minnesota Historical Society; http://collections.mnhs.org/cms/web5/media.php?pdf=1&irn=10279612.

14. Walton and Rockoff, *History of the American Economy*, 514–15 and Greenspan and Wooldridge, *Capitalism in America*, 225 and 254.

15. "The New Home Decorator", Sherwin-Williams catalogue, 1934.

16. *Minneapolis Star*, September 18, 1934.

17. Walker, *American City*, 214.

18. Weber, "Gentiles Preferred."

19. Carey McWilliams, "Minneapolis: The Curious Twin," *Common Ground*, Autumn, 1946, quoted in Weber, "Gentiles Preferred."

20. *Minneapolis Star Tribune*, November 7, 1946, 16.

21. Valelly, 148.

22. Weber, "Gentiles Preferred," 172.

23. Rosen, *Saving the Jews*, 51.

24. Rosen, *Saving the Jews*, 25; Daniels, *Guarding the Golden Door*, 77; Robert N. Rosen, *Franklin D. Roosevelt and the Holocaust* (New York: Thunder's Mouth Press, New York, 2006), 18–19, 25.

25. Rosen, *Saving the Jews*, 45.

26. Weber, "Gentiles Preferred," 400.

27. Brodkin, *How Jews Became White Folks*, 33.

28. "Egg Weighing Scale," United States Patent Office, 2205917; June 25, 1940, https://patentimages.storage.googleapis.com/ff/30/ee/ac2afe67df05cd/US2205917.pdf.

29. *Minneapolis Star Tribune*, July 21, 1938.

30. Book of Psalms, *The Holy Scriptures*, Jewish Publication Society, Tanakh 1917 edition (Philadelphia, 1917).

CHAPTER 29

1. Weber, "Gentiles Preferred," p. 172; and Laura Weber, "Jewish Community Relations Council of Minnesota and the Dakotas," MNopedia, http://www.mnopedia.org/group/jewish-community-relations-council-minnesota-and-dakotas.

2. See Zac Frber, "Politics of the Past: Anti-Semitic red-baiting swayed '38 governor's race," *Minnesota Lawyer*, September 22, 2016; and Hyman Berman, "Political Antisemitism in Minnesota during the Great Depression," *Jewish Social Studies*, Vol. 31, no. 3/4, 1976.

3. MacGowan, "Interview with Elmer A. Benson."

4. www.poetrynook.com/poem/goodbye-christ.

5. Berman, "Political Antisemitism in Minnesota," p. 257; and Weber, "Jewish Community Relations Council."

6. Donna T. Haverty-Stacke. *Trotskyists on Trial: Free Speech and Political Persecution Since the Age of FDR (Culture, Labor, History, 1)* (New York: New York University Press, 2016), p. 25.

7. Berman, "Political Antisemitism in Minnesota," p. 258.

8. Livia Rothkincher, *The Jews of Bohemia and Moravia: Facing the Holocost* (Lincoln: University of Nebraska Press, 2012), pgs. 60, 69, 72, 78.

9. Holocaust Education Archive and Research Team, 'The Jews of the Sudetenland, Bohemia & Moravia,' http://www.holocaust researchproject.org/nazioccupation/sudetenland .html.

10. Rothkincher, *Jews of Bohemia*, p. 110.

11. Ibid, pgs. 91–92.

12. Ibid, p. 110.

13. Ibid, p. 112.

14. Ibid, p. 136.

15. National Council of Jewish Women, "History Folder," Berman collection, #0039-001.

16. Anonymous, "'The Jews in the Nazi State: Their Position As It Is Today," *Hebrew Jewish Tribune*, March 8, 1935, p. 353, 363.

17. Rogan, 174, and "Fate of Political Refugees Rests with Labor," V.R. Dunne, Socialist Appeal, Vol II, No. 36, September 1938, p. 4.

18. James Grossman, 'Bigotry Stopped American from intervening before the Holocaust . . .' *Los Angeles Times*, April 29, 2018.

19. Rothkincher, *Jews of Bohemia*, p. 112.

20. Wyman, 19–62.

21. David S. Wyman, *The Abandonment of the Jews: America and the Holocaust 1941–1945* (New York: The New Press, 1984/1998), p. 5.

22. Daniels, *Guarding the Golden Door*, p. 88.

23. http://www.jewishvirtuallibrary.org /report-on-the-acquiescence-of-fdr-govern ment-in-the-murder-of-the-jews-january-1944.

24. Holocaust Encyclopedia, 'The Holocaust in Bohemia and Moravia,' https://www.ushmm .org/wlc/en/article.php?ModuleId=10007323.

25. 8. US Code β2385.

26. Ibid, p. 42.

27. Rebecca Hall, "The History of the Smith Act and the Hatch Act: Anti-Communism

and the Rise of the Conservative Coalition in Congress," in Robert Justin Goldstein, editor, *"Little 'Red Scares:" Anti-Communism and Political Repression in the United States, 1921–1946,* (Farnham, England: Ashgate, 2014).

28. Bryan D. Palmer, 'Red Teamsters,' *Jacobin*, October 14, 2014, www.jaobin.com/2014/10/red -teamsters, and *Winona Daily News*, December 22, 1950.

29. Haverty-Stacke, *Trotskyists on Trial*, p. 73.

30. Ibid, p. 141

31. Ibid, p. 163.

32. Ibid, p. 86.

33. Ibid, p. 113.

34. Anja Witek, 'Smith Act Trial,' MNopedia, http://www.mnopedia.org/event/smith-act-trial; *Gitlow v. People of New York*.

35. Haverty-Stacke, *Trotskyists on Trial*, p. 137.

36. Ibid, p. 150.

37. *Schneiderman v. the United States*, 63 Sup. Ct. 1333 (1943); and Ibid, p. 159.

38. Haverty-Stacke, *Trotskyists on Trial*, p. 165.

39. Ibid, p. 205.

40. Millliken, 'Where's The Working Class at the Mill City Museum?' (and 'National Affairs. Barrel No. 2', *Time Magazine*, June 23, 1947, http://content.time.com/time/magazine /article/0,9171,797962,00.html.

41. www.equalrightsamendment.org/history .htm.

42. *Star Tribune*, November 12, 1939, p. 60.

43. Dedicatory plaque, quoted in "History Folder, NCJW, Greater Minneapolis Section," Box #0037.001 Berman Collection.

44. Mary V. Wrenn, 'Surplus Absorption and Waste in Neoliberal Monopoly Capitalism,' *Monthly Review*, Vol. 68, no. 3, July–August 2016.